Understanding youth and crime

Second edition

CRIME AND JUSTICE
Series editor: Mike Maguire
Cardiff University

Crime and Justice is a series of short introductory texts on central topics in criminology. The books in this series are written for students by internationally renowned authors. Each book tackles a key area within criminology, providing a concise and up-to-date overview of the principal concepts, theories, methods and findings relating to the area. Taken as a whole, the *Crime and Justice* series will cover all the core components of an undergraduate criminology course.

Published titles

Understanding drugs, alcohol and crime
Trevor Bennett and Katy Holloway

Understanding youth and crime 2nd edition
Sheila Brown

Understanding crime data
Clive Coleman and
Jenny Moynihan

Understanding white collar crime
Hazel Croall

Understanding victims and restorative justice
James Dignan

Understanding justice 2nd edition
Barbara A. Hudson

Understanding crime prevention
Gordon Hughes

Understanding social control
Martin Innes

Understanding violent crime
Stephen Jones

Understanding risk in criminal justice
Hazel Kemshall

Understanding psychology and crime
James McGuire

Understanding community penalties
Peter Raynor and
Maurice Vanstone

Understanding criminology 2nd edition
Sandra Walklate

Understanding youth and crime

Listening to youth?

Second edition

Sheila Brown

Open University Press

Open University Press
McGraw-Hill Education
McGraw-Hill House
Shoppenhangers Road
Maidenhead
Berkshire
England
SL6 2QL

email: enquiries@openup.co.uk
world wide web: www.openup.co.uk

and Two Penn Plaza, New York, NY 10121-2289, USA

First published 2005

A catalogue record of this book is available from the British Library

ISBN 10: 335 21678 1 (pb)   0 335 21679 X (hb)
ISBN 13: 978 0335 216789 (pb)   978 0335 216796 (hb)

Library of Congress Cataloging-in-Publication Data
CIP data has been applied for

Typeset by RefineCatch Ltd, Bungay, Suffolk
Printed and bound by CPI Group (UK) Ltd, Croydon, CR0 4YY

Contents

Series editor's foreword

The first edition of *Understanding Youth and Crime*, which appeared in 1998, was the fourth book in the Open University Press *Crime and Justice* series. It maintained the high quality of the first three and helped to further cement the series as a key resource in universities teaching criminology or criminal justice. The aim throughout has been to produce short but intellectually challenging introductory texts in key areas of debate, which will give undergraduates and graduates both a solid grounding in the relevant area and a taste to explore it further. Although aimed primarily at students new to the field, and written as far as possible in plain language, the books are not oversimplified. On the contrary, the authors set out to 'stretch' readers and to encourage them to approach criminological knowledge and theory in a critical and questioning frame of mind. The books have also, in many cases, contained original thinking and – unusually for textbooks designed for teaching – made substantial contributions to the literature in their own right.

Sheila Brown's book explores the discourses that surround the social construction of childhood and youth, and especially the role of the media in creating a strong association of young people with crime and disorder, which sustains processes of marginalization and exclusion and leads to frequent 'panics' about youth crime. She also explores the importance of representations of gender in these processes. Within this framework, she critically examines recent developments in youth justice policy, which she characterizes as increasingly politicized and punitive. As in the first edition, she argues that the construction of 'youth' as a special object of knowledge and policy should itself be questioned, and we should instead 'listen' to young people as equal citizens with a legitimate voice. In this new edition, Dr Brown has not only substantially revised and updated the original text to take account of new political events and legislative developments, but has added two important new chapters on issues of growing concern.

The first explores the phenomenon of 'cybercrime', where the risks of exploitation of children are weighed against the positive potential of the internet as a resource for the autonomy and safer participation of young people in social life. The second looks at the impact of globalization on young people, going beyond discussions of conventional criminological topics to raise major issues concerning poverty, war and the commercial exploitation of children. At the same time, young people are regarded as having social agency, and we are warned against adopting an overly passive view of children, or a solely western view of childhood, in attempting any global criminology of youth.

Other books previously published in the *Crime and Justice* series – all of whose titles begin with the word 'understanding' – have covered criminological theory (Sandra Walklate), penal theory (Barbara Hudson), crime data and statistics (Clive Coleman and Jenny Moynihan), crime prevention (Gordon Hughes), violent crime (Stephen Jones), community penalties (Peter Raynor and Maurice Vanstone), white collar crime (Hazel Croall), risk and crime (Hazel Kemshall), social control (Martin Innes), psychology and crime (James McGuire), victims and restorative justice (James Dignan), and drugs and crime (Trevor Bennett and Katy Holloway). Three are already in second editions and other second editions are planned. Other new books in the pipeline include texts on prisons, policing, social attitudes to crime, criminological research methods, race and crime, 'cyber-crime' and political violence. All are topics which are either already widely taught or are growing in prominence in university degree courses on crime and criminal justice, and each book should make an ideal foundation text for a relevant module. As an aid to understanding, clear summaries are provided at regular intervals, and a glossary of key terms and concepts is a feature of every book. In addition, to help students expand their knowledge, recommendations for further reading are given at the end of each chapter.

Mike Maguire
University of Wales, Cardiff

Acknowledgements

Thanks to Mike Maguire, and Mark Barratt at Open University Press/ McGraw-Hill for their encouragement. John Macmillan's original contribution remains central to Chapter 4. Many thanks to Fabio Reis for inspiring me to be concerned about the online exploitation of children, a testament to the rich link between teaching and research. Thanks to Lou for all her support, and to Is for the positive energy.

Introduction to the second edition

I was delighted when I was asked to produce a revised edition of *Understanding Youth and Crime*. Whilst none of the original questions had gone away, a lot more had emerged. Perhaps most dramatically in the intervening six years has been the increasing centrality and visibility of globalization and cyberspace in the spaces of academia, policy and popular talk. Criminology in particular has been brought rudely up against very large and rather unfamiliar landscapes, and in more than one sense it is currently straining at the edges to accommodate so many new challenges to its traditional (western) ways of seeing 'crime' and 'justice'. No more is this so than in the field of understanding youth and crime.

What happens when we try to somehow change the prism of youth criminology to accommodate cybercrime, global conflict, transborder crimes, children's rights or the impacts of (g)localism on young people's experiences as 'deviants' or 'victims'? From thinking about anything from children as victims of human trafficking, to girls and boys' experiences as combatants in lethal warfare, to young women selling sex on the net, the traditional Anglo-American notion that 'youth and crime' can ever again be all about a view from the (dysfunctional) boys is gone. Diversity has finally been forced on to the conceptual map of criminology simply by the fact that it is impossible to ignore it any longer; and along with it comes a need to recognize youth criminology as a product of colonialism that must inevitably become dispersed and rethought, or fragment altogether. Accordingly, Chapter 1 of this edition has been reframed somewhat to emphasize the implications of the western criminological legacy for non-western youth (a theme that will reappear in Chapter 8); whilst Chapter 2 retains its emphasis on a critical evaluation of postwar Anglo-American criminology and identifies some refreshing challenges from 'cultural criminology'.

Also in this edition I have retained the original insistence upon the centrality of young people themselves as the point of youth criminology, rather than adults' concerns about what young people should be. The latter is only of interest as a research topic in itself, to which end I retain a strong emphasis on understanding how the packaging and repackaging of 'youth' in popular, policy, political *and* academic discourses operates to silence and subjugate the young as 'other', to demonize, differentiate and disenfranchize, to exploit and to displace anxiety. The continuing importance of this 'appropriation' of youth for adult purposes, especially cynical political populism, is seen in an expanded Chapter 3.

I have updated Chapter 4 substantially to allow for changes in UK policy and political contexts (contexts that may well have twisted and turned again by the time this book comes into print), as well as to reflect more recent research and the interesting work that has emerged from areas of 'quasi-criminological' analysis, particularly discourses of social in/ exclusion and social policy.

Following from this, Chapter 5 continues to consider children and young people as victims of crime, but is more emphatic in its consideration of the ambiguities and weaknesses in responses to children and young people constructed as 'abuse cases', and in supporting the policy critique of a notion of child abuse that serves to mask the reality of institutionalized, criminal and violent victimization of the young in families and in social care settings. 'True' victims, it seems, are to be differentiated from the more ambiguous victimizations of the family or the peer group, and the stranger is differentiated from the known adult – a position that serves only to further strengthen the mythology of 'innocent childhood' and 'deviant youth'; but more importantly, a position that leaves many children unprotected in dangerous settings.

Chapter 6 on 'beyond the boy zone' remains the same, in recognition of two things. It has been retained because of the distinctive contribution made by feminist criminologies and their deserved 'right' to a special chapter in the history of youth and crime but is also unaltered since the first edition because – partly due to the paradigm-shifting contribution of feminist voices and some 'masculinities' writings – I now consider that we *have* gone beyond the boy zone. Girls are no longer a 'special case' and gender is at the very heart of the diverse criminological global enterprise – nowhere is that clearer than in the issues raised in the new material throughout this edition: criminology is gendered through and through.

In the end, what is of real importance is the experience of young people themselves, and the diversity of that experience. In that respect I place a great deal of importance on the question mooted by academics involved in childhood studies: one childhood or many? What is the 'yardstick of the West' in relation to crime, deviance, justice and victimization, and why is it still assumed so often that there is a universal 'childhood' or 'youth', and that an equally universal 'deviance' is possible?

Here the reader will find two completely new chapters, on cybercrime and on global youth and crime. These attempt to cover a very wide range of material indeed, and especially given their still formative status in criminology 'proper', it will be necessary to make use of non-criminological resources and to be imaginative in the use of the internet as a search tool. I have tried to provide pointers in the right direction: whatever direction that may lead you to is an interesting question! The cyber-crime chapter questions the notion of the net as a place of danger for the young and suggests the possibility that adult concerns over young people and the internet arise at least partly from the freedom that it allows young people. At the same time the extent of child victimization, especially through child abuse images on the internet, is recognized and explored, with the very strong point underlined that whatever the 'technology' may enable, the images on the net frequently derive directly or indirectly from incidents of abuse in the child or young person's own close relationships with male relatives. Similarly, the enormous market for such images attests to the wide cultural support, especially among adult males, for child sexual abuse. There is no kind way of saying this, so I am afraid that some male readers may find this chapter rather 'insulting'. Given the abuse suffered by young people, and the knowledge that the images of their damage remain circulating indefinitely in cyberspace, I remain unrepentant.

Finally, in Chapters 8 and 9, I challenge the very boundaries of youth criminology and ask whether we are witnessing its demise. In this my aim is positive, not destructive: the challenges of the global (and virtual) landscape offer an opportunity, a necessity, to throw off disciplinary straitjackets. Should criminology be concerning itself with children as victims of armed conflict, with children as illegal child soldiers, as slave workers, as street dwellers subject to unregulated homicide or 'cleansing', as smuggled 'goods' in human trafficking for labour and sexual exploitation? International relations, human rights, legislative campaigns, the work of non-governmental organizations and intergovernmental organizations, child and youth groups, the popular media *and* criminology – all of these domains have leaky boundaries, and they are all resources for formulating the questions, whether definitional or substantive, surrounding youth and crime.

Overall, the book attempts to reassert the strengths of existing youth criminology, but also to push at its self-imposed boundaries, including the ones between 'the academe' and other areas of action and knowledge concerned with young people's voices. It does not attempt to be objective; 'objectivity' is usually a smokescreen for sequestered knowledges, seeking to be impervious to challenge except on their own terms. In so far as youth criminology is concerned, I lay no claim to an ability to be 'objective' about the sexual trafficking of 10-year-old girls and boys, for example, or about indiscriminately imposing anti-social behaviour orders on young teens, for that matter. What I do hope to achieve is to encourage the reader – whether in agreement or not with whatever they read – to be critical and inquisitive about 'youth and crime', and never to be satisfied with hand-me-down knowledge.

chapter one

Constructing the other: childhood and youth

Age and the social
Childhood and the Victorian lament for innocence
Youth and adolescence, masculinity and nation
Beyond the margins: non-western childhood and youth
Childhood, youth and exclusion
Further reading

In this chapter we employ a historical approach to demonstrate the origins of present-day perceptions of childhood and youth as 'problem' categories for the adult world. As we move into the twenty-first century, childhood and youth become increasingly controversial and confused notions. In order to understand why this might be, we need to reconsider the nature of these states as they have been constructed historically, and their place within a more general theory of the life course as a social and cultural phenomenon. In this chapter we will also make some inroads into understanding the relationship between concepts of age and concepts of deviance and 'otherness'. Only then can we begin to address, as we do in subsequent chapters, the seemingly inextricable relationship between youth and crime.

Age and the social

Many of us will be used to thinking of the categories of age as fixed and natural. We think of certain attitudes, behaviours or lifestyles as being 'only natural at that age'. We often have taken-for-granted common-sense notions about what to expect of childhood, youth, adulthood, middle age, old age and so on. Indeed, it is not to go too far to suggest that when people deviate from the social expectations attached to their age group our sense of social order is subtly outraged. Children acting 'like adults' pose, somehow, a threat; similarly, perhaps some of us do not like to see 'mutton dressed as lamb'. The problem we are introducing here is that in truth neither 'age' nor 'generation' (Pilcher 1995) are simple or natural categories.

The only 'truth' we have is that we are born, we grow older and we die. The attributes attached to the intervening years ('childhood', 'youth', 'adolescence', 'middle age', 'elderly' etc.) are largely social. By this we mean that the expectations attached to age are culturally produced and sustained. Whether through academic/professional languages (science, psychology, psychiatry), popular media (such as film, TV, music and the newspapers), the statements of public commentators or politicians, or the interactions of everyday life, the individual's passage through society and history – their life course – is enacted through a web of socially produced notions of age-appropriate behaviour and identity.

The theory of age as a cultural rather than a natural category is a relatively new field of inquiry in western social science. Developed through anthropological studies of non-western societies (see e.g. classics such as Margaret Mead's (1929) *Coming of Age in Samoa*), recent work has focused on the ways in which supposedly age-appropriate behaviours and identities are *representations* of how we should feel, and be, at different chronological points in our life span (e.g. Hockey and James 1993; Pilcher 1995; Jenks 1996). We turn now to consider some examples of these representations and the ways in which they may be *deconstructed*.

How do we think of childhood? How do we think of youth? How do we think of middle age? And how do we think of old age?

On childhood, Young (1996) captures one essential part of this process when she talks of 'imagining' age-appropriate behaviour in her discussion of the murder of 2-year-old James Bulger by Jon Venables and Robbie Thompson, two 10-year-old boys. We will discuss this important case in more detail later, and the significance it has had for definitions of crime and justice. For the moment, the point to focus on is that the Bulger killing was seen as, above all, an abrogation of *childhood*. How could children behave like this? The innocent and angelic 2-year-old, horrifically – that is, violently and 'deliberately' – killed by two boys who were themselves children. Suddenly, the whole notion of childhood seemed to have changed, and with it, a sense of belief and stability in the world around us. It is no coincidence that the journalist David Smith, in his chronicling of the Bulger case, quotes Jean-Jacques Rousseau's *Emile* of 1762. Remember, Rousseau tells us, that 'childhood is the sleep of reason'; a time of innocence, simplicity, irrationality; we should 'hold childhood in reverence' (cited in Smith 1994: ix). The real violence of the Bulger case is arguably the violence it did to adult notions of childhood.

Holland (1997) points to the significance of the way in which the mass media focused disproportionately on Thompson and Venables' viewing of

Child's Play 3, the horror movie series in which Chucky dolls (outwardly cute and innocent) are transformed by the demon within, upon which they begin speaking in guttural adult voices. It is not, she argues, so much a question of whether the two boys were incited by *Child's Play* to commit the act they did, but of the sense in which the media coverage fed on the horror dimension of the case: why was the Bulger killing like a horror film come true? Because, perhaps, the media representation of it conjured up images of childhood as no longer innocent but demonic. Hence, as Holland argues, 'The Exorcist, The Omen, Carrie ... the *Child's Play* films, are stories about the nature of child*hood* ... and have very little to do with actual child*ren*' (1997: 50). Holland likens this slippage to a 'confusion of tongues' (p. 50) in which the social representation of something (children) is conflated with a cultural discourse which refers to them (childhood). The demonic child implies the loss of the innocent child and is therefore a threat to adult notions of control and power.

Youth, on the other hand, is contemporaneously *expected* to be an age of deviance, disruption and wickedness. When teenagers behave badly they are typically fulfilling negative stereotypes about them. We are bombarded with images of idle, anti-authoritarian, subversive – and inevitably criminal – teenagers, as opposed to the minority of well schooled, clean, respectful, sporting and disciplined teenagers; the former of course spending their time hanging around on street corners 'causing trouble', and the latter in their bedrooms doing their homework. One group is destined for the dole queue and the boot camp, the other for college and career. The vast bulk of criminological writing, indeed, has been about these very distinctions (Tierney 1996).

Imagine now a different scenario: middle age. Mid-life is portrayed as a time of maximum respectability, maximum productivity: the age of the solid, respectable, law-abiding citizen. Life is therefore portrayed as a problem *for* those in mid-life, rather than the middle-aged being portrayed as a problem for society. Rarely do we imagine middle-aged people as corporate or white-collar criminals, embezzlers or orchestrators of sleaze in politics. The fact that most serious crimes of theft and violence are perpetrated by this age group (Box 1983) is concealed by our cultural notions of respectable middle age and our concomitant fear and suspicion of the young.

Certain images also abound about the elderly: that they are – or should be – passive and vulnerable members of society is illustrated endlessly by press coverage. Hence, both the 'novelty' and the 'comic' value of the following:

A judge told two elderly brothers yesterday to make peace in what are their 'few remaining years' after a family dispute ended in court. After giving Maurice Berger, 75, a 30 month suspended sentence for a 'vicious and potentially lethal' assault with a metal bar on his 81-year-old brother, Judge Timothy Pontius told him: 'Heaven knows, we have a short enough time on this earth – you and your brother rather less than most' . . . he told the defendant, who bowed repeatedly when sentenced, 'I am rather more used to dealing with young thugs and drunken hooligans for offences such as this, not respectable and law abiding pensioners . . . you could have killed your own brother'.

(*Daily Telegraph* 24 February 1996)

Is, then, this very serious assault, which could easily have ended in death, in murder, in fratricide, to be treated as little more than a joke?

In order to understand this apparent anomaly in the way in which we regard the crimes of the youthful and the elderly, we must distance our-selves critically from the assumptions we hold about old age. The crucial notion here is that of the *infantilization* of old age (Hockey and James 1993). This involves the ascription of child-like qualities such as vulner-ability, imperfectly developed reasoning, deficiency in knowledge and understanding, and so on, to chronologically older adults. One of the clearest illustrations of this in contemporary discourse is in magazines aimed specifically at retired people. Free with *Yours* ('Britain's leading news-stand magazine for retired people', February 1996) came a 'Tell the Story of Your Life' booklet: a special 'nostalgic booklet and kit' including 18 stick-on title lines, 36 decorative motifs, a 12-page 'nostalgic look at landmarks of our lives' . . . and so on:

> Dear Reader,
> With the help of this booklet you can re-live moments of your life, write them down and produce a beautiful book . . . the only materials you will need to begin is [*sic*] some plain A4 paper (preferably with two punched holes in one side . . . Please have a go . . . don't be put off by feeling you can't express yourself very well, or that your spelling is a problem.
>
> (*Yours* February 1996)

One could be forgiven for assuming that this is addressed to 6-year-olds. Nauseatingly twee stickers entitled 'My Favourite Things' are interspersed with patronizing instructions and injunctions 'not to be shy'. Thus, as Hockey and James (1993) show, infantilism 'should' be a property of old age. Deviance is as much about overturning cultural expectations as it is about a general conception of right and wrong in themselves; the life course, as a cultural construction, is no different. Age, more than anything, is about the expectations – morally and behaviourally – which we place on a person's chronological positioning in the life span, the sense in which age-stages are 'conceived and articulated in particular societies into cultur-ally specific sets of ideas and philosophies, attitudes and practices' (James and Prout 1990: 1).

As we will see in later chapters, we cannot sensibly move towards a fuller understanding of youth and crime until we jettison our search for the holy grail of what causes the 'youth of today' to commit heinous acts. We need to concentrate on the interrelationship of cultural representations of age with institutionally framed power relationships. Pilcher (1995) emphasizes three essential tasks in considering this question: the historical variability of the notion of childhood, the cultural specificity of notions of childhood, and the analysis of the relationships between adults and children in terms of power, control and dependency (p. 32). We shall attempt to touch upon all three of these dimensions in our discussion below.

Childhood and the Victorian lament for innocence

By tracing some important aspects of the history of discourses of childhood, we may begin to see how this supposedly natural stage has gone through various stages of interpretation and mutation. This, to reiterate Holland's (1997) point, demonstrates the dissonance between adult conceptions of childhood and the real lives of children.

The notion of childhood as a specific, special and distinctive state – as a historical and cultural product rather than as a biological necessity – is typically attributed to Philippe Aries' *Centuries of Childhood* ([1960] 1973). Although very difficult to distil (the Penguin edition runs to some 339 pages of closely argued historical evidence), his argument is commonly paraphrased to posit that in medieval society, the idea of childhood as we know it did not exist: 'Medieval Art until about the Twelfth Century did not know childhood ... it seems probable that there was no place for childhood in the medieval world' (Aries [1960] 1973: 31). This is not to say that *children* did not exist, but that the idea of child*hood* came into being alongside other historical changes. Aries focuses on the emergence of schooling and the transformation of family relationships during the sixteenth, seventeenth and eighteenth centuries as the institutional sites which were crucial in producing discourses of childhood (James and Prout 1990). Children were no longer treated as small adults, but as a distinctive category of beings (see Jenks 1996 for a good synthesis of these arguments).

It was in Victorian society, however, that the 'cult of childhood' reached its height and laid down a marker for all the subsequent debate of the twentieth century on the nature of the child. Nowhere is this clearer than in the proliferation of literature of all kinds both for, and about, children in Victorian society. Alongside the printed word came images, commercial and artistic, educational theories and practices, a burgeoning of markets in the production of special clothes and toys for children, and heated political and philanthropic debate over the special nature of the child (James and Prout 1990; Hockey and James 1993). Thus a clear distance was established between childhood and adulthood. The child was to be protected, trained, but not to have autonomy (Ennew 1986).

With a schizophrenic dualism so redolent of the Victorians, childhood was at the same time idealized, worshipped and protected, feared, regulated and punished, and debased, exploited and appropriated (Hendrick 1990). It is this process that we must first explore to understand the subsequent fate of the notion of childhood in the twentieth century.

Hendrick (1990: 37–47) identifies no less than five versions of childhood which were articulated during the Victorian era: the Romantic child, the Evangelical child, the Factory child, the Delinquent child, and the Schooled child. All emerged between 1800 and 1880, to be followed by the Psycho-medical child and the Welfare child as life swung into the twentieth century and the Edwardian era. Similarly, Jenks depicts the 'natural' child, the 'social' child, the 'Dionysian' child and the 'Apollonian' child (1996). The major point here is that all these different 'versions' of childhood may be identified as reflecting the social conditions of the time rather than as natural or intrinsic qualities of a universal state of childhood.

What, then, were the delineating features of these constructions of childhood (or, one should rather say, child*hoods*) in the Victorian age?

Victorian literature and art depict a romantic and obsessive concern of middle-class adulthood with the notion of childhood. The discourse of the Romantic child presents a psychologically disturbing picture, at once emptying childhood of sexuality and knowledge, by imputing innocence and virtue as quintessential qualities of the child; while at the same time making that very innocence and virtue sexually charged. As Hockey and James note, at first glance sexuality and innocence 'make strange bedfel-lows' (1993: 69). Jackie Wullschlager, in a fascinating essay on children's literature, encapsulates the apparent contradiction in a quotation from the Victorian clergyman and diarist Francis Kilvert. While extolling the essence of childhood as innocence and purity, he noted: 'One beautiful girl stood entirely naked on the sand . . . there was the supple slender waist, the gentle dawn and tender swell of the bosom and budding breasts . . . and above all the soft and exquisite curves of the rosy dimpled bottom and broad white thigh' (Wullschlager 1995: 12). Wullschlager locates this convoluted vision of childhood in the fantasy of the middle-class Victorian man, living in a society where the overt expression of sexual desire was castigated, where suppressed desire resurfaced as an obsession with innocence. As Michel Foucault would have it, the apparent absence of sexuality in Victorian middle-class culture was always a myth, for sex was everywhere (1990). Nowhere is this clearer than in the case of the cult of the Romantic child. From the personal lives of epochal children's writers such as Lewis Carroll to the paintings of John Everett Millais, the softness, tenderness and inno-cence of children was the focus of a heady passion. Carroll – lonely, celibate, intellectually and practically divorced from the coarse grain of everyday life – channelled his energies into inventing *Alice in Wonderland* and photographing 9- and 10-year-old girls in as few clothes as possible.

'At *any* rate', wrote Carroll to a wife of a colleague, 'I trust you will let me do some pictures of Janet naked; at her age, it seems almost absurd to even suggest any scruple about dress . . . My great hope, I confess, is about Ethel . . . If the worst comes to the worst, and you won't concede any nudities at all, I think you ought to allow all three to be done in bathing drawers, to make up for my disappointment' (cited in Wullschlager 1995: 37).

The importance of these constructions of childhood is not so much whether we consider (from the vantage point of the twentieth century) figures such as Carroll to be 'paedophiles', which has been a common critical assumption of the 1970s onwards, but the way in which the 'Romantic' (sexualized-de-sexualized) child had little to do with the lives of young people *per se*, and everything to do with the nostalgia, longings and social life of adults. Eric Griffiths, Fellow of Trinity College Cambridge, commented in an interview with the *Guardian* (26 April 1996), 'That his [Carroll's] writing is paedoerotic in a certain sense is absolutely true. Yet surely the point is that the evidence of the books wanting to preserve the state of being both an adult and a child is stronger than any . . . biographical data could be.'

The narrow outward conventionality of Victorian, patriarchal, middle-class official morality, and the rapid pace of social change occurring at the time, formed the conditions for this construction of childhood. It was reproduced in the whole genre of the Victorian literary idealization of childhood, whether in the figure of Charles Dickens' Little Nell, or in moral stories in the flourishing periodical market of innocent children on their deathbeds. Similarly, the use of childhood innocence as a way of idealizing high rates of infant mortality (s/he has gone to a far better place, atrophied in innocence and uncorrupted by becoming an adult) preserved the Victorian middle classes from the harsh realities of the world they were creating.

They lamented, because this very world – the heyday of industrial capitalism and empirical science – was also a world where machines mechanized the people who worked them, the town overgrew the country and the secular ousted God. As Murdock writes, referring to the 'archaeology of popular anxieties',

> As Nineteenth Century observers knew very well, the dynamics of modernity called all pre-existing moral and social relations in to question. As Marx put it in 1848 . . . there was an 'uninterrupted disturbance of all social conditions . . . all fixed, fast frozen relations are swept away . . . All that is solid melts in to air, all that is holy is profaned . . . What Marx celebrated as a liberation others mourned as a loss. They saw established and social restraints crumbling away. They were haunted by the spectre of moral decline amidst material plenty.
>
> (Murdock 1997: 70)

Childhood became one reference point among many in which the tensions and contradictions of the age could be managed and anaesthetized. It was paralleled in an idealization of womanhood, an idealization of the rural idyll and a lament for lost simplicity. As we will argue later, it is this adult nostalgia and fear which is projected onto the lives of young people. This will be seen to form a recurrent theme in the way in which we have responded to childhood and youth throughout the twentieth century, and which, as we shall also argue, has informed adult society's largely irrational responses to the 'youth crime question'.

What of the other Victorian 'childhoods'? The Factory child is, of course, the inverse of the Romantic child. Contemporaneously with the world of childhood innocence, masculine middle-class fantasy and longing, and the cosy world of the nanny and the nursery, as many as 80 per cent of workers in English cotton mills were children (Muncie 1984: 31). Muncie provides a clear account of the construction of the Factory child. In the early stages of English industrialization, child labour was both common-place and economically necessary. Without the employment of children as young as 5, families would have starved and profits would have dwindled. Not here had children ceased to be regarded as small adults. Economic vicissitudes would not have permitted it. Until the 1830s, argues Muncie, 'the use of child labour remained unquestioned, not only by families who relied on their income, but also by factory owners who were keenly aware of this ever increasing source of cheap labour' (1984: 31).

A number of factors affected the subsequent history of the Factory child. Economic and technological developments in production processes were one important dynamic. Manufacturing industries became concentrated in urban centres, the size and complexity of machinery increased and the division of tasks within the production process changed. Whereas in the early stages of industrialization, production had more nearly mir-rored family structures, with whole families being employed as units, the Victorian era saw the breakdown and anonymization of tasks. Children were increasingly seen as too small and too little skilled to take a full part in the production process. Parallel with these developments were the growing strength of a Labour movement dominated by adult males, which sought to preserve wages from the downward pressure of cheap child labour, and a swelling religious and philanthropic movement based in the middle classes which sought to save children from the debasement of factory life in the interests of civilization. Hendrick notes the appalled reactions of middle-class reformers to the impact of industrial urban manufacturing, and particularly to 'the violence which it was felt was done to the nature of "childhood" itself; the Factory child seemed to symbolise profound and often little understood changes in British society, changes which seemed to threaten an imagined natural order' (1990: 40).

The innocence of 'Romantic' childhood and all that it stood for, was seen as under siege from the brutalization of children. Most importantly, the state of childhood gathered force as a barometer of social order, linked as it was to the cult of the domestic ideal. Civilization and social order were seen to inhere in the Christian, disciplined, family life of the middle classes where the woman was portrayed as the 'angel of the hearth' and the patri-archal, authoritarian but benign father as the guardian of his 'castle'. The reconstruction of the Factory child was thus born of forces of social class, gender and religious belief, as well as more purely technical or economic imperatives.

These kinds of forces are well portrayed in the literature of the time, particularly in the writings of philanthropists and novelists such as Elizabeth Gaskell, who depicts explicitly and with passion the perceived effects of factory life upon the social order. The Factory Act of 1833 is commonly cited as the watershed of these developments. The Act virtually prevented the employment of children under 9, and limited working hours for those aged between 9 and 13. Subsequent Acts throughout the century progressively marginalized children from the workforce and the centre of economic production (Pinchbeck and Hewitt 1973 cited in Hockey and James 1993) and reinforced the notion of the child as 'other' and 'special'. By the late 1840s, revolutions in Europe had also strengthened the middle-class conviction that the very social order of England was under threat from brutalization. Gaskell wrote in the preface of the 1848 edition of *Mary Barton*,

> If . . . the woes, which come with an ever returning tide-like flood to overwhelm the workmen in our manufacturing towns, pass unregarded . . . it is an error . . . bitter in its consequences . . . the idea which I have formed of the state of feeling among too many of the factory people in Manchester . . . has received some confirmation from the events which have so recently occurred among a similar class on the continent [i.e. the 1848 revolutions].
>
> (Gaskell [1848] 1981: 38)

This must be linked into the transformation of public space and the spectre of the mass or the crowd. The overcrowding of the rapidly expanding urban conurbations (such as Manchester, where Gaskell was writing), the relatively short distances between the houses of the bourgeois and the poor, produced fears such as those voiced by commentators like Matthew Arnold, of a 'vast residuum', a murky mass of people outside the bounds of respectability and control (cited in Murdock 1997: 71).

In the unnatural child, the brutalized child, lay the terrifying potential for these 'dangerous classes' to reproduce themselves. Schooling came to be seen as the only hope for the salvation of civilization. Alongside reforming zeal came educating zeal, as the middle classes came to perceive that with the exclusion of children from factories, the Devil would be rapidly making work for their idle hands. No longer fully enclosed within the factories, the children of the labouring poor would be spreading the seeds of disorder and debauchery on the streets. The increasing numbers of street children, child prostitutes and beggars consequent upon the changes of the 1830s became the next spectres of urban life: 'In 1848, Lord Ashley, veteran campaigner for factory reform, referred to more than 30,000 "naked, filthy, roaming, lawless, and deserted children", in and about the metropolis. Edwin Chadwick warned of such children's "perpetual tendency to moral as well as physical deterioration" . . . In 1840 police in Manchester reported that 3,650 children were sleeping rough in the city' (Cockburn 1995: 72).

While the prisons became a repository for some – Muncie (1984) notes that in 1835 nearly 7000 young people were in prison, and in 1853, 12,000 – this could not form a practical solution to child regulation, nor did it accord with the idealization of the nature of the child. That 'solution' arose in the form of the Schooled child, and by extension the Reformatory, or the Delinquent child.

Thus another duality surfaced in the troubled waters of Victorian bourgeois sensibilities; hand in hand, the Delinquent child and the Schooled child began to form (Hendrick 1990). While the notion of 'delinquency' was only fully to take shape with the invention of adolescence later in the century, the writings of the philanthropist Mary Carpenter clearly linked the discourses of deprivation, depravation, social disorder and the need for 'education'. The title of her book, *Reformatory Schools for the Children of the Perishing and Dangerous Classes and for Juvenile Offenders* (1851) is sufficiently clear. Although, as Hendrick correctly points out, the history of the creation of delinquency and the history of education are separate and different (Hendrick 1990: 45) in many respects, the ideological origins of both forms of regulation are similar. Both focused on the special nature of the child; both saw social and physical regulation as integral to both the moral health of the child and the moral health of society, and both were ultimately concerned with the symbolic and practical threat of the unregulated child to the sustenance of social order. The discourses of the Delinquent child and the Schooled child came to form the conceptual domains for the construction of the child as 'other' and opened up new public sites for the regulation of childhood: 'there was nothing coincidental in mid-century penologists and social investigators seeking to return children to their true position (to their nature), as it also involved making them more amenable to the classroom' (Hendrick 1990: 46).

This institutional and discursive framing of childhood within the school and the reformatory has had long and profound consequences for the interlinking of youth and crime. We may juxtapose two excerpts from contemporary writers – Mary Carpenter and Henry Worsley – to consider the importance of Victorian history:

> The child must be placed where . . . he will be gradually restored to the true position of childhood . . . He must perceive by manifestations which he cannot mistake that this power, whilst controlling him, is guided by interest and love; he must have his own affections called forth by the obvious personal interest felt in his well being by those around him; he must, in short, be placed in a family.
>
> (Carpenter 1853 in Muncie 1984: 37)

> A bane to society, which, like an ulcer on the body, is continually enlarging, and distributing far and wide its noxious influence . . .

a general and latent depravity, which a large extent of juvenile depravity seems to indicate, is a state under which the manufacture of a society must eventually decline, agriculture languish, and commerce disappear.

(Worsley 1849, in Pearson 1983: 157–8)

The construction of the child as a particular kind of social category in Victorian society thus culminated in a series of linked, if often confused and contradictory, conceptions of childhood identity. These focused on the potential and hope represented by childhood to restore a sense of lost order, innocence and simplicity; and the potential and threat represented by childhood to undermine ideals, moral health and social order.

We encounter here a central dilemma facing the student of childhood, youth and crime. This is the tension between 'fact' and 'myth'. If conceptions of the childhood or adolescent as 'other', 'deviant' or 'threatening' to the fundamental social order could be shown to derive strongly from the general anxieties of (middle-class) adults about the nature and pace of change in society – that is, as a projection of adult anxieties – then the validity of the accusations made by adults about the decline in standards of youthful behaviour must also be called into question. It is through exclusion of others that we include ourselves; that we draw the boundaries between the indoor (safety) and the outside (threat), suggesting that there is indeed a 'deeply rooted formation of social fear which presents the vulnerable, suggestible, and dangerous as living outside the stockade of maturity and reasonableness that the rest of "us" take for granted' (Murdock 1997: 83).

The consequence for children's real lives of these constructions is less often considered, and will form an enduring theme of this text. In the 'emptying out' of children's lives and the 'filling in' of adult concerns, crucial directions were set for history whose repercussions have gathered strength, rather than diminished, into the twentieth century. Ironically the quest for the rediscovery of the 'true' nature of the child led to an increasing marginalization and silencing of the actual voices of children. Muncie comments upon this from a more class-based point of view in his argument that the concept of juvenile delinquency did not so much represent a more humanitarian attitude towards young offenders as 'justify an increased surveillance and regulation of both [young offenders] and their working class families' (1984: 40).

Hendrick frames the problem in a more child-centred and 'liberal' way. The school, he argues, 'threw aside the child's knowledge' and required a sense of dependency (Hendrick 1990: 47). The practical benefits of the discovery of modern childhood in some respects can hardly be contested. This is particularly so in relation to the removal of children from the life-threatening physical conditions of industrial labour. But these humanitarian benefits are countered by the economic dispossession of children; enforced and prolonged dependency on adults; the discrediting of their views and experiences; and above all, by ensuring the role of young people as an enduring scapegoat (and contingently a whipping post) for the collective neurosis of a society (Holland 1997).

Thus, as Pearson comments in his lively and detailed history of these developments, the most 'remarkable' feature of early Victorian perceptions of the criminal question was 'the way in which juvenile lawlessness was believed to foreshadow the possibilities of political insurrection amongst the lower orders' (1983: 159).

This extended increasingly, as we trace our history towards the beginning of the twentieth century, to insecurity about the maintenance of British economic prowess globally. This period also sees, not entirely coincidentally, the emergence of the construction of 'adolescence'.

Youth and adolescence, masculinity and nation

The extension of the period of childhood dependency through legislation and institutionalization, and the development of more sophisticated modes of surveillance of the working-class urban poor (through philanthropy, schools, the development of police forces and the regulation of popular culture), made children at once more problematic and more visible. It also formed the backdrop against which the development of a construction of youth and adolescence, rather than childhood, was to take place. Indeed, throughout the latter part of the nineteenth century, a number of histories were unfolding which were to have an even greater impact upon the subsequent construction of childhood and youth as 'other'.

Griffin (1993) suggests that we must consider the interactions between discourses surrounding 'race', sexuality, gender, class, nation and age if we are to understand the discourses surrounding youth which were in place by the end of the century. As Wullschlager comments, by the turn of the century, the Romantic obsession with the girl child had been obscured by the Edwardian cult of (male) youth. The broad context here has to be located in the 'impact of Empire'. Harris's statement is hardly too sweeping when he writes that 'British economic and political power in the wider world was in itself a major determinant of the character of domestic society throughout the period [1870–1914]' (1993: 4). Two interlocking developments were occurring during this period. On the one hand, 1870–1914 saw the heyday of the extension and consolidation of imperial power; while on the other, the failure (or refusal) of Britain to restrict free trade and the take-off of German and French industrial capitalism had begun to result in internal insecurities and threats as early as the 1880s (Harris 1993). While Empire reigned abroad, the development of the notion of the masses at 'home' was the order – or rather the disorder – of the day. Despite this apparent 'golden age',

British society was vulnerable to the perpetual changes and collapses wrought by the collapse of world markets . . . in the 1880s, Britain . . . chose not to protect British home producers against American wheat, with a consequent collapse of . . . rural communities, an explosion of migration to the cities, a rapid rise in living standards for those in secure employment . . . but it could be seen also more diffusely in a certain latent instability throughout the industrial world . . . society was having to adapt to new forms of economic life and thought, long before it had . . . absorbed the social consequences of industrial change and agrarian decline. The result was increasingly a society in which people felt themselves to be living in many different layers of historical time.

(Harris 1993: 5)

Once more the complex insecurities of the era come to bear upon the young; but this time on 'youth' rather than 'childhood'. For the middle classes, education came increasingly to be a focus for the preparation of their sons for colonial rule and trading success; the teenage sons of the poor were concomitantly focused upon as the origin of domestic disorders in the cities and the source of industrial failure. The preconditions for a universalizing discourse of youth were in place: a youth which was either to be the standard bearer and upholder of a Great Nation, or the scourge of the future and the harbinger of doom. In particular, concern was turned to the perceived problem of young men in gangs on the streets. In part, of course, this reflected reality: youthful street disorder formed an aspect of everyday urban life. Some of this may be described as 'political', at least to the extent that it represented the response of the urban working class to the increasing regulation of their lives and modes of popular culture. Since the modern police force itself may be seen in part as the middle-class answer to the fear of disintegration in the Victorian city, it is hardly surprising that resistance was generated among those who were to be policed (Storch 1980). More broadly, however, the popular culture of youth, whether overtly political or not, was increasingly regulated in public places, so that by the latter part of the nineteenth century, 'the distinctive styles and subcultures of working class youth were well established as a highly visible, much remarked upon . . . feature or "problem" of the urban scene' (Davis 1990: 44).

Yet again, however, the important point is the way in which youthful behaviour constitutes the locus for much broader fears.

The emergence of the hooligan in the late nineteenth century was thus no historical accident; it was an Irish term for what was seen as an unprecedented eruption of youthful disorder on Britain's streets (Pearson 1983: Ch. 5), which was above all to be regarded as un-British, and 'the name of the Hooligan . . . provided a crystallising focus for any number of overlapping anxieties associated with imperial decline, material incapacity, the erosion of social discipline and moral authority, the eclipse of family life, and what was feared to be the death rattle of "Old England" ' (Pearson 1983: 107).

The solution to the problem was seen to lie in adopting the methods of the public school used to prepare middle- and upper-class youth for rule and Empire. The existing system of elementary education, in place since the 1870 Education Act extended schooling to the age of 13, was now seen as inadequate to cope with the growing crisis. Sporting and military languages and practices came to be the clarion call. Again Pearson notes the dualism in this response, for the 'hooligan' was seen at once to be a source of recruitment for imperial armies, and therefore to represent the future salvation of the Empire, and as a threat to its survival as a source of degeneracy and slackness.

Thus Davis (1990) points out that the discussion of hooliganism was explicitly linked to discourses on the state of the nation, the rising supremacy of Germany and the poor showing of Britain in the Boer War. Imperial anxieties were projected onto youth through the discourse of hooliganism.

It will be of little surprise by now to learn that the response was the proliferation of more institutions for the regulation of young people, further delineating them as 'special' and marginalizing them as 'other'. This phenomenon cannot be understood without reference to the development of social theory and science in late Victorian society, for a powerful alliance in the construction of youth and its regulation was made between social and scientific discourse and social 'reform'.

Within the framework of genetic psychology, G.S. Hall (1904) defined adolescence as a 'physiological stage triggered by the onset of puberty' (Griffin 1993), which concomitantly involved a period of 'transition' to 'normal adulthood' via a sexual 'awakening'. We have come largely to accept these categories as constitutive of some real state of adolescence; what Griffin is able to do in her detailed history of ideas is to show that the emergence of adolescence had as much to do with Hall's own interests and background as they did with the 'discovery' of a new life phase. Hall was concerned to establish psychology as an expanding, medicalized discipline and to shift the emphasis from the spiritual and the religious realm to the sexual and biological domain. This in turn may be seen as part of the general growth in power of psycho-medical discourses in the nineteenth century, attendant upon the influence of Darwinian notions of evolution. It is important to underline at this point the gendered and racialized nature of the concept of adolescence, for here we are able to see how social and scientific discourses danced in step to the music of Empire.

In its emphasis on masculine heterosexuality, Hall's concept of normal adolescence was coterminous with contemporary concerns for the health of the nation: 'one of his main concerns was the need to control masturbation, especially amongst young men . . . homosexuality, especially amongst young men, was also a potential danger which had to be controlled and channelled into "normal" adult heterosexual relationships' (Griffin 1993: 17).

The concern, of course, was not just that 'slack morals' would undermine the backbone of the nation, but the declining birth rate of the time, and the threat of 'race suicide' contained therein. Women were seen as less of a threat to the nation than young men because they were not seen, in general, as sexually driven or active independently of childbirth; nor was lesbianism recognized. Women were perceived as more naturally obedient to their biological destiny, which was to ensure the survival of the 'race'. The main concern with regard to adolescent girls was to ensure the regularity of their menstrual cycle and in other ways to ensure their physical fitness for childbearing (Griffin 1993).

Hence the categories 'white', 'masculine', 'heterosexual', are moved centre stage as key indicators of the 'health' of adolescence. This had two crucial impacts upon the later development of studies of youth and crime.

Firstly, the subsequent history of the study of delinquency was inordinately obsessed with the behaviour of young white males (their 'normality' after all was to be the indicator of the state of the nation). Secondly, the voices of non-white, non-heterosexual and non-male young people were to become marginalized and excluded even further than those of their white male peers.

Beyond the margins: non-western childhood and youth

The preceding discussion has shown how the modern conception of childhood and youth, centring as it did around the concerns of western industrializing nations, gave birth to the notion of youth as 'other' in western societies. This was a doubly complex process however, because in creating idealized conceptions of white western childhood and youth, the lives and experiences of non-western 'childhoods' were discounted. Western writers, philanthropists and pedagogues were both egocentric and ethnocentric in their concerns. The legacy of imperialism for non-western children was one of an existence not even on, but beyond, the margins: they were exploited by the West for cheap (or slave) labour, and within their own cultures were vulnerable to a range of practices from institutionalized infanticide and sexual abuse to the vicissitudes of famine, poverty and war. At the same time, indigenous cultures of subjected peoples were the loci of fear and of missionary zeal – 'savages' or 'primitives' must be tamed, disciplined *and* saved.

In order to grasp the significance of this for later (western) framings of the youth-crime nexus, we have to try and imagine ourselves inside the imperial/colonial mind; as Singh puts it in relation to India, a 'language of colonialism' within a trope of 'discovery' (Singh 1996). Since the early modern period, Singh suggests,

this discovery motif has frequently emerged in the language of colonization, enabling European travelers/writers to represent the newly 'discovered' lands as an empty space, a *tabula rasa* on which they could inscribe their linguistic, cultural, and later, territorial, claims . . . the trope of discovery took on shifting, multiple meanings within British colonial discourse, being constantly refurbished and mobilized in the service of other colonizing enterprises, such as *civilizing*, *rescuing*, and *idealizing* or *demonizing* their Indian subjects as 'others'.

(Singh 1996: 1–2)

It is important to remember that whilst we are primarily concerned with British imperialism here, colonialism is a distinct concept representing a broader history: before Britain became a major player, Spain and Portugal had virtually divided up the world between them, attempting with varying degrees of success to impose their own cultural and religious orders across the globe (Neill 1966). British imperialism was thus following a long historical precedent in its exercise of subjection, but nevertheless the British also had a distinctively ambiguous (or less charitably, hypocritical) relationship with their subjects. In economic and political oppression, they were ruthless, yet in cultural discourse, the primary language was one of 'civilization'. This extended to popular culture, such as the export of British theatre to Calcutta, so that 'the Victorian colonists in India, whilst apishly promoting Shakespeare's works in colonial Calcutta, were, in effect, reproducing the metropolitan culture as part of the "civilizing mission" of the British Raj' (Singh 1996: 122).

'Civilizing' is thus a term that demands pause for thought. In effect it involves *exclusion* at the same time as *assimilation*. Thus, indigenous cultures were to be 'civilized', or purged of their own characteristics; indigenous peoples were expected to 'assimilate' western culture, yet at the same time, to remember at all times their inherently subservient position in relation to the imperial rulers. A 'special' relationship was possible between the British and elite Bengalis because of the latter's willingness to adopt (and financially support) British mores; but when rebellion came, as with the Sepoy Mutiny of 1857, not only was the military reaction swift and vicious, but the cultural representations of the time (e.g. contemporary novels) revealed the core assumptions of the British rulers: India was 'decadent, backward, and in need of civilization' (Singh 1996: 82).

For indigenous childhoods, the effect of western colonization was to be profound and long-lasting. As Balagopalan argues, 'the contingency of culture is linked to the histories of modernity, colonialism, and capitalist expansion. A majority of the countries in the Third World are former colonies of Europe, and therefore the multiple childhoods we seek to study have been affected by the significant break that colonialism, modernity and the spread of capitalism engendered in these lives' (Balagopalan 2002: 20).

Thus as conceptions of 'childhood' were universalized in western Europe, these colonial nations also sought to export – to *globalize* – idealized western childhood as a normative standard against which non-western childhoods would be judged and found wanting. 'Civilization' and 'development' produced a number of discourses and strategies in relation to non-western children in endeavours to (re)produce the latter as compliant bodies, as social actors 'willing and able to function in complementary ways within [colonial projects]' (Stephens 1995: 16).

Thus if poor white western (male) children were constructed as deviant and threatening, poor non-white, non-western (male) children were doubly so; whilst non-white non-western (female) children were doubly 'at risk' from immorality and the savagery of the (male) native. Stephens relates de Alwis' work in relation to missionary-sponsored boarding schools in the nineteenth century: girls would often receive a new western name; they were taught Christian scripture, needlework, orderliness, thrift, and cleanliness (Stephens 1995: 16 deriving from de Alwis 1991). In inverse proportion, non-western males – particularly black South Africans – were feminized and infantilized through western discourse, being seen as falling short of the true qualities of (western) manhood. Qualities of irrationality, immaturity and uncontrolled emotionality were typically imputed to them (Stephens 1995: 18). Nevertheless, this non-western male was a constant source of latent threat in his potentiality for unbridled, uncivilized savagery. As Baden-Powell, the founder of the Boy Scout movement, was to put it as late as 1930: 'there are men, and there are White men' (Baden-Powell 1930: 227). It was important in this context to harness non-western boys from poor families early to subservient labour in the colonies – not just for economic reasons, but to ensure that they might be tightly surveilled and controlled. Anxieties grew in proportion with nationalisms in the latter half of the nineteenth century, resulting in both expansion of the colonial penal system and of a kind of 'colonial criminology' – or, as Sen (2000: 36–7) puts it in relation to India, 'by focusing the discursive power of the colonial enterprise upon these criminals, it generated a substantial body of knowledge about Indian crime . . . a vision of criminality that was predicated on political insubordination and on concepts of private and public disorder'.

Such complexities of the 'civilizing process' moreover had general implications for the rule of law. Fitzpatrick (2001) identifies the sense in which law as cultural practice was a tool for establishing the permanence of 'discovery': the discovery of territory was an 'extraversion' of a specific imperial nation, but it could only attain an effective, recognized, international presence to the extent that the colonizing nation successfully established commonality. This latter was an homogenizing process that represented (in the present case) British law as 'the' law, the legal discourse of civilization in the face of the savage other. Culture was to be *essentialized* through law (Riles 1993). Hence Fitzpatrick (2001: 19) comments that 'the supreme justification of imperial rule was that it brought order to chaos, reined in "archaic instincts" and all this aptly enough through subjection to "laws". Looked at another way, the violence of imperialism was legitimated in its being exercised through law.' The primary effect of imperial law was thus to define and contain the subjected culture as *different*. Even where concessions were made to customary or aboriginal laws, the law of the colonizers was to be the supreme, the superior arbiter, the normative standard against which the effectiveness and quality of all other law was to be judged (Fitzpatrick 2001: 21). T.B. Macaulay, asserted by Sen (2000: 3) to be the 'true "law giver" of modern India', wrote of his desire to 'raise and encourage a manly spirit among the people' (p. 4). Hence the civilizing mission and the rule of (western) law was seen as a predominantly benevolent process, seeking to secure subjection through ideology as much as through force. 'Tradition' and 'backwardness' were the problems for law-makers; immorality had its locus in *native* society.

Whilst it would be wrong to over-generalize across a process that occurred unevenly in very different regions, countries and continents – for example, India, Africa, Australia, New Zealand, China – the 'colonial idea' (Neill 1966) as filtered through the prism of imperialism remained broadly consistent in its 'civilizing', universalizing, essentializing and globalizing tendencies; and the rule of law equally filtered through this prism, discursively embodied in the western idealization of 'normality'. Thus along with prisons in the colonies came asylums, also exported from the West to become an international enterprise (Porter 1991). Asylums focused on problems of 'difference' that could not be easily subsumed under the criminal code, but which were troubling for the colonial peace of mind: various problems of disorderliness from 'idiocy' to 'excitability', 'immorality' and drink, and opiate-induced behaviours were dealt with by means of the asylum (Colebourne 2001). Indeed, the methods of panoptic (all-seeing cellular confinement) and medicalized containment detailed in Michel Foucault's work (1977) made the colonies offshore laboratories for the development of domestic western penal and psychiatric regimes (Sin 2000), and 'lessons' from the colonial criminology referred to above were imported back to Britain. This was reflected in the languages used to define criminality at 'home'; it was frequently Orientalized, creating a difference between the Christian/English (good, law-abiding) and the Arab/Indian (criminal/heathen) – hence child pickpockets were 'street Arabs' (Sin 2000).

Children and young people in non-western cultures were, then, situated in relation to a complex world order. The 'tabula rasa' of discovery meant also that indigenous cultures of the young became tabula rasa for the universalization of the 'western child'. This hegemonic force of western notions of childhood and youth, of western discourses of law and normality, and the tying together of 'civilizing' and 'developmental' processes, had in particular two lasting consequences. One was that all issues relating to childhood – whether subsumed under discourses of legality or normality – would from the nineteenth century onwards be framed by the notion of a universal (western) child. Another was that the everyday lives of non-western children and young people would be judged against a yardstick that was frequently senseless in relation to their own life worlds. From the 'hegemonic social reform' represented by the Age of Consent Act 1891, introduced into the Indian penal code by the Supreme Legislative Council (Bannerji 2002), through to twenty-first century discourses on child labour, the 'problem' of street children, the iniquities of exploitation and the need for and nature of children's rights, legality and normality typically came not just from above, but from outside. There is a construction of a 'double other' at work here: if western youth is silenced and distanced from auto-nomy, then non-western youth is doubly distanced and doubly silenced in an 'identity politics . . . where we see projected binary identities of inferior "others" *and* of the "enlightened self" of Europe' (Bannerji 2002: 94). Hence Balagopalan concludes that unless we are able both to study Third World childhoods within their own social, cultural and economic realities *and* take into account the 'disjunctions' caused in their histories by colonial control, then an unrealistic 'bourgeois western construct' of the civilized ideal will continue to hold sway with real consequences for the lives of children and young people (Balagopalan 2002: 20–1).

Matters are further complicated because there is an inherent possibility within an overly crude critique of colonialism and western universalism that children's experiences of labour exploitation, sexual victimization, conflict and violence could be theorized back out of sight through, for example, an attack on the westernized assumptions embedded in the *United Nations Convention on the Rights of the Child*. As Ennew and Morrow point out, 'the child envisioned by the Convention belongs to a conception of childhood constructed during the development of capital-ism in Europe and North America, a construction that implies becoming an adult (and in need of socialization to do so) rather than being a social actor' (Ennew and Morrow 2002: 10). If children's agency and their indigenous cultures are taken seriously, this may well lead to conflict with western discourses of 'rights' and 'protection': the case of street children is now a much cited instance of this, where a phenomenon that is seen from one position to represent an abhorrent state of affairs may be seen from the perspective of street children themselves to be a way of life which they actively wish to retain (see e.g. Glauser 1997; Skelton and Allen 1999). Similarly, the Age of Consent Act (raising the age of consent to sexual intercourse for Indian girls from 10 to 12 in 1859) is shown by Bannerji to be in many ways a racist attempt to control sexuality and reproduction and suppress agency because of western paranoia about 'native' 'breeding'; moreover, it 'created for the state a space for conduct-ing research in the areas of sex and reproduction in the name of science and civilization' (Bannerji 2002:84), leading to a *patholigization* of girls through an obsessive focus on sexual activity and reproduction. Whether through welfarism or criminalization, it is clear that western legal and rights discourses *can* undermine further the agency of young people and abet in their silencing, acting as a reflection of adult desires to control rather than young people's own experiences, and so such discourses *should* be a legitimate focus for critique.

Nevertheless, as Jenks (2004: 6–7) identifies, the recognition of the existence of 'many childhoods' (James and Prout 1998) does contain an 'inevitable paradox':

> If children . . . have agency, then one set of consequences following from this new found status is a new set of responsibilities. Childhood is no longer a mitigation . . . children who commit crimes are responsible for those crimes 'as if' they were adult social actors . . . But this cannot be right, are children no longer dependent or vulnerable in any sense? Are children's relationships with paedophiles equivalent and consensual? . . . The ideal of childhood as a universal category does not meet the real experiences of children across the globe; it does however, produce a moral position from which it can be claimed that children should claim a unity of treatment rather than simply succumbing to their found material conditions.

We shall see in Chapter 8 how important this becomes for understanding youth and crime: for taking into account non-western childhood and youth is a precursor to understanding processes of crime and globalization in the contemporary world. Recognizing the existence of 'many childhoods' means taking seriously the particularities and voices of young people in their experiences of 'crime', 'exploitation' or 'victimization'. To imagine a global 'criminology' that comprises a grasp of both local and global (or (g)local – see Featherstone *et al.* 1995) contexts is both immensely difficult and the most necessary element in the future of childhood and youth criminologies. Conversely we shall also see how the colonial legacy has produced a universalized (and frequently racist) western 'criminology' that continues to be a part of, as much as a critique of, the exclusionary processes of the twenty-first century, compounding the absence of children's voices in the episteme. It will also be necessary to examine the often contentious notion of children's agency and a discourse of 'rights' which may exist in tension with this – bringing in the controversial issue of a victimology of childhood and youth.

Childhood, youth and exclusion

Children and young people are constituted as 'at risk' or as 'a risk' in contemporary western legal and welfare discourses (Stephens 1995); this is a phenomenon of late modernity and its preoccupation with riskiness (Beck 1992) but is importantly also a phenomenon with its roots in the uneven development of European colonialism and British imperialist capitalism.

The above account charts historically a process of *exclusion*: the setting apart and differentiation of some social groupings by others. What is notable about processes of exclusion is that they typically involve marginalizing the excluded groups: that is, denying their right to be self-determining, to have direct access to the general forms of power and resources in society, to have a voice in the making of decisions about their lives. Other histories of exclusion have focused on, for example, discourses of race, gender or disability; here we have taken the rather less usual focus of age gradation and the exclusion of childhood and youth as *cross-cut* by other forms of exclusion.

The making special of certain groups by defining them as representing childhood or adolescence may no longer be seen as simply a benevolent process based upon the special needs of a biologically driven life cycle. The coincidences of history and discourse are too many. That certain young people may have benefited in substantial ways by their constitution through the discourses of childhood and adolescence is not in question. Our concern is rather to identify the senses in which their delineation as 'other' leaves them open to a projective process whereby their own voices are lost and the anxieties and angers of a social formation may come to rest upon their shoulders (Young 1999). Such exclusion is rarely beneficial to the reputation and status of the excluded social grouping. It has very practical and often catastrophic consequences for particular individuals and groups. The effects are seen in a myriad of social phenomena from the vigilantism of extreme 'moral panics' (Critcher 2003), to material inequalities compounded by exclusionary social policies (Young 1999), to late modern global upheaval and devastation (Stephens 1995; Machel 2001; Brown 2003). Indeed, Young (1999) has highlighted the need for a 'criminology of intolerance'.

Theoretical explanations for the tendency of societies and individuals to create a discourse of difference range from the psychoanalytical through the anthropological and the more conventionally sociological. What remains more or less constant through different disciplines and accounts is the threat posed by the notion of marginality. This is fundamental to understanding how age operates in relation to criminality and criminalization.

Mary Douglas (1994a) frames her discussion of difference-exclusion-otherness through a study of the concepts of pollution and taboo: 'granted, disorder spoils pattern, it also provides the material of pattern . . . this is why, though we seek to create order, we do not simply condemn disorder. We recognise that it is destructive to existing patterns; also that it has potentiality. It symbolises both power and danger' (Douglas 1994a: 195). While Douglas is writing here from a somewhat structuralist perspective, writers closer to the psychoanalytic tradition have focused on the importance of exclusion to the maintenance of self-identity. In this sense the stereotype of the bad person enables us to 'split the world into good and bad objects, and the bad self, the self associated with fear and anxiety over the loss of control, is projected on to bad objects. Fear precedes the bad object, the negative stereotype, but the stereotype – simplified, distorted, and at a distance – perpetuates that fear' (Sibley 1995: 15).

Discourses of childhood and youth as 'projection screens' of adult fear

(Davis 1990) need to be considered at both these levels of explanation. Psychoanalytic discourses, themselves a product of the Victorian age, present us with a form of reflexivity – a kind of self-examination – of that era. Discourses of hierarchized difference take away power and legitimacy by denying the importance and competence of social groups to take a full part in social life and at the same time they attribute powers of danger to 'otherness'. We place ourselves in a constant state of ambiguity towards otherness, firstly by creating it to ensure our own psychic survival and secondly by fearing it, as a threat to our survival. In neither part of this tortuous equation can we honestly declare that we are taking seriously the need to understand the groups upon whom our fears are projected. This is the crucial background to understanding youth and crime.

Further reading

James and Prout (1990) is an edited volume which contains a number of interesting essays on the social construction of childhood; see in particular the piece by Hendrick. Pilcher (1995) provides a brief introduction to age and generation in social context. Jenks (1996) is a rather more complex text on childhood. It is never too soon to get acquainted with Pearson (1983) and Davis (1990), both of whom provide essential further reading for this volume. Griffin (1993) is rather difficult, but may be useful to those readers with some background in sociology or psychology. Chapter 2 of Muncie (1999, 2nd edition 2004) is useful on the emergence of a 'youth crime' problem in Britain. Stephens (1995) provides a good range of readings on children and the colonial/postcolonial world. James and Prout (1998) is a good volume on theorizing childhood: see Chapter 7 on issues in the comparative study of children and childhood. The journal *Childhood* (Sage) publishes a wide range of work within childhood studies. Young (1999) presents some key arguments on the construction of the 'other' and on general exclusionary processes from a criminological perspective, but is limited to the British and North American context: see Chapter 4 on 'Essentializing the other'.

chapter two

Problem youth meets criminology: the formative decades

Criminology meets 'problem youth': a long-term relationship
Early British criminology: causes, correlates and delinquents
Transatlantic crossings: the prewar American legacy
After the war: the youth obsession revisited
Postwar reconstruction: a cult of youth?
A merging of histories: criminology and youth in the postwar era
Critical criminologies: resolving the paradox?
Presence and absence: voices and silences
Further reading

The task for this chapter is to assess in what ways criminology and some of its associated fields of inquiry – in particular, sociology and cultural studies – have constructed 'youth' through the academe, concentrating on what we have termed the 'formative decades' of the 1920s through to the 1970s. The intention is not to provide a comprehensive overview and assessment of specific theories and studies. These are covered thoroughly in the cited textbooks and suggestions for further reading. Rather, the aim is to understand how and why 'youth' became intertwined with the study of crime to the extent that 'delinquency' and 'youth culture' as areas of knowledge production have historically dominated academic fields which might otherwise have displayed much more diversity. Did academia, in its attempts to provide a rigorous method of interrogating the social, transcend the exclusionary and mystifying practices of media and popular discourse? Or did it, albeit using a more elaborate language, reflect rather than challenge the processes we have discussed in Chapter 1? What kinds of link may be made between the unfolding of academic studies and the social contexts of their development?

Criminology meets 'problem youth': a long-term relationship

Firstly, it is necessary to make some preparatory comments about the nature of criminology as an academic enterprise. In this section we are concerned to sketch in briefly some of the conjunctions and alliances between academia and wider societal and institutional developments.

It is widely recognized that criminology is an eclectic project, rather than a 'discipline' in the strict sense of the word. Some writers would characterize it as essentially a 'raider' discipline, having no inherent philosophy of inquiry, aims or methods but, rather, drawing on a broad range of other disciplines, including law, sociology, psychology, psychiatry, forensics, statistics, geography – potentially almost any area of academic practice which seeks to make sense of human behaviour (see e.g. Cohen 1988 and Tierney 1996 for a discussion of this). Others, while acknowledging the diversity of the field, would emphasize the unifying themes in criminology – most obviously its concern with crime as an object of study, and within this its use of systematic empirical research as a starting point for understanding crime (Garland 1994). It is not our immediate intention to engage with these debates. However, it is important to understand that 'criminology' does not stand in an impartial, separate relationship to either other academic fields or to policy and practice. Its history has been one of institutional development within government agencies and academic organizations. It has been concerned in some cases principally to further understanding of the social phenomena defined as 'crime', but it has more often been harnessed to other imperatives – for example, to manage better the prison population, to inform legislation and policies governing the nature of the criminal justice system or social welfare systems, to provide a critique of existing social arrangements, to further particular political ideologies or even, the cynical may argue, to secure economic security and institutional power for criminologists (see e.g. Downes and Rock 1988; Garland 1994; Tierney 1996). Moreover, and partly because of this, we shall use the term 'criminology' loosely to include the sociology of deviance and the cultural studies of the 1970s, which have had a particularly close relationship with the criminological project (Redhead 1995: Ch. 3).

Above all, we must seek to understand something of the fortunes of academic ideas and the social conditions under which they flourish or perish.

It is with this in mind that we begin to explore the long relationship between criminology and young people. Indeed, it is hardly an exaggeration to claim that British criminology embraced young people with fervour while other areas of potential criminological inquiry lay fallow for most of the discipline's history. White-collar crime, corporate and fiscal crime, gender and crime, race and crime, and police crime could, up until the 1970s, boast only a small crop of publications compared with the vast literature on 'problem youth'. Why should this be so?

We have already seen the origins of this preoccupation in Chapter 1, the construction of childhood and youth as 'other' providing a social and cultural context for the general obsession with the young as a locus of anxiety. Small wonder that this should be reproduced in the academic and developing institutional base of criminology during the twentieth century. Griffin (1993) charts the subsequent story of academic youth research as one of 'bad boys and invisible girls' (Ch. 4), a translation of general anxiety and official concern into a *pathologizing* discourse. A historical conjunction occurred in the early decades of the century between, particularly, the growing strength of the 'human sciences' and the already existing construction of youth as a 'social barometer'. Specific conditions both in the inter-war and postwar eras can be seen to feed a relentless strengthening of criminology's focus on youth. Below, we will juxtapose the conventional 'map' of youth and crime with broader historical developments in an exploration of this focus.

Early British criminology: causes, correlates and delinquents

The first conjunction between problem youth and academia began, chronologically speaking, with the influence of biological, psychological and sociological *positivism*. These discourses, notwithstanding their differences, typically sought to explain the origins of deviant or criminal behaviour, utilizing a 'scientific' logic. The primary concern was to identify a group of 'delinquent' young people and to ascertain the dimensions along which key features of their biological make-up, psychological functioning or social environments supposedly differed from those of 'normal' young people. By identifying and measuring these differences between the normal and the abnormal, it was assumed to be possible to predict the incidence of delinquency within a given population.

Cyril Burt's *The Young Delinquent* (1925) is commonly given the dubious accolade of being a milestone in this type of study. Accounts of Burt's work may be found in Muncie (1984), Davis (1990), Griffin (1993), Garland (1994) and Tierney (1996). Burt's approach, stemming from within a medical-psychological paradigm, was to correlate individual psychological differences between 'normal' and 'pre-delinquent' or 'delinquent' schoolchildren, thereby claiming to identify the causal bases of delinquency. As Garland notes, almost everything was 'tested': 'Biometric measurement, mental testing, temperament testing, and psychoanalytical and social inquiries, together with the most up to date statistical methods . . . its findings were expansively eclectic, identifying some 170 causative factors which were in some way associated with delinquency' (1994: 53).

This must itself be seen within a broader impetus of the growth of scientism in modern western societies – everything may be controlled if only we can measure it – and an administrative concern within state bureaucracies to control deviant populations through a more effective use of policing, punishment and incarceration (Muncie 1984; Davis 1990; Garland 1994). Having its roots in positivism, Burt's study was to prove an academic inspiration because of its method of searching for causal correlates of delinquency and non-delinquency. It therefore marked a watershed because it stretched back to the scientific appropriation of youth in the late nineteenth century (see Chapter 1), and looked forward to generations of subsequent correlational studies into the late twentieth century. Hence, 'The scientific criminology which developed in Britain between the 1890s and the Second World War was thus heavily dominated by a medico-psychological approach, focused upon the individual offender and tied into a correctionalist penal-welfare policy' (Garland 1994: 53).

Young people were to constitute the hapless population upon which much of the emphasis of 'scientific criminology' and 'administrative criminology' was to come to rest. Garland notes the expansion of criminological teaching in universities from the late 1930s onwards, 'catering to the needs of the fast growing social work and probation professions' (p. 54). The title of Britain's first criminology journal, launched in 1950, was no coincidence: the *British Journal of Delinquency* (only renamed the *British Journal of Criminology* in 1960). This was the 'official organ' for the Institute for the Study and Treatment of Delinquency based at the London School of Economics. The development of academic criminology in the UK was from its inception inextricably linked with concerns to regulate and supervise the children of the poor through social work, education and the organization of juvenile justice. It was never simply a concern with 'art for art's sake', but had explicit orientations towards social control of populations seen as potentially problematic to the maintenance of social order through what has been termed in the French context the 'policing of families' (Donzelot 1980). Thus from an early stage, criminology was centrally defined by its concern with the very ill-defined concept of delinquency, and with the control of the supposed 'problem population' of the young.

Transatlantic crossings: the prewar American legacy

Meanwhile, a rather different tradition of research was developing in the USA, most significantly in the sociological writings of 'Chicago School' in the 1920s and 1930s and the work of Robert Merton in the 1930s and 1940s. These were to have an enduring legacy in relation to the subsequent development of British criminology in the postwar period (Pearson 1994; Tierney 1996).

The Chicago 'School' in fact represented a series of often diverse and disparate studies, based at the University of Chicago but also allied to numerous policy initiatives such as child guidance clinics, housing projects and early versions of social crime prevention projects (Tierney 1996: 76). The focal concerns of the Chicago School were initially with understanding the impact of rapid urban growth, economic development and multi-ethnic immigration on residential areas and cultures in the life of the city, particularly the extent to which social cohesion and community might be affected by the spatial dislocations attendant upon such changes. The School had a wide-ranging mission centring around understanding the city as a whole culture, using in particular the anthropological method. Downes and Rock summarize this eloquently: 'Chicago sociology was to become the sociology of Chicago itself, a detailed anthropological mapping of the social territories that made the city . . . an exploding mosaic of contrasting social worlds . . . Urban life resembled a phantasmagoria, a welter of shifting scenes and identities' (1988: 62).

For a number of reasons, these very diverse projects often ended up focusing on 'problem youth', a fact which was to have a far-reaching impact upon UK criminology. Firstly, the whole point of anthropological and ethnographic method was to capture the culture of the city as it was lived, using, for example, observation and life-history techniques; only then would researchers interrogate the data from the point of view of more formal or abstract theory. Ironically, however, the emphasis upon these methods narrowed down the scope of the studies and slanted them toward youthful delinquency. This was because in practice, despite the scope of the research interests – gangs, organized crime, prostitution, taxi-dance halls, real estate offices, local newspapers, the rooming house district, hobohemia, the central business district and specific ethnic groupings, are all listed by Downes and Rock (1988: 67) as foci of distinct studies – the insistence upon ethnography and life-history interviews made the study of visible cultures of the street – relatively 'undefended' cultures, as Downes and Rock put it (p. 70) – much easier than the study of the powerful and often invisible domains of the business sectors. Quite simply, it was much easier to gain access to groups of visible young people on the streets than it was to infiltrate the crime of the suites.

Secondly, there was a link between the activities of the academic researchers and the practical policy initiatives: funding provided by the policy organizations was to be directed toward the solving of social problems, seen in terms of the 'saving' of problem youth. Thirdly, the focus on an ecological approach (see Glossary) to the study of a city in flux encouraged a concern with the transmission of cultures in the 'deviance-rich' zone of transition, a transmission which was seen to occur through socialization processes among young people themselves and via the passing on of deviant cultures from older to younger age groups.

As a result, the far-reaching potential of the Chicago School's study of social change and social processes in the ecological system of the city in general – its concern with 'the human costs of capitalism' – became linked inextricably with a gaze directed at the 'deviant' responses of young people to the exigencies of urban life.

Merton (1993) provided a second avenue of American academic inquiry which was later to become a staple of British criminological textbooks, and which equally fastened upon youth. Contextually this related to an American preoccupation with the potential consequences for social democracy of blocked opportunity structures. Frustrated, lower-class young people were seen as the potential seedbed of a threat to the ideological consensus around the USA as the home of the 'American Dream', the land of opportunity for all. The evident inability of many lower-class young people to gain access to the 'avenues of success' led Merton, in a reworking of Emile Durkheim's concept of 'anomie' (Pearson 1994) to the disturbing implication that the disjunction between cultural goals and structural means rendered the land of opportunity inherently criminogenic (i.e. 'crime-producing'). Delinquency could be seen as an almost inevitable solution to the strains between the culturally desirable and the structurally attainable.

It was to be these influences which would be most strongly taken up in postwar criminology, both in the USA and in Britain, so that by 1940 the transatlantic paradigm was already predominantly constructed around 'youth', blinkering subsequent generations of academics as they sought to develop their research by engaging with what had gone before.

After the war: the youth obsession revisited

In the postwar period the American tradition continued with the study of the responses of adolescent boys to inequality, in particular utilizing the notion of delinquent subculture as 'deviant adaptation' (Cohen 1955; Cloward and Ohlin 1960; see overviews in Downes and Rock 1988; Pearson 1994; Tierney 1996; and any number of sociological textbooks). The notion of subculture, despite significant differences between studies, was used to denote the coping mechanisms adopted by lower-class young males in a social system which denied them legitimate access to the material and status rewards enjoyed by the affluent. This was not just about money, but about masculinity: 'trouble, toughness, smartness, and excitement' (Miller 1958), a creation of status and hierarchy within the gang sustained through delinquency, a kind of parody of the 'parent culture' achieved through resistance to, rebellion against, or retreat from, respectable middle-class values.

A further important resource for UK criminology was to be the critique of this genre by David Matza and Gresham Sykes (1961). Their critique related to the over-determinism of the subcultural theorists, in particular charging them with differentiating too sharply between the 'normal' and the 'deviant'. Matza in particular developed his analysis subsequently in the books *Delinquency and Drift* (1964) and *Becoming Deviant* (1969), where firstly he criticizes positivism (and therefore the notion that 'the delinquent' could be meaningfully distinguished from 'the non-delinquent') and secondly he attacks the conception of 'becoming deviant' which rests on subtle processes of the everyday interaction of the individual with other actors around them. For Matza, most delinquency was not so much a 'statement'; it was usually trivial and incidental to a broader and far less structured passage through life by young people. Young people, then, sometimes drifted into delinquency in particular contexts and under particular conditions, but their activities were not characterized by an adherence to 'delinquency' as a 'core value'. These critiques, although going some way to challenging the notion of youth subcultures as typically criminogenic, nevertheless continued to add to the intensity of academia's scrutiny of young people's lives, rendering them ever more visible and ever more defined as the object of criminology's gaze. Again, it was to be youthful delinquency which was to form the resource for the development of postwar British criminology. In order to understand fully the way in which the American studies were taken up and remodelled in the British context, it is first necessary to revisit the broader context of postwar Britain and the development of what has been termed a 'cult of youth' (Davis 1990), which provided an all too fertile soil for the ever more vigorous propagation of delinquency studies.

Postwar reconstruction: a 'cult of youth'?

A number of quite specific historical factors framed the extent to which, and the way in which, academic narratives of youth and crime from the USA were to be taken up and reworked in the UK in the 1950s and 1960s.

The process of postwar reconstruction had a number of far-reaching consequences, leading, as Davis argues, to the rise of 'youth as a category of particular sociocultural significance' (1990: 86). Davis summarizes these factors as a series of demographic, social institutional and social structural/economic changes which carried both practical and metaphorical significance (1990; see also Lury 1996: Ch. 7).

Firstly, there was a concern with the instability of wartime childhoods, seen as arising from the dislocating effects of war on young children (evacuation, disrupted education, the absence of fathers). Davis cites T.R. Fyvel's classic, *The Insecure Offender*, where it was argued that high rates of teenage delinquency in the 1950s stemmed from 'the expression of a particularly disturbed generation, a delayed effect of the war' (Fyvel 1963: 51 cited in Davis 1990: 89). Once more the barometer of the nation's health preoccupation surfaced in relation to youth. How could Britain rebuild her global position and recuperate from the ravages of war if her youth were hurtling out of control?

Secondly, this interlinked with the focus on education as a pivot of reconstruction. The Butler Education Act of 1944 was a central plank of general social reform under Beveridge, and introduced for the first time a system of universal secondary education while raising the school-leaving age to 15.

This further placed young people centre stage and institutionalized further the 'state of youth' within state control. Thus in an interview with *The Times*, Geoffrey Crowther, author of the Crowther Report of 1959 which lamented the inadequacies of secondary education, claimed that a 20-year programme of education was as necessary to reconstruction as a programme of railway modernization or the atomic generation of nuclear power (Davis 1990: 98).

This ideological focus had its parallel in the scrutiny of the youth service (see the Albermarle Report of 1960, proposing a 'ten-year plan' for reform and expansion of the youth service based on the notion that 'the problems of youth' were 'deeply seated in the soil of a disturbed modern world' – Davis 1990: 111). Similarly, Mary Morse's study of 'the unattached' concluded that young people's 'inability' to join a youth club was no more than part of 'a much wider pattern of unstable behaviour' (Morse 1965: 75 cited in Davis 1990: 112). Indeed, the Albermarle Report itself made explicit reference to 'a new climate of crime and delinquency' and 'crime in affluence' (Davis 1990: 114).

This leads to the third strand in the 'youth obsession': a preoccupation with economic changes and the implications for the adult world of young people as producers and consumers. On the 'production' side, the growth of the technological and scientific sectors of the economy led to calls for trained and technical 'manpower', perceived as lying dormant in the unrealized potential of young people. At the same time, almost full employment, despite the supposed skills shortage, helped fuel a high labour turnover that was seen as further evidence of instability among the young. These labour market factors, allied with the educational debates, produced another 'problem': that of the transition from school to work, which was then seen as in need of support, training, and – again – moral education (see Carter 1966). On the consumption side, young people were also to be highlighted. The notion of affluence in relation to young people, as noted in Chapter 3, formed one more focal point of adult unease about young people. Abrams's (1959) *The Teenage Consumer* has been termed 'the first major study of youth culture in Britain' (Willis 1990: 29). Essentially a consumer survey, this work – both at the time and subsequently – has formed an obligatory reference point in academic youth studies. Although (as Garratt 1997 correctly points out) this study focused upon the role of young people within an expanding cultural sector of the economy rather than young people as a problem, it nevertheless both reflected and provided fuel for a further separating out of youth as a distinct entity: 'young people became set apart simply by their market choices, and were defined in terms of leisure and leisure goods' (Garratt 1997: 145). By the late 1950s, soaring disposable teenage incomes provided a mass market for records, make-up, clothes and magazines, and resulted in a general explosion of popular cultural activity among young people. This inevitably sparked off a minute scrutiny of youthful lives by adults, specifically in terms of life*style*. Once more, this scrutiny produced a 'problem' of young people. Either the young were viewed by adults as passive consumers of commercialized 'pop' culture – which was construed as problematic because of its connotations of brainwashing, the unthinking adoption of the mindless hedonistic values supposedly purveyed by the sellers of pop culture – or, if young people were seen as actively constructing popular culture through their appropriation of commercial goods and services in the production of 'style', then this was disturbing because of its implications for subversiveness: a rebellion against 'establishment' (i.e. adult) notions of moral order.

Having yet again made youth stand proxy for the condition of Britain, it is hardly surprising that the impact upon academic study was profound. This was as much so in criminology and sociology as elsewhere, in fact, more so, since the growth of UK universities – itself a product of reconstructionism – bound social inquiry ever more tightly with the concerns of an expanding postwar welfare state.

A merging of histories: criminology and youth in the postwar era

Thus, as Tierney comments, 'An emphasis was placed on the social basis of various defined social problems, among which was crime . . . One striking characteristic of the sociological studies of crime carried out during the 1950s and the first half of the 1960s . . . is that they all concentrated on young people and their delinquencies' (Tierney 1996: 73). The Anglo-American academic legacy and the conditions of postwar construction in the UK produced a peculiar concern in British criminology and its associated disciplines with 'problem youth' which was to have a double axis: the enduring 'causes and correlates' school reaching back to Burt, and the emergent 'British subculturalist tradition' of the 1960s drawing upon the US studies (Pearson 1994).

While our major focus will be on the subcultural tradition, chiefly because of its huge impact on academic criminology, we must first note that despite subsequent criticisms, Burt's work was never to become quite an anachronism. Griffin (1993: Ch. 4) provides an extensive litany of comparable 'origin stories' into the 1980s. These 'updated' accounts, while utilizing more sophisticated statistical techniques, and in some cases embracing sociobiology and modern genetic theory, nevertheless still have in common with Burt the 'elision of statistical correlations with causal relationships between demographical characteristics and criminal behaviour' (Griffin 1993: 103). Similarly, Rutter and Giller (1983) provide an overview of many psychosocial correlative studies, and Farrington (1994) provides a comprehensive overview of psychosocial correlates in relation to criminal careers developing from Farrington and West's (1990) study of 'delinquent development'.

For present purposes our interest is in the methodological orientation of correlative research rather than in a detailed account of the respective merits and demerits of particular studies. Located within the search for a 'science of causes' (Tierney 1996), the concern of the studies is firmly with the key variables in the propensity to, causation of, maintenance of and desistence from, offending behaviour. It is therefore not of relevance to give a voice to the young person's own account of their lives, for the causes of delinquency are seen to lie either outside the individual – in particular in the family background and the role of the mother – or inside the individual, but out of their control – such as for example in genetic dysfunction or psychological malfunction. Such studies thus distance young people as an object of study, rather than addressing them as meaningful or rational subjects. 'The problem' is one posed *by* the young person for society and for scientific inquiry. Similarly, the definition of the 'problem' – delinquency or pre-delinquency – is not considered as in itself problematic. The question as to why particular categories of young people, or particular kinds of behaviour engaged in by young people, are *defined* as problematic (or anti-social, or criminal) in the first place is not relevant to this type of study. The conclusion by Farrington (1994: 569) is illuminating:

> As with offending and anti-social behaviour, investigations of the causes and prevention of heart disease often require . . . the identification of risk factors and developmental sequences, and randomised clinical trials to evaluate the success of methods of prevention and treatment . . . It is clear that problem children grow up in to problem adults, and that problem adults tend to produce more problem children . . .

This has led to the critique that such studies in fact contribute to the construction of youth-as-other rather than in any way providing a critique of the marginalization and scapegoating of young people in society. Griffin, indeed, terms this kind of research 'victim blaming' (1993: Ch. 4). 'Victim blaming', although an emotively charged term, does convey the sleight of hand in such research: adult researchers define 'the problem' (what is anti-social, what is 'delinquent', what is socially unacceptable), relegate young people to a zone of exclusion where they represent 'the problem', and then seek to explain why these young people stand 'outside' of society – without, of course, authenticating the voices of young people themselves.

However, it is the British subculturalist tradition, having its roots strongly in the post-Beveridge liberal desire to advance social progress through an 'understanding' of youth, which was to become the most potent force in the conjunction of criminology and youth.

Downes (1988: 177) captures succinctly the melding of postwar reconstructionist perspectives, the American tradition and the equation of criminology with youth, and is worth quoting in full:

> The appeal of American theory was that it addressed a problem, and

seemingly furnished a framework for its intellectual resolution, of the persistent rise in official crime rates despite the appearance of both greater affluence and diminishing inequality in the major Western industrial societies. Anomie theory and its subcultural variants seemed to supply the answer in terms of the frustration of rising expectations among socially disadvantaged youth ... Research in this tradition corresponded to the social-democratic reformism of the Labour Government in Britain and ... with the reformism of the Democratic Party in America ... Sociology was seen as capable of furnishing a 'vocabulary of motives' for delinquency.

It was in fact Downes's own study, *The Delinquent Solution* (1966), which formed a crucial conduit for the meeting of these histories, for as Pearson (1994: 1176–7) notes:

> It was not ... until the appearance of David Downes' 'The Delinquent Solution' ... that British sociological criminology came of age. Undertaking a thorough review and critique of the North American legacy, and interrogating it against the British experience, this work constituted both a path breaking study of the social and economic contexts of juvenile delinquency in London and a rare example of comparative criminology.

The real importance of this work, then, lay not just in its academic quality but in its crucial, catalytic role in the subsequent 'development and ratification' of the subculturalist tradition in the UK (p. 1177). In comparable vein, the British 'area studies' of the 1950s and 1960s (Downes 1988) drew upon the Chicago School in a modified sense to focus upon juvenile offending and social deprivation in urban neighbourhoods and housing areas. Consequently, 'the intersections of youthful crime, subculture, and local definitions of territory have thus been understood as central issues in both British and North American criminology' (Pearson 1994: 1177).

Thus, reviewing the field in 1988, Downes observed that from the late 1950s through to the 1970s (and including his own 1966 study in this): 'Morris began what became successive plunderings of American sources ... Britain became the offshore laboratory for the distillation of ideas fermented in the USA' (Downes 1988: 176).

The UK development of US perspectives became in effect a dual-edged sword in terms of its construction of young people. On the one hand, high quality ethnographies and carefully designed area studies brought to the discipline a previously unheard of sensitivity of analysis to the understanding of youth and crime. In particular, the according of primacy and authenticity to young people's own accounts of their activity fundamentally challenged the positivist legacy (see e.g. Parker's *View from the Boys* of 1974); young peoples' voices were to be accorded a sympathetic legitimacy. Studies of 'delinquent areas' were able to highlight the complex interactions between local cultures, housing policies and local economies in producing the criminality and the criminalization of young people. These studies challenged the simplistic notion within the 'science of causes' that the 'delinquent' could be simply differentiated from the 'non-delinquent' or that 'delinquency' itself could be seen as a simple or monolithic category (see e.g. Baldwin and Bottoms 1976; Gill 1977).

On the other hand, however, the feeding on the US subculturalist and areal traditions continued to lock many studies into a focus on young, lower-class males, and arguably closed more doors than it opened. What of adult crime? What of young women? What of the mundane rather than the spectacular? In shackling 'youth' to 'crime' in this way the academe continued to impede a fuller conceptualization of either, and ironically provided a support to the processes of 'repackaging reality' discussed in Chapter 3. Lacking an explicitly formulated critical framework as to how and why such young people come to be constructed as 'folk devils' in given social formations and in particular historical contexts, it is arguable whether such studies are part of the problem or part of the solution.

Critical criminologies: resolving the paradox?

Two institutional contexts in the study of youth crime and youth cultures were to provide a further 'transposition' (Young 1988: 163) of American ideas, this time into radical and critical criminologies through the National Deviancy Conference (NDC), formed in 1968 and based around the University of York, and the Centre for Contemporary Cultural Studies (CCCS) at the University of Birmingham in the early 1970s. Both groupings were to prove important for the way in which 'youth' was to be constructed.

As with our discussion of the reconstructionist period, an understanding of these requires historical context. This context was framed by two significant and related histories. Firstly, the 1960s saw an unprecedented expansion in the university sector, and of funding for research, particularly in sociology and criminology departments. This produced what has been dubbed the 'fortunate generation' (Downes 1988) of social science graduates who could find relatively easy access into teaching and research posts. The economic transformations of the 1950s and 1960s impacted upon higher education to produce levels of job security and academic confidence which will almost certainly prove unique. Hard to imagine from the vantage point of the late twentieth century, these decades facilitated a massive output from scholars who were themselves young and critical. Allied with this was the mood of student radicalism which produced a fusion between the politics of the left and the nature and content of academic analysis. The 'you've never had it so good' rebels of the 1950s were the new generation of academics of the 1960s and 1970s – or, one should rather say, male academics, a point to which we shall return.

This heralded the formation, firstly, of a 'breakaway' movement in

British sociology of deviance which, stemming from a sweeping dismissal of positivism, was to transform the subject area through the activities of the National Deviancy Conference (NDC). While still drawing upon the North American scholars, NDC studies (themselves constituting a diverse array of subject matters and personalities) approached things in a quite different way. The American influence in this case stemmed principally from the critical approaches of Matza and the 'labelling' perspectives of Becker and Lemert, embracing wholeheartedly a qualitative methodology which explicitly sought to accord authenticity and appreciation to the 'deviant': 'Radical criminology was the main torch carrier against reductionism. It was critical of any attempt to see the offender as a denatured, determined creature without conscious will and was insistent on granting meaning to the act of deviancy. It was, in the vernacular, *appreciative* of the deviant act' (Young 1988: 162).

'Appreciation' in this sense, however, did not simply stop at the offender's own motivations and accounts; it situated the 'meaning' of the act within the wider social relations of a class society: 'It is that part of the discipline which sees the causes of crime as being at core the class and patriarchal relations endemic to our social order and which sees fundamental changes as necessary to reduce criminality' (Young 1988: 160). (In fact, the extent to which the NDC scholars approached any sense of a critique of patriarchy is highly doubtful – this seems to be added in to Young's 1988 memoir with the benefit of hindsight, reflecting much labour in the intervening two decades on the part of feminist criminologists: again, we shall return to this issue later.)

Thus, under the banner of the NDC and the 'new criminology' (Taylor *et al.* 1973) a plethora of studies emerged which embraced a critical analysis of capitalism and emphasized ethnographic methods: 'interpretive sociology on the side of the underdog' (Downes 1988: 177). It is at this point, however, that we are brought to a halt. For, in the list of papers given at the National Deviancy Symposium between 1968 and 1973 (numbering some 69 in total: see Taylor and Taylor 1973), less than 5 specifically addressed 'youth'. Topics ranged from mental illness to con-men, transvestism to prisons, suicide to pornography, but only Phil Cohen's *Youth Subcultures in Britain* (1970 unpublished) substantially returned to the ground of young people. Laudable, of course, in the light of our criticism of criminology's obsession with youth deviance, but a clear case of babies and bathwater: precisely where a forceful critique could have been launched against the criminalization and demonization of the young in modern capitalist societies, silence reigned. It seems that criminology was still only interested in young people as problems, not as problematized.

In contrast, the CCCS was to provide a fertile meeting ground for radical cultural studies, criminology and the sociology of youth: it was to be cultural criminology (Redhead 1995) which was to effect the most fundamental transformation of the era. Drawing as heavily on European theory as on North American 'new deviancy' (Downes 1988), it was from the 'Birmingham School' that the most interesting studies of youth were to emanate. Diverse in nature, a key thread throughout the youth studies of the CCCS was an essentially celebratory stance toward youth subcultures, locating them within a critique of capitalist economic structures and ideologies.

Loosely, the starting point for these analyses may be located in Phil Cohen's paper published in the Centre's *Working Papers in Cultural Studies Two* in 1972 (reproduced as a shorter version with an introduction in Cohen 1997: Ch. 2). Utilizing a quite different – and theoretically far more sophisticated – approach to the question of youth subcultures than the former transatlantic models, Cohen argued for 'subcultures' to be seen as a complex symbolic expression of the relationship between class structure, social change and actors' meanings. Based on a study of the East End of London, Cohen charts a series of dislocations brought about by planning decisions in the reconstructionist era. Slum clearance programmes brought about the depopulation of the East End's 'traditional' communities of white working-class people to new towns and estates on the outskirts of the area, and a subsequent repopulation through an influx of West Indian and Pakistani peoples into the vacated inner residential zone. This was followed, as the implications dawned on planners (the increasing dilapidation of the central area due to the predominance of private landlords), by further attempts at redevelopment by building new high rise, high density housing on old slum sites in the inner area. What resulted, argues Cohen, was a disintegration of community through the disappearance of communal space and the disruption of kinship networks; high rises represented nothing better than 'prisons in the sky' (1997: 52): 'the working class family was thus not only isolated from the outside but also undermined from within' (p. 52). During the same period, the postwar economic growth in high technology industries, and the accompanying transformation of production techniques to large-scale, highly automated plant, substantially eroded the localized trade and craft economies formerly indigenous in the area, compounding dislocation. It was young people who were, according to Cohen, worst affected by these exigencies of capitalist development: lacking the traditional supports and sources of identity of kinship and community, and economically vulnerable and atomized in the new industries, the 'crisis' in the working-class community emerged in subcultural form among the young:

> The internal conflicts of the parent culture came to be worked out in terms of generational conflict. One of the functions of generational conflict is to decant the kinds of oedipal tensions which appear face to face in the family and to replace them by a generational specific symbolic system, so that the tension is taken out of the interpersonal context, placed in the collective context, and mediated through various stereotypes which have the function of defusing anxiety . . . *It seems to me that the latent function of subculture is this: to express*

> *and resolve, albeit 'magically', the contradictions which remain hidden
> or unresolved in the parent culture* ... Mods, parkas, skinheads,
> crombies, all represent in their different ways, an attempt to retrieve
> some of the socially cohesive elements destroyed in their parent
> culture.
>
> (Cohen 1997: 56–7, original emphasis)

Despite the difficulty (and sometimes downright strangeness – e.g. the
use of Oedipal references) of some of the language and concepts in this
work, its departure from former accounts of youth subcultures is clear
enough. It locates young people squarely as the victims of wider structural
processes in class society, and sees subcultural formations as essentially a
positive exercise in the recovery of some sense of community, rather than
as a product of 'deviant' personalities.

This orientation was further developed in a theoretical essay on 'subcultures, culture, and class' by John Clarke, Stuart Hall, Tony Jefferson
and Brian Roberts in the CCCS collection on the subject, *Resistance
through Rituals* (Hall and Jefferson 1976). This again is a definitive piece
which merits close attention for the radical way in which it constructs the
relationship between youth and culture. It is here that the theoretical influences of the 'new deviancy' interactionist and labelling perspectives are
explicitly acknowledged, except operating within a western Marxist
framework (Hall and Jefferson 1976: 5–6). This explains the importance
of the concept of hegemony within the work of the school, and is what
renders this work distinctive. For here, at last, is a clear recognition of the
ideological role which the category 'youth' had been made to play in postwar reconstruction: ' "Youth" provided the focus for official reports,
pieces of legislation, official interventions. It was signified as a social problem by the moral guardians of the society – "something we ought to do
something about". Above all, Youth played an important role as a corner-
stone in the construction of understandings, interpretations, and quasi
explanations about the period' (Hall and Jefferson 1976: 9).

In a critique of the notion of youth culture used in the postwar media
and policy discourses, Clarke (1976) reveals the ways in which the
anxieties surrounding social change in the era of reconstruction were
projected onto young people, thus positioning themselves outside the
youth obsession. Instead, they emphasize the importance of youth
subcultures as subsets of young people, 'distinctive groupings, both from
the broad patterns of working class culture as a whole, and also from the
more diffuse patterns exhibited by "ordinary" boys (and to a lesser extent,
girls)' (Hall and Jefferson 1976: 14).

These subsets were seen to occupy a position of 'double articulation':
firstly, as necessarily sharing some values of the parent culture (e.g. 'working class-ness'), and secondly, being subordinated to the dominant culture
(i.e. the dominant – hegemonic – values of class society). Dismissing the
generalized notion of youth culture as a theoretically bankrupt and

ideologically loaded one which (as we exhaustively argue in this volume) does little more than reflect the preoccupations of certain socially dominant groups of adults, their plea is for an analysis of the specific focal concerns of youth subsets ('activities, values, uses of material artefacts, territorial spaces etc. which significantly differentiate them from the wider culture': p. 14) in relation to their 'deeper social, economic, and cultural roots' (p. 16). The endeavour, then, is to 'replace the concept of "Youth Culture" with the more structural concept of "subcultures", in terms of their relation . . . to "parent cultures", and, through that, to the dominant culture, or better, to the struggle between dominant and subordinate cultures . . . we try to show how youth subcultures are related to class relations, to the division of labour and to the productive relations of the society' (Hall and Jefferson 1976: 16).

This theoretical framework, then, formed the broad context (while acknowledging numerous differences of emphasis and intra-critiques within the approach) for a series of ethnographic studies ranging from the 'cultural responses of the Teds' as a defence of 'space and status' (Jefferson 1976) to a critical analysis of young people 'doing nothing' (Corrigan 1976), reported upon in the same volume.

The distance travelled by the CCCS in relation to earlier traditions of youth research, then, is measured by:

1 the adoption of a European Marxist perspective stressing the important role of youth subcultures in the relationship between capitalist economic structures and the domination of 'ruling' ideologies legitimating and supporting these structures;
2 the concept of 'resistance' to hegemonic structures and ideologies through subcultural focal concerns: expression and style as 'resistance through rituals';
3 a detailed attention through ethnographic research to specific forms of cultural expression, rejecting generalized notions of youth culture and the generic 'youth = delinquency' equation.

Certainly, in moving determinedly from a focus on 'youth as problem', through the critique of generalized 'panics' surrounding young people as a metaphorical projection of adult anxieties under postwar reconstruction, and in the framing of class society as a problem for young people rather than vice versa, as well as in the insistence on detailed ethnography, the CCCS tradition was important. It went much further in challenging the stigmatizing, generalizing and exclusionary tendencies which had characterized many of the previous forays of criminology into 'youth' (partly, of course, by shifting the focus away from crime, as noted above).

The main problem was that in debunking one set of mystifying practices, the CCCS substituted another: the 'symbolic reading' of young people's lives, accounts and experiences in terms of their 'imaginary' relationship to relations of production has left successive generations of students somewhat agog. The 'analysis' bolted onto the ethnography resulted in statements such as: 'The Skinhead style represents an attempt to recreate through the "mob" the traditional working class community as a substitution for the real decline of the latter' (Clarke 1976: 99).

Quite clearly, it is the ethnographer who is to supply the cultural meanings. Of course, the job of the social scientist is to interpret, which means that all social research is by definition carried out at one remove (otherwise there would be no analysis, only reportage); but carried to the extent where young people's own meanings are subordinated to abstract notions of 'imaginary relations' between constructions invented by the same social scientists, any notion of actually listening to, rather than simply appropriating young people's voices recedes very quickly. Willis's *Learning to Labour* (1977), probably the most widely acclaimed study within this genre, demonstrates this problem. Despite a sensitive ethnographic study and an excellent account of the development of oppositional subcultures among schoolboys destined for the factory floor, his attempts to theorize the complex relationship between the boys' own perceptions of their culture and its structural significance leads Willis to the conclusion that they have a 'partial penetration' (recognition) of class relations which finds expression in their focal concerns ('having a laff', e.g. winding up teachers and more middle-class students).

Finally in this section I would like to focus on an important study from within critical criminology that centred on a more specific concern with the genesis, form and maintenance of moral panics about young people within an analysis of class and *race* relations, shifting attention to the criminalization of certain groups of young people under particular conditions of capitalism. Although criminalization will be discussed in detail in Chapter 3 of this volume, it is important to consider here the seminal work of Hall *et al.* (1978). Their book, *Policing the Crisis: Mugging, the State, and Law and Order*, offered a more complex and historically informed account of 'youth crime' than had previously been attempted. Crucially, it offered the first study that really paid attention to race and colonialism in considering youth and crime. Finally, youth criminology was about more than just white male delinquency. Whilst retaining the Gramscian-Marxist focus on the centrality of the capitalist state, this work also introduced careful analyses of social and political developments that both took account of colonial history and tackled the issues current to 1960's and 1970's policy contexts and the mass-mediated 'structures of feeling productive' of peculiar exclusionary impulses in relation to black urban youth. Hall *et al.*'s interpretation of the 'mugging' panic of the 1970s hinges on the notion of the 'exhaustion of consent', a crisis of hegemony for the state whereby continuing economic recession from the late 1960s onwards undermined the essential legitimacy of capitalist-state authority in postwar Britain. A renewed 'law and order' agenda was the product of this, appealing to the idea of 'England' and a universalized 'Englishness' that depended in turn on the unification of 'public consciousness' around the other-ness of young black males. Thus, although Hall *et al.* argue that there was indeed a deterioration in relations between black youth and the police, to the extent that a Select Parliamentary Committee was set up on the issue during 1971–2, the task of criminology was to examine the historical and structural conditions under which this occurred, and was exacerbated by the state response in the form of more repressive policing and more draconian laws, in complex concert with the public arena of media and opinion. A 'politics of mugging' (Hall *et al.* 1978: 39) is mooted in a passage worthy of careful attention:

> Crises can dislocate the 'normal' mechanisms of consent and sharpen the class struggle over how and where the costs of crisis management are to be borne. Crises have to be remedied . . . They also have to be controlled . . . they have to be *policed* . . . The construction of an authoritarian consensus over a wide range of social issues has already provided the platform on which, if necessary, such an initiative could be launched with public support . . . Thus, in its location, the crisis now bears down directly and brutally on the 'colony' areas and the black population . . . so the crisis of the working class is reproduced, once again, through the structural mechanisms of racism.
>
> (Hall *et al.* 1978: 341)

Put simply, the 'problem' of mugging (representing a crisis of order among poor, black, urban populations in Britain) was a crisis *waiting to happen*. It did not suddenly come into existence when an elderly man was stabbed to death in Waterloo on 15 August 1972 and the *Daily Mirror* headlined with 'As Crimes of Violence Escalate, a Word Common In The United States Enters Our Vocabulary: Mugging . . .' (Hall *et al.* 1978: 3). The subsequent racialized moral panic and repressive policing tactics is only explicable, for Hall *et al.*, through a study of the complex linkages between colonial history, state, youth, urbanization, 'Englishness', class, capital, and the processes and contradictions of the striving of the state for legitimacy and consensus under conditions of economic recession.

In the present context, what interests me most about Hall *et al.*'s work is that although it did not set out to give young people a 'voice' in the sense of the ethnographic studies of the CCCS, and despite its heavy reliance on an overarching framework of 'class struggle' and Gramscian Marxism, it represents one crucial step forward: it insisted on the *particularity* of young people's experiences in relation to the *historicity* of their construction as 'problems' with a focus on the *specificity* of their position as young black males in 1970's Britain. Despite the looming Marxist framework, enough is left of the complexities of the era for the reader to grasp some sense of what these young people might actually have been experiencing; a sense lacking, despite the ethnography, in much of the unwieldy theorizing of the *Resistance through Rituals* collection. Pitts (1993) is somewhat unfair in his dismissal of all radical criminological analysis of race as 'thereotyping'; *Policing the Crisis* (Hall *et al.* 1998) endures as perhaps the best thing the 1970s had to offer by way of understanding youth and crime as a complex, historically grounded phenomenon of structure, culture and lived experience. Nevertheless, it has to be said that the undoubted potential of radical and critical (cultural) studies for providing an authentic and appreciative voice for young people is ultimately subverted, as 'youth' are made to stand proxy for yet another series of adult longings and preoccupations with the 'class struggle', a form of generalized politicized criminology as potentially alienating as the conservative universalizing of early criminology.

Presence and absence, voices and silences

In conclusion, the lengthy engagement of academics with 'youth and crime' between the 1920s and the 1970s undoubtedly went far in providing a rigorous critique of the construction of 'youth' as 'problem' and 'other'. In approaching questions of economic inequality and cultural exclusion, a legitimizing 'voice' was accorded to the young which was consistently denied in other fields, supported by often painstaking and detailed methodological techniques. Some young people were accorded a 'presence' within criminological analyses which could never have been achieved without the critical distance available to the academe. Nevertheless, massive absences remained, and many voices continued unheard as a result of academia's own preoccupations with institutional success and academics' preoccupations with their own biographies. Beyond the discussions already engaged with in this chapter are other, fundamental absences. Most notable is the almost complete characterization of 'youth' as male (and usually white); and the almost breathtaking assumption that adult academics can – and should – appropriate young people's experiences in the pursuit of their own (subcultural?) focal concerns.

These absences will be addressed in subsequent chapters, where we examine the developing directions and concerns of youth criminology. It will be seen that 'race' and gender were problematized in youth criminology throughout the 1980s, frequently within an apparently more grounded paradigm of 'new' left realism; whilst in the 1990s an important focus on youth victimology emerged. Also in the 1990s a 'new' cultural criminology developed, which has become highly fashionable in the twenty-first century and yet still owes much (perhaps more than its proponents would like to admit) to the legacy of 1970's radical/cultural criminology. There is a long journey between the white, malecentric postwar period in understanding youth and crime and the late modern, post-industrial, and arguably post-modern, landscapes of acid house, ecstacy and 'deviant dancing' (see e.g. Redhead 1990, 1997; Thornton 1995), cybercultures, global conflicts and global markets – populated by a diversity of young people (and a concomitant diversity of exclusionary experiences); and it is a journey characterized by both continuity and disjunction.

Before embarking upon this journey, however, we turn to a consideration of the construction of 'problem youth' through the popular media and through public policy.

Further reading

Tierney (1996), Pearson (1994), and Muncie (1999, 2004) provide good accounts of the development of youth criminology. Downes (1988) also provides a useful contextualized survey of the development of criminology; and Downes and Rock (1988) is, as it claims, 'a guide to the sociology of crime and rule-breaking'. Davis (1990) is important for the postwar context. Some foray into the original 'classics' is strongly recommended: Matza (1964), Parker (1974), Hall and Jefferson (1976) and Hall *et al.* (1978) are excellent examples of their genre. Cook and Hudson (1993) is a good edited collection on racism and criminology although only part of it concerns itself with the period covered in this chapter.

chapter three

Representing problem youth: the repackaging of reality

We argued in Chapter 1 that the states of childhood and youth are socially produced categories, projection screens upon which the fears and longings of the adult world are cast, a locus of the creation of difference and the playing out of adult insecurities under modernity. We saw how the universalization of western concepts of 'childhood' and the foundations of youth as 'other' were laid and how exclusion and marginality developed during the era of colonialism and imperialism. In Chapter 2 we examined the formative role of criminology in both consolidating and challenging this history. In this chapter we explore the crucial role of media and cultural representation in the construction of problem youth. We will begin with a general consideration of the nature of the relationship between representation and society, followed by a specific consideration of different strands of the packaging and repackaging of problem youth. Finally we will address the question of whether children and young people have any hope of media representation which is not dominated by the problem youth paradigm, and the role which young people are being made to play in the media in the twenty-first century.

Messengers, messages: the power of word and image

If childhood and youth are social categories, then, as we have seen, they are discursively framed. That is to say, our understandings of those categories are always refracted through the prism of public knowledge about them. In the Victorian era this may have been paintings, printed literature, newspapers, poetry, novels and so forth. From the nineteenth century onwards – coterminous with the growth of discourses of 'risky' and 'at risk' childhood and youth – the growth of the media was inextricably tied up with fears of 'troublesome populations', of the 'urban mass', and with urban myths of violent and sexual crime. Thus 'the media were at once the primary producers of crime news and crime narratives . . . and the chief mourners of the supposed ill effects of popular culture on public morality. Hence the media won both ways; both selling fear, and lamenting it' (Brown 2003: 26). The rapid pace of urban change, the fear of the unruly mass, the growth of the population and its concentration in the cities and in factories, the 'chic by jowl' effect of the affluent middle classes crushed in the urban sprawl with the mass of the poor everywhere around, produced the *embeddedness* of crime as a theme in popular discourse (Sparks 1992). It also produced the notion of moral contagion explicated so well by Pearson (1985).

Publicly produced 'versions' of childhood and youth have therefore long been at the heart of public perceptions about the 'youth problem'. With the advent of 'saturation media' in the twentieth century, public discourse became an even more universalized source of understanding. We should be careful here to note that this is not simply a question of the influence or impact of media representations upon our opinions or beliefs, but rather a broader and deeper question about the relationship between representation and reality in modern societies; about how our ways of knowing about or making sense of the world around us can never be derived simply from direct experience. This state of 'mediated being' is further contingent upon that most modern of transformations: the globalization of electronic media. Giddens points out that while the advent of printing was one of the main influences on the rise of the early modern state,

> when we look to the origins of high modernity it is the increasingly intertwined development of mass printed media and electronic communication that is important . . . the visual images [of] television, films, and videos . . . like newspapers, magazines, and printed materials of other sorts . . . are as much an expression of the disembedding, globalising tendencies of modernity as they are the instruments of such tendencies.
>
> (Giddens 1991: 25–6)

In other words, there exists a complex reciprocal relationship between media and society which cannot be distilled into a simple cause-effect dichotomy. Our very identities, our senses of ourselves and who we are, even who we might or should become, are constantly refracted through media images. This leads to the problem of ever accessing unmediated 'reality' *out there* somewhere, for in modernism, *out there* is always *in here* (Giddens 1991: 27). Distant events on the other side of the world are instantaneously in our living rooms; the internet scatters its rainshower of websites across the globe; we may sit in electronic chat rooms and discuss the latest atrocity. This was most dramatically and startlingly seen in the images of the destruction of the World Trade Center on 11 September 2001, which were instantaneously harnessed by politicians and the global media as the universal icons of 'terror' in the western world.

Thus words and images in the public domain are dissolving many of the distinctions between our private subjectivities (our internal selves) and objectivities (or external realities); a kind of media version of the statement that 'you are what you eat'! Some theorists would even go so far as to say that we are engaged in a transition to a state of being where there is no longer much distinction to be made between the virtual and the real, the fictive and the documentary (Kidd-Hewitt and Osborne 1995; Brown 2003: Ch. 2). A vision of constant 'inter-textuality' is invoked, whereby fiction becomes embedded in 'factual' television programmes (e.g. *Crime-watch UK*) through dramatic conventions such as crime reconstructions. Then, with the widespread distribution of images of *cause célèbre* trials via satellite TV and the internet, real trials become mass drama and instant-aneously fuel public, policy and political debate. As dozens of satellite vans park outside the courtrooms, the electronic landscapes (Morley and Robins 1995) of the internet blaze with furious debate of every possible kind (see Ferrell 1996; Greek 1996; Hunt 1999 on the 1995 O.J. Simpson trial) and the coverage of the trials subsequently affects the 'real' legal process. This is what Nichols (1994) has called the question of 'blurred boundaries', where the almost implosive relation between media por-trayals and reality obscures real events, or indeed almost dissolves them, into the mediascape. There is also of course the now-ubiquitous reality TV, whose editors determine to forge dramas out of the most mundane of events, including crime no matter how petty (e.g. *Traffic Cops*, *Rail Cops*, *Police, Camera, Action* and so on ad nauseam). Brutality is catered for too, in 'harder' reality/documentaries such as *Anatomy of a Crime*. Meanwhile the entertainment value (e.g. the macabre, the voyeuristic, the violence) of human suffering infuses the movie genre, while the movie genre infuses the presentation of news (Kidd-Hewitt and Osborne 1995; Brown 2003: Ch. 2). In this constant blurring of boundaries, the misconception that the representation of childhood and youth could ever have been a simple reflection of the 'real' is finally laid to rest (Jenks 1996).

If taken crudely, these kinds of approaches to the importance of the media could of course end up by implying that the mass of individual human actors are little more than zombie-like creations of global totalitar-ian forces, a kind of orientation for which much earlier writings on culture and media were correctly criticized (Inglis 1993; Brown 2003). They could also be misinterpreted as giving credence to the 'video nasties cause children to murder' species of moral panic with which we are all now so familiar, and which we shall be discussing further (Barker and Petley 1997; Critcher 2003). The key to avoiding such misinterpretations lies in the notion of reciprocity; for no media representation is passively received by a mere audience. Whether reading, listening, watching or typing at a keyboard, we are engaged in activity. Consumption is *active* by definition. It requires choice (to take part), interpretation (to create an understanding from the word, image etc.), comprehension (to produce an overall pattern of understandings from the interpretative process) and so on. We may be what we eat, but we do not eat, taste or enjoy without the cultural and subjective meanings which we place upon eating. In turn, of course, the words-images so consumed further add to our bank of meanings with which we confront the next word-image . . . and so on. Moreover, in an era of interactive technologies from digital TV to the internet, there is no longer an unquestioned division between who 'produces' and who 'consumes' mediated images. You are invited to vote on any number of news items in 'media referenda' by text, phone or email, from whether Tony Blair should have authorized the UK involvement in Iraq to whether athlete Paula Radcliffe should or should not have dropped out of a race in the Olympic Games of 2004! Crime-related 'vote-ins' have included everything from opinions on curfew orders for young people to whether 'life should mean life'. So, then, internet debates rage incessantly across the wired landscape on every conceivable topic. I have written extensively on this elsewhere (Brown 2003); suffice it to say here that some notion of 'mediatization' is required that encapsulates this reciprocity and recognizes its relationship to 'the pains of modernity'.

This is a complex debate, and we cannot hope to cover it here; but essentially what is required in the present context is an understanding of the representation of childhood and youth that includes an inquiry into the kinds of reciprocities involved between the media and society. These are both questions of *why* and *how*. Why is it that certain representations are popular, powerful, influential? From where do they gain their popular power? Why are certain types of content and images selected over and above others? Why are certain kinds of representation 'fashionable' at any given time? And how do these things happen; by what social, cultural and technological processes?

Because of the extent of change in the cultural and media landscape since the original moral panics of the 1960s, and the constant evolution of what a panic may usefully mean, such questions also need to be considered in their historical context. In this sense, we reflect both sociocultural change and changes in criminologies. The following sections will thus discuss the packaging, repackaging, and re-repackaging of youth in relation to such changes. Nevertheless, we also need to keep in mind the continuities. Although the wired world of the 2000s may seem (and in some senses is) incomparable to the quaint black and white footage of the 1960s, fundamental issues also remain the same. By the same token, 'vintage' theories and research remain important. The following sections therefore present the material in the form of epochs (a dangerously false distinction!).

Moral panics and problem youth: the study of media representations from the 1960s to the 1980s

News stories and young people have rarely made happy reading since the advent of print media. As Pearson (1983) has chronicled, the news media have consistently given a high profile to the detrimental effects of popular culture on the decline of young people's – and thereby the nation's – moral fibre. Mass media, from its inception, have been closely associated with mass anxiety about young people (Förnas and Bolin 1995). However, the emergence of the notion of 'moral panics' as a way of conceiving of the relationship between the media and young people was to prove an analytical watershed. We shall explore these earlier studies before considering how children and young people are 'repackaged' in contemporary media.

The now famous (or infamous) term 'moral panic' emerged as a key concept in the sociology of deviance in the 1960s, and has since been much appropriated, and some would say, misappropriated, until it has become a part of everyday language. In its original formulation, presented in Stanley Cohen's *Folk Devils and Moral Panics: The Creation of the Mods and Rockers* (1973), 'moral panic' was used to characterize a specific phenomenon in the context of a specific study.

Cohen chronicled a particular set of events – disturbances between groups of youths over a bank holiday weekend in small seaside towns in the South and South-east of England in 1964 – from his own research. He then juxtaposed these alongside the news media's representations of the events. The first point to emerge from this was the discrepancy between the two types of account.

The news media characterized the events in terms of clashes between rival gangs of mods and rockers, seen as scooter and motorbike gangs respectively; the 'gangs' were described as deliberately terrorizing local residents and 'innocent' holidaymakers, as wreaking mass havoc and destruction (particularly arson), causing other serious criminal damage, and carrying out assaults using weapons. The disturbances were presented by the media as being a result of unfettered, undisciplined young people with too much time and money, corrupted by popular music and the values of consumption (see e.g. Abrams 1959).

By contrast, Cohen found that in the original disturbances, the conflicts were largely based on regional rivalries rather than identities of mods and rockers; most of the young people involved were unskilled and semi-skilled workers and not particularly affluent; most did not own scooters or motorbikes; and serious criminal damage and violence were on a considerably smaller scale than the news media claimed. What started out as a fairly modest piece of sociology became obligatory reading in academic circles because of its description of a deviancy amplification spiral which news coverage set in motion. In this process the media characterization of events was seen to arouse public concern on a mass level about the threat of violent young gangs of affluent teenagers threatening the very fabric of society. Not only the misrepresentation of 'facts' is at issue here, but the language and imagery deployed: 'There was Dad asleep in a deckchair and Mum making sandcastles with the children, when the 1964 boys took over the beaches at Margate and Brighton yesterday and smeared the traditional postcard scene with blood and violence' (*Daily Express* 19 May 1964 cited in Cohen 1973: 127).

The public perception thus took hold that the 'mods 'n' rockers' subculture did indeed exist, was growing in strength, and 'something must be done about it'. The result was increased police surveillance and arrests, perceptions by the courts dealing with cases that they were facing a 'new' threat, which then appeared to confirm the 'accuracy' of the initial media prophecies. Along the way this also created an identity which young people in some cases began to ascribe to themselves, leading to more incidents which would be classed under the same heading, leading to more reaction . . . and so on. Thus a 'moral panic' arises (see Cohen 1973; also many accounts of his work in e.g. Muncie 1984; Förnas and Bolin 1995; Kidd-Hewitt and Osborne 1995; Muncie and McLaughlin 1996).

From Cohen's perspective, then, 'news' representations neither simply reflect reality nor simply invent it, but are produced through a complex set of social relationships between the general public, institutions of social control such as the police and the courts, and young people themselves. Certain groups in society, at certain times, become the scapegoats of wider social pressures. Cohen terms these groups – in this case young people dubbed as mods 'n' rockers – folk devils. This is designed to invoke parallels with the demonization of certain groups and individuals who become symbols of society's ills. Hence, for example:

> For years now we've been leaning over backwards to accommodate the teenagers. Accepting meekly on the radio and television it is THEIR music which monopolizes the air: That in shops it is THEIR fads which will dictate our dress styles . . . we have watched them patiently through the wilder excesses of their ban the bomb marches. Smiled indulgently as they've wrecked our cinemas during their rock and roll films . . . But when they start dragging elderly women around the street . . .
> (*Glasgow Sunday Mail* 24 May 1964 cited in Cohen 1973: 59)

Cohen (p. 60) also reports an interview by the Margate MP: 'It spreads like a disease. If we want to be able to stop it . . . we must immediately get rid of the bad children so that they cannot infest the good.'

The broader question must then of course be why particular panics arise at particular times, and why certain groups are focused upon as the folk devils of society. This requires us to go somewhat further than Cohen's account, since although Cohen provided some analysis of the deeper social origins of moral panic, he was basing it on one type of case study and was rather more concerned to chart and describe the process than to explain it fully.

Through the 1970s, further key analyses were produced within the 'new deviancy' tradition (Tierney 1996) which in various ways developed ideas contained within Cohen's work. Young (1974) identified an 'institutionalized need' within the media to create moral panics to 'create good copy' (discussed in Muncie and McLaughlin 1996). Young's by now much-quoted formulation that 'newspapers select events which are atypical, present them in a stereotypical fashion and contrast them against a background of normality which is overtypical' (1974: 241) led to a focus on the structures and interests of news media organizations. Chibnall's (1977) *Law and Order News* went further by producing a typology of the news media's handling of violent crime in the form of 'news values'. The professional cultures of journalists were seen as involving informal 'rules of relevancy', around which 'news values' are built, which in turn influence the selection (of what facts or events to include and exclude) and presentation (the language, imagery, layout etc.) of news stories. Thus Chibnall's original 'rules of relevancy' highlighted the importance placed by journalists, in the context of violent crime, on visible and spectacular acts, sexual and political connotations, graphic presentation, individual pathology, and deterrence and repression. The main point for the present discussion is that Cohen, Young and Chibnall all produced work which was of crucial importance, both in undermining the notion that the news media reflected reality and in building understandings of the kinds of social imperatives which resulted in the selection of working-class young men in particular as the focus of moral panics. These works were subsequently drawn upon in Hall *et al.*'s (1978) *Policing the Crisis*. This, however was a far more wide-ranging work, as discussed in detail in Chapter 2 of this volume. It is also a very significant 'moral panic' analysis of youth, media representation and crime in that it situated the media repackaging of 'youth as problem' firmly within a systematic, complex analysis of representation and the ideological, political and economic structures of a modern society in crisis. We shall consider this in some detail.

Emanating from the CCCS at the University of Birmingham, the authors begin with an account of the way in which the term 'mugging' suddenly, and apparently randomly, emerged in British culture to describe street robbery: a form of crime which has a history spanning centuries. They relate the robbery of an elderly widower by three young men in August 1972 which culminated in the victim being stabbed to death. Based on the phraseology used by a police officer that it was a 'mugging gone wrong', the press precipitated to fame a term which was, in fact, imported from America. However, along with the importation of the term came the importation of its connotations. Britain became seen as under siege from the 'American pattern of urban violence'. Jill Knight, MP, is quoted from the *Birmingham Evening Mail* of 20 March 1973 as saying: 'I have seen what happens in America where muggings are rife . . . It is so absolutely horrifying to know that in all the big American cities, coast to coast, there are areas where people dare not go after dark. I am extremely anxious that such a situation should never come to Britain' (cited in Hall *et al.* 1978: 26).

Hall *et al.*'s point here is that 'mugging' does not simply imply the crime but a whole series of images about the kind of society we are living in, imported from America but applied in the British context (p. 28). Following the initial event (the stabbing), as with Cohen's mods 'n' rockers, both the media and the control agencies seized upon 'mugging' as a new phenomenon. In fact, of course, street robbery had been an endemic aspect of crime in Britain (Pearson 1983). In accordance with Cohen's mode of analysis, Hall *et al.* placed the media account of 'mugging' next to a different kind of account – this time using statistics on street robbery. They concluded that 'mugging was out of all proportion to the actual level of threat', and therefore the moral panic must have arisen out of a perceived or symbolic threat. As with Cohen's study, the media characterization of the phenomenon produced higher levels of public awareness and alarm, and fostered an increasing level of punitive and authoritarian responses from the police and the judiciary, which in turn produced apparently higher levels and seriousness of street crime, which in turn escalated media and public attention . . . Thus far, the argument is familiar. Here, however, Hall *et al.* take a distinctively different turn. While Cohen's account is in some senses compatible with the argument that 'The key role of the media cannot be treated in isolation . . . it can only be analysed together with those other collective agencies in the "mugging" drama – the central control of apparatus in the state: the police and the courts' (Hall *et al.* 1978: 30), *Policing the Crisis* parts company with Cohen's interpretation. It substitutes an account which places the police and the courts, the 'apparatuses' of the state, in a far more crucial position. The strength of the media panic, they argue, could only have had the force it did in a social context of a backlash by an authoritarian state against the liberalizing influences of the 1960s: 'The factor which seems of greatest importance in shaping the "judicial attitude" in this period is anxiety about growing "social permissiveness" . . . there was undoubtedly a feeling . . . that the erosion of moral constraints . . . would in the end precipitate a weakening in the authority of the Law itself' (Hall *et al.* 1978: 34).

In particular, the moral panic surrounding mugging made young black males its 'folk devils', and this again was seen as no accident. Youth, as we have seen, is the recurrent focus of social anxiety in modernity; exacerbated in this case because the 1960s had seen inroads into the liberalization of the juvenile justice system. Thus the Children and Young Persons Act (CYPA) of 1969 proposed to decriminalize juvenile crime almost entirely.

That the CYPA was never fully implemented was itself a reflection of the 'moral backlash' which was to characterize the 1970s (see Pitts 1988, 1995, also Chapter 4 in this volume). 'Youth', again, landed squarely in a tussle over the moral fabric of society, with the police, the judiciary, the politicians and the media carving up the delinquent body in their attempts to recoup a perceived loss of authority in the 1960s. The 'new' ingredient, however, was the focus on black youth. Hall *et al.* placed this in the context of heightened racial tension in this period: worsening police – black relations, the growth of Powellism, the growth of the National Front and increasing restrictions on immigration.

However, neither the 'youth' nor the 'black' issues are characterized by the authors simply as a backlash. Rather the backlash was seen to arise from the place of the police and the judiciary as central institutions of the state in a capitalist socioeconomic formation experiencing the beginnings of a period of economic instability. The vision of the world presented by Harold Wilson in the early 1960s had been, as Pitts observes (1988: 3), a vision in which the 'white heat of the technological revolution' would 'eradicate poverty and iron out social inequality', and in which, with the expansion of educational opportunity and an enlarged welfare state, full employment would be secured. But by 1970 poverty had been rediscovered, industrial unrest had taken hold as traditional manufacturing industries declined in the international markets, and powerful shop steward actions in the relatively strong motor industries threatened industrial relations. Sterling was weak, inflation was rising and so was unemployment. A Conservative government was elected under Edward Heath.

It is these developments which Hall *et al.* present as the crucial backdrop to the resurgence of authoritarianism and the scapegoating of black youth, producing, as they did, 'deep structured paradigms about crime in our society', 'English ideologies of crime' (1978: 138) which drew upon the unifying hegemonic ideology of nation. In this context, the moral panic of mugging was able to draw upon the longstanding structures of feeling surrounding youth and nation described in Chapter 1. Once again, young people become the locus of anxiety, this time deflecting attention as the government presided over a crumbling economic infrastructure in which the consensus politics of welfarism were already under threat, if not yet siege.

One need not accept the Marxist analytical framework used in *Policing the Crisis* to appreciate its contribution to an understanding of the framing of 'problem youth'.

Hall *et al.*'s. study expanded the scope of 'moral panic' analysis, not only because it explicitly linked the representation of 'problem youth' to a broader analysis of the social relations of a declining capitalist imperial nation and to the structures of the state, but also because it depicted an important shift in the representation of 'problem youth' more generally. This shift may be characterized as one from 'discrete' moral panics to 'generalized' moral panics. Unlike the specific focus on a single, identifiable 'folk devil', such as the teddy boy, or the mods and rockers, the Hall *et al.* treatment of the mugging panic demonstrated how the image of problem youth was locked by the media into a generalized 'climate of hostility to "marginal" groups and racial minorities' (Muncie 1987; Muncie and McLaughlin 1996). Moreover as Critcher (2003) points out, in the Hall *et al.* model, agents of the state or 'official agencies' were not seen as just reacting to the media process, but as precipitating it. In Critcher's summary this means that the label did not *follow* the emergence of 'muggers' as folk devils but rather *preceded* it, because it was a police officer who first coined the American term – in relation to *already* heightened activity by police against black youth crime and black young people in general; and this itself was a product of an *already existing* deterioration in relations between young black people and the police (Critcher 2003: 15), all *before* the media entered the fray. In this 'signification spiral', hegemony is at the centre because it is the legitimation of the state in crisis that is the core issue. The media process is seen as one aspect of the whole, imbricated within the complex of class-state-race struggles. Whereas Cohen's model is concerned with the specificities of 'panic', Hall *et al.* are concerned with the production of hegemony, wherein 'moral panic' sits as one strand (Critcher 2003: 16).

This elasticity of the concept of moral panic has led to the accusation that it is not a useful concept to characterize the mode of 'repackaging reality', that it 'lacks a precise theoretical grounding' (Muncie 1987). At the same time Hall *et al.*'s contribution has been critiqued for *over*-theorizing the term and thus losing the vital specificity of Cohen's more detailed processual model (Critcher 2003). What may rather be the case for our present purpose is that the media representation of 'problem youth', reflecting the uneven processes of historical development, varies historically in its nature and extent. As such, any 'model' must be flexible to acknowledge changing social conditions. Given the complexity of the world, a little lack of precision may well be a good thing.

The 1980s is an interesting decade in this respect. After the success of the Conservatives in securing a landslide victory under Margaret Thatcher (largely on the 'law and order' ticket) in 1979, the beginning of the decade saw ever more deteriorating relations between black urban communities and the police. The 'hegemonic crisis' it seemed, was deepening. Indeed, much of the decade can be read as a struggle to maintain public legitimation for worsening economic and social conditions, in which the media played a crucial part. Significant episodes of urban unrest occurred in 1980 (Bristol) and 1981 (Toxteth, Brixton), attracting the sobriquet 'riots' in the press, which presented a looming image of the American ghetto arriving in England (Crowther 2000). Here, responses to the 'riots' were directed to the breakdown of social discipline in general, toward a racialized notion of lawlessness in particular and in more liberal circles toward a breakdown in police race relations in the inner cities, as evidenced in the Scarman Report of 1981. Lord Scarman's report, the result of an inquiry into the Brixton disorders, focused on the deterioration of police-community relations, notably through saturation 'hard line' policing exemplified by the Special Control Group which in 1981 conducted an operation known as 'Swamp 81' to operate blanket surveillance in Brixton, stopping and arresting any supposedly 'suspicious' persons on the streets and removing them for inter-rogation (possible under the Vagrancy Act of 1824, showing that 'sus' laws have a long history!). Thus despite the politicians' condemnation of young people involved in urban unrest as 'riff raff' spreading a disease of moral degeneration (Beynon and Solomos 1987), and the endorsement by the tabloid press of these pronouncements (Beynon and Solomos 1987), the concern at this time was rather with urban disorder, the disenfranchise-ment of racial minorities in the deteriorating inner cities, and policing, than with youth *per se*. Caution again is needed however. For example, the *Observer* newspaper produced a 'Race in Britain' special report on Sunday 19 April 1981 emblazoned with *The Observer* leader view: 'We cannot afford to let British citizens conclude that riots are the only hope of improving their lives,' and presented a picture of generalized breakdown of relations between black 'communities' and the police. It also linked those events explicitly with race discrimination in general, especially in relation to employment (http://observer.guardian.co.rac/story/0,11255,603735,00.html). This illustrates the broadening out of the issue of 'riots' toward more general concerns. The TV news coverage however, placed emphasis on the activities of black *youths* (http://news.bbc.co.uk/onthisday/hi/stories/april/11/newsid_25230000/2523907.stm), who were located at the hub of 'flashpoints' in contemporary chronologies of events 'which turned part of London into a battleground of burning buildings and looted shops' (http://www.urban75.org/brixton/history/riot1.html). The importance of this is that whilst the 'youth panic' may temporarily have receded in the face of more widely cast anxieties, the iconic figures of (angry) black young males remained locked implacably in public images of social uprising. It seems this concern with the rioting body of the black (young) would not go away.

More complexity: at the same time the 1980s saw on one level a relative *diminution* in interest in the 'youth problem' in relation to white males. On one side of the monetarist coin was the 'black youth in the ghetto' figure; but the coin had another side, the 'get rich quick city kid'. This was the era of the 'yuppies' (young urban professionals). Greed was good: so one sec-tion of the population benefited from the temporary property boom ori-ginating in the South of England and based on the bubble of financial deregulation. The deregulation of the market opened up opportunities for quick fortunes to be made. 'Problem youth' in the media vied with images of 'kids in the City', the dog-eat-dog world of the 20-something barrow-boy-turned-share dealer, ambitious young Conservatives hungry for power. This was echoed at the level of popular culture: rather than the cult films of rebellious, anarchistic youth such as depicted in Derek Jarman's epochal

Jubilee (1978), we see an emphasis on slick Hollywood productions following the lives of rich college kids or the traumas of urban go-getters such as Jamie (Michael J. Fox) in *Bright Lights, Big City* (1988, based on the 1984 novel by Jay McInerney). If popular imagery were to be believed, rebellion had been replaced by consumption, 'punk' by the 'new romantics'. Was this the death of the moral panic around problem youth?

Not so. For seething underneath the veneer of affluence and ambition was monetarism's other face: a much deeper crisis waiting to happen, bigger and wider than the unrest of the 1980/1 disorders. By 1982 unemployment had already reached 3 million – an unprecedented level in the postwar era – and had been increasing dramatically. For, while financial deregulation may have produced an illusion of affluence, the manufacturing infrastructure had of course been rapidly disintegrating. While the yuppies of the South of England babbled hectically into their mobile phones, the tracts of the urban North were populated by young people who were to be the first cohort of post-Beveridge long-term unemployed. Nor were the middle classes exempt: graduate unemployment reached a high in 1982 unrivalled until the 1990s. By the mid-1980s Thatcherite government policy had firmly embraced the rhetoric of the 'skills gap' among our youth, and a 'victim-blaming' culture once again emerged which depicted surging youth unemployment as a crisis 'of' rather than 'for' young people. This was the birth of the 'training scheme' panacea with which the New Right sought to deflect attention from the deep and serious economic decline which had settled in for a long visit. Hence, as Griffin (1993: 67) argues, many academic representations of youth unemployment in the 1980s 'were marked by a combination of moral panic and paternalistic concern, and constructed mainly through the language of crisis. This reached a crescendo by the middle of the decade ... much of the debate centred around rising official unemployment levels and speculations about whether youth unemployment represented a cause or a symptom of this "crisis" ' (Griffin 1993: 67).

Endemic unemployment and its disquiets must be explained. The notion of a racialized 'underclass' emerged, connecting media, academic and official discourse (Crowther 2000). This was in its rightist version essentially a theory from the ghetto: that there was emerging a flotsam and jetsam stratum who inhabited poor inner-city areas and areas of public housing, whose unemployment and criminality was a consequence as much of their own culture (promiscuity, family breakdown, poor attitudes to work and discipline, antipathy to law and order) as of structural economic conditions or politicians' actions – another import from the USA. The notion was 'racialized' largely because of the stereotyping of black family life as pathologically disorganized and 'matrifocal' (Crowther 2000).

Current in the UK from the mid-1980s onwards (although it had been used in the USA for decades), it was Charles Murray in *The Emerging British Underclass* (1990) who made the term famous in the UK. (Young) single, unmarried mothers were the root cause of the problem according to Murray, producing a generation of fatherless and rootless children. This led to indiscipline, a breakdown in morals, fecklessness and exclusion from the labour market – and a concomitant rise in (youth) crime. Children and young people were once more at the centre of lawlessness; perhaps even more so than in the nineteenth century, for they were being held responsible for the decline of the social fabric *in general*, even for structural disintegrations of the economy. The interaction of this mediated crisis with crime policy was interesting, and will be discussed further in Chapter 4.

At the turn of the decade the British media were once more poised for a fully-fledged apoplexy surrounding youth. Something else again was about to happen to the 'moral panic'. The panic was speeding up, and it was spreading. We turn now to examine this transformation in more detail.

A total panic? The media and young people in the 1990s

The history of panic in the 1990s may be characterized less as the 'generalized' panic described by Hall *et al.* (1978) and more as a 'total' panic: a series of discourses of fear reaching out to almost every aspect of the lives of young people, at the same time expanding the catchment age of 'problem youth' downwards to encompass ever younger age groups. There are several distinct 'stories' within this history which it would be wrong to attempt to synthesize overly into a deterministic 'model' of panic. We should be quite clear also that we are in no sense attempting to utilize Cohen's phrase in the sense in which he originally coined it. We continue to use the term 'panic' to suggest the continuity in the demonization of youth under modernism, not to retain its specific sociological application. In suggesting that the 1990s have seen the emergence of a 'total' panic surrounding youth, then, we are seeking to sketch out some general tendencies in the diffusion of fear which may prove to have profound consequences for the understanding of 'youth as problem'.

First came a resurgence of specific narratives of fear in the form of urban unrest. The 1990s 'riots' appeared to 'erupt' in Cardiff and Oxford at the beginning of September 1991. In the first case, the trigger of this narrative seemed to be an attempt by angry crowds to force out a Pakistani shopkeeper after he won a court injunction to stop the shop next door selling bread. The *Wales on Sunday* reported that 'more than one hundred police in riot gear fought to control a mob', and 74 arrests were made (cited in Campbell 1993). In the second case, following police attempts to control 'joyriding' (riding around in stolen cars) and 'hotting' (competitive driving displays in stolen cars) among young men, a cordon was thrown around the area, clashes ensued, and 83 arrests were made (Campbell 1993).

Days later, Dale Robson, aged 17, and Colin Atkins, aged 21, died in a stolen car at the end of a 125 m.p.h police chase on the Meadow Well

Estate in Tyne and Wear. The deaths provoked anger among other young people on the estate, some of whom in one notable statement painted: 'POLICE ARE MURDER'S DALE 'N' COLIN WE WONT LET'THEM GET AWAY' (*sic*) on the wall of a community centre. This event, following a build-up of tension in the preceding weeks as police had moved onto the estate to investigate a series of 'ram raids' (a form of burglary on wheels where thieves drive into stores or warehouses through windows or doors), was to form the focus for a media bonanza.

'Violent night shocks "the Bronx" ' (*Independent* 11 September 1991) was one headline, apparently referring to a local nickname for the area. The subsequent disturbances – or 'riots' – resulted in the burning out of the community centre, smashing of shop windows and more arson. Days later, more disturbances took place in the Elswick district, eight miles away. 'Flames of Meadow Well riot spread around the Tyne' declared the *Guardian* (12 September 1991), and 'Youths take to streets in new out-break of rioting': 'A jeering mob of up to 300 strong set fire to a derelict pub in the Elswick district. Youths performed handbrake turns on cars in front of a crowd outside the blazing building . . . Two fire engines were forced to withdraw after being severely damaged by missiles' (*Guardian* 12 September 1991).

It was the Newcastle incidents, with their strong visual imagery of macho young men, spectacular displays of stunt driving, burning buildings and rampant lawlessness (even the fire engines were 'stoned'), which were really captured by the media to frame a narrative of despondent, aggressive, lawless young men in a *fin de siècle* crisis careering inexorably to the destruction of urban society. Almost any disturbance, small or large, through 1991 to 1993, was to become a 'Meadow Well'-style riot. The regional newspapers, not to be outdone, carved out their share of the 'riot culture'. 'Anarchy on the estates' proclaimed the *Northern Echo* (25 October 1993), providing a map of the North East showing map-pin type fireflashes and with the anarchist logo superimposed. To the right of the graphic, a mini-chronology of 'riot history' in the region is shown, beginning with Meadow Well, and followed by:

28 February 1992: police stoned by youths in South Shields
27 August 1992: disturbances on Blue Hall Estate in Stockton
25 May 1993: youths riot on the Sherburn Estate in South Durham
14 July 1993: police car stoned on the Edenhill Estate in Peterlee
31 July 1993: large brawl in Ferryhill market-place
4 September 1993: Ragworth Estate sealed off when car is set on fire
24 October 1993: vandals throw stones at houses and fires started on the Skerne Park Estate in Darlington

In true 'moral panic' genre, the application of the term 'riot' extends to cover every incident or disturbance suspected of involving young people. Urgent measures are called for, from policies to tackle unemployment, to more youth clubs, to harsher penalties. Indeed, a twin-track mentality inhabits the media throughout the coverage during this period, on the one hand claiming that starving the estates of money and long-term unemployment produces 'the problem', on the other denouncing the actions of the 'rioters' and calling for harsher penalties and a remoralizing of Britain. What the 'riots' left behind them, however, was a longer lasting media legacy: the spectre of disillusioned urban youth with no foreseeable end beyond the shattering of the social fabric. Visually, the photographs accompanying newspaper articles and the footage on television news on almost any aspect of 'youth' (crime, drugs, alcohol, unemployment . . .) are characterized by tracts of urban wasteland, de-industrialized landscapes, with groups of aimless boys in baggy jeans and hooded tops in the foreground; or run-down council estates, graffiti ridden, with burned-out cars and again the obligatory aimless boys.

Within these sorry tales of lost generations high on music and drugs or abandoned to mindless urban wrecking, portrayals of macho subcultures rise and bubble for a while: panics within panics. 'Joyriding' took pride of place. The crusading journalist cum self-styled sociologist Bea Campbell clamped the 'macho car culture' onto urban unrest as if it were part and parcel of the same phenomenon (Campbell 1993). 'The macho men who wreck lives' declared Campbell in the *Northern Echo*, referring to her book *Goliath* (1993). In fact, TWOCCing (taking without the owner's consent) and its predecessor TDA (taking and driving away) have a history as long as the motor car, and TDA is referred to as a popular pastime among the teenage boys in Wilmott's classic *Adolescent Boys of East London* (1966). TDA was still common in the 1970s, and when this author first researched in the North East in 1985, TWOCCing was popular enough to have street 'raps' composed about it. Campbell's inventive if inaccurate 'theorizing' of the youth crime problem provides a typical example of the dangers of creating categories and pouring people into them. In the 1990s, 'joyriding' was to become the symbol of the ultimate destructiveness of dispossessed 'bully' male youth seeking to assert his macho-ness through spectacular posturing in a car he could not afford. This led to wild tales in local, and sometimes national, media reports of children as young as 6 or 7 taking cars.

Our next narrative of panic shows the net of anxiety spreading from youth culture, through car culture, to the mounting wickedness of ever younger children. A 10-year-old Hartlepool boy made national headlines when he 'swaggered free' from court wearing an SAS mask (a balaclava without the hole for the mouth), leading to cries for clampdowns on ever younger criminals. The seamless web grows again, this time with the added horror of children 'as young as 6 or 7' joining in the anarchistic attack on societal values.

And into this scenario came Robbie Thompson and Jon Venables. The facts are now well known: in February 1993 two 10-year-old boys abducted 2-year-old James Bulger from a Liverpool shopping mall, took him on a 2½ mile walk to a railway line, and battered him to death.

There was no rational 'motive' available for the killing. On Monday, 1 November 1993, the murder trial began and the politicians and the press immediately made the case stand proxy for all the evils of society on the verge of dystopia. This link is made nicely by David Smith (himself a journalist) in his painstaking chronicle of the 'Bulger case', *The Sleep of Reason* (1994), and is worth quoting at length:

> The front page of Thursday's edition of the *Sun* gave a single left hand column to Michael Howard. SUN SPEAKS ITS MIND: YES; CRIME MINISTER . . . 'It was', said the *Sun*, 'a joy to hear a tough talking Home Secretary say he couldn't give a damn if more people ended up behind bars. Never mind three cheers, he deserved one hundred and three for yesterday's declaration of war on the muggers, robbers, and rapists who made our life hell. Bail bandits, young yobs the law couldn't touch, guilty men freed because they stayed silent in court. They were all about to be whacked with a very large stick' . . . The rest of the . . . front page, alongside this column, was consumed by a photograph of Jon, carrying a lollipop, being led in to Preston Crown Court by a policeman with his hand on Jon's shoulder, taken the previous Sunday . . . Page 12 described in spurious detail the boys' luxurious lives in their units as they awaited trial . . . Page 13 was two more photographs [*sic*] . . . One of Bobby, another of Jon, again with their faces obscured. They were, respectively, captioned 'Good Life . . . one of the boys, charged with Jamie's murder . . . has put on weight . . . Sweet treatment . . . the second accused lad clutches a lolly as he is led in to court' . . .
>
> (Smith 1994: 191–2)

Smith argues that the newspaper had waited four days to use these pictures alongside the comment on the Home Secretary's speech. He further notes that throughout the whole trial of the two boys, perhaps '20 minutes out of 17 days, was the full extent of the trial's inquiry into the boys' mental health' (p. 211). In his summing up, the judge told the court, 'It is not for me to pass judgement on their upbringing, but I suspect that exposure to violent video films may in part be an explanation' (p. 227). Smith comments:

> It was unclear why the judge had made reference to violent videos. There had been no mention in evidence of any videos. Had he heard the rumours about *Child's Play 3*? . . . If he had wanted to provoke a public debate it was, perhaps, surprising that he had singled out violent videos as a possible explanation for the killing, with no mention of any other issues that might be a factor in young people committing serious crime.
>
> (Smith 1994: 227)

In truth, no one appeared to be concerned with a serious consideration of the aetiology of the crime. Yet of course 'public debate', if it may be graced with the term, certainly ensued: Holland (1997: 49) relates how in the last months of 1993, the face of Chucky Doll, 'a terrifying face, super-human and unreal, yet freckled and somehow childish', was reproduced over and over again on the front pages of the *Mirror*, the *Sun*, and other newspapers, 'now staring out at a wider public, their millions of readers' (p. 49), until, on 26 November the *Sun* showed the image of Chucky consumed in flames, declaring: 'For the sake of all our kids . . . BURN YOUR VIDEO NASTIES'.

Fast-forward now to April 1994: a report is published by Professor Elizabeth Newson, co-signed by 24 child 'experts' comprised of psychologists, psychiatrists and paediatricians. The Newson argument begins with the 'Bulger case'. Thompson and Venables are 'depicted as exemplars of a new cruelty in children . . . something exceptional must explain this new viciousness' (Barker 1997: 15). The Newson Report claimed that the ever easier availability of films containing sadistic images in which the viewer is invited to identify with the perpetrator had led to a sea change in violence among children (p. 16). Despite the equal and opposite claims of many other 'experts' and academics, criticizing both the arguments and the evidence of the report, virtually no media attention was paid to dissenting voices. Efforts by the dissenting academics to reach representatives of the major political parties and individual MPs failed, and only the *Times Higher Educational Supplement* published the contrary statement (Barker and Petley 1997: 3). The 'child villain', innocence polluted by video nasties, is here to stay. And not just video nasties: the Newson Report makes further links with computers and video games, indeed all forms of 'vicarious viewing'. In their critique of Newson, Barker and Petley point out that the conception of childhood is so 'empty as to be manipulable' (1997: 6; see also Chapter 1 in this volume); they pertinently suggest that 'we need to ask questions about real children as an antidote to these sorts of scare' (p. 6).

Our next narrative of this era concerns a resurgence of the anxiety surrounding youthful consumption of popular culture. Bridging the end of the 1980s and the beginning of the 1990s the spectre of youthful hedonism through popular culture reappeared in the form of music 'n' drugs. This was not however, a simple continuance of every other packaging of music 'n' drugs panics. Many pop journalists saw it like this, but the wider media did not. Thus, writing of the pop chroniclers' reaction to Acid House music in the late 1980s, Redhead (1990: 1) comments, 'The tale was that Acid House was nothing new; it was merely another, much lauded, link in the subcultural chain, replaying and reworking the 1950s, 1960s, or 1970s.'

The tabloids did not share this view on Acid House and the 1988 'summer of love' was encapsulated in headlines such as 'Evil of Ecstasy', 'Ban this killer music', 'Drug crazed Acid House fans' and so on (Redhead 1990: 2). Why was this not 'just another moral panic' about youth culture?

We were about to witness something very different from the earlier representations of problem youth cultures, starting with the creation of a seamless web of anxiety more far-reaching than the long-hair-equals-hippy-equals-psychedelic-drug-taker formula of the late 1960s. A series of overlapping formations surrounding youth consumption and youth behaviour paved the way to the 'post-industrial panic'. Mindless hedonism became portrayed as the new 'culture' of a lost youth. This partly reflected the increasingly intertwining associations of different forms of consumption, each making reference to the other. To begin with there was 'psychedelia, Acid, smiley, beachwear, Lucozade, fluorescent paraphernalia, and so on' (Redhead 1990: 2), and increasingly into the decade, 'sportswear, football, Britpop, Britlit, Britfrocks, Alcopops . . . Movies of novels, soundtracks of movies, soundtracks of novels, novels of football, music of drugs, novels on drugs . . .' and so on. Irvine Welsh catapulted to fame with the hedonist-nihilist novel *Trainspotting*, a novel-on-drugs, followed by the film and the soundtrack, and subsequently by Welsh's rise to further giddy heights as an icon reading to thousands in packed clubland venues.

Nor did the panic any more restrict itself to spaces of the inner-city poor, for 'media publicity on acid house refocused attention on the city, but only the outskirts, the margins on the urban environment, not the inner city which Margaret Thatcher has targeted as ripe for political conquest through policies of "regeneration" ' (Redhead 1997: 59). Indeed, both Redhead and then Thornton (1995) argue against the notion of 'sub-culture' in the CCCS sense of 'authenticity'. The commodification of youth styles in speeded-up 'pop' time means that the minute a 'subcultural' style emerges, it is absorbed and re-sold to young people as a marketized commodity. As media pressure racked up public (adult) opinion against this widespread 'menace', resultant criminalization was aimed at a whole market segment, not a 'subculture'. Thus, holding unlicensed 'acid house' parties became illegal in 1990 (this was directed at controlling *venues*) – although as Redhead (1997: xi) points out, by the time the Act came into force, acid house was out of fashion! Then came the infamous 1994 Criminal Justice and Public Order Act. Under Section 63 ('Powers to Remove Persons Attending or Preparing for a Rave') it was the first attempt 'to enshrine in law . . . a criminalization of certain forms of *music*' (Redhead 1997: x, emphasis added). No account of criminalization could be complete without reiterating the gloriously funny and also 'chilling' section 63(1)(b), defining rave music as 'sounds wholly or predominantly characterised by the emission of a succession of repetitive beats'.

This was not, then, 'moral panic' in the original sense. The mass (global) marketization of cultural hedonism ('hedonism in hard times' as Redhead 1993 would have it) and the disintegration of discrete 'cultures' into a plethora of postmodern sampling of styles, rob the notion of its specificity but highlight a tendency that was to become typical of the 1990s. The youth culture vista was increasingly portrayed as encompassing every feature of consumerism, but without a narrative, without a central theme of conflict, dissent, rebellion or politics. Increasingly, media and political attention turned to the 'problem' of how to regulate a whole, 'lost' generation and a *whole field of cultural practice.*

The irony in this particular narrative is that such a notion of 'total panic' is in itself a form of commodification, a re-repackaging of problem youth, for the 'panic' is courted by the music industry itself in order to attract young people. Problem youth, always a highly saleable commodity in media terms, seems to have lost any referent in real life. As Thornton (1995: 122) acerbically notes, 'from the point of view of clubbers and ravers, in particular, micro, niche, and mass media have remarkably different cultural connotations . . . with mass media for instance, affirmative coverage of the culture is a kiss of death'. Thornton is critical of the whole notion of moral panic in relation to club cultures: ' "Moral panic" is a metaphor which depicts a complex society as a single person who experiences sudden groundless fear about its virtue . . . its anthropomorphism and totalization mystify more than they reveal. It fails to recognize competing media, let alone their reception by diverse audiences. And, its concept of morals overlooks the ethics of abandon' (Thornton 1995: 136).

This is an interesting point because the assertion we have made above that the 1990s heralded the dawn of a 'total panic' about young people does of course suggest a 'totalizing' process. That is, it suggests the idea that many different media representations of many different phenomena and cultural events proliferate ever more quickly, gesturing vaguely to an assumed audience who consume and – literally – buy anxiety by the bucketful from a rather monolithic media. However, our argument here is not about theories of moral panics *per se*, but about precisely how the forms of media most forceful and visible in relation to the most number of people, under certain social conditions, sit in an inextricable relation to late modernity. Within this relationship between media and late modernity, the real and highly differentiated experiences of young people *appear* from an adult-centric view as an ever-expanding vista of troublesomeness. This vista – in so far as people take it on board – precisely subsumes 'young people' as one problematic entity. It is, in other words, an ideal projection screen for adult anxiety. There is not a single message, but a mosaic, an explosive proliferation of messages about youth and crime, which is obfuscating and revealing at the same time: obfuscating, because it hides young people, and revealing because it tells us much about the adult-centricity of the re-repackaging of youth. It can be read as a barometer of what 'we' the adults feel.

Other commentators have suggested that there is nothing new about the panic over hedonism in hard times, and that the media packaging of phenomena such as acid house, rave and ecstasy was not indicative of any sea change in cultural form and criminalization (see Critcher 2003: 58–9). This seems strange given the extent to which criminology has been centrally concerned in recent years with the concepts of late- and postmodernity and the complex transformations that have occurred across societies globally, suggesting that we are in an era of extremely rapid change. In this the discipline has drawn on key social theorists to examine the relevance of changing concepts of self and society (Giddens 1991), the risk society (Beck 1992) and globalization (Featherstone *et al.* 1995).

It is these latter analyses that may help inform our understanding of the proliferation of anxious images and dissatisfactions within which public representations parcel up young people in the twenty-first century.

New millennium, new panics?

In this context perhaps there is nothing very new about the new millennium, at least in the context of public representations of young people in the UK. (Globally there is a different issue, as we shall see in Chapter 8.) If the 1990s saw the coming of age of the 'repetitive beat generation', the 20/30-somethings who had been raised on the harms of hedonism and translated it into 'new fiction' (Redhead 2000), the 2000s are rapidly becoming the age of the repetitive complaint generation, raised on a diet of late modern risk and anxiety. Giddens (1991: 28) put it most succinctly: 'to live in the "world" produced by high modernity has the feeling of riding a juggernaut. It is not just that more or less continuous and profound processes of change occur; rather, change does not consistently conform either to human expectation or to human control.' For Giddens, apocalypticism is a central feature of late modernity and a preoccupation with risk and risk control is inevitable. Ulrich Beck, in the contemporary classic *Risk Society* (1992), famously argued that modernity, having produced uncontrollable risks (scientific, technological and social developments, which as in Giddens' 'juggernaut' cannot now be stopped or necessarily foreseen), results in intensive political concentration on the distribution and control of risks. For our present purposes, the interesting point about these two strands of analysis from social theory is, as Mary Douglas (1994b) has pointed out, that in these analyses, and in political and popular discourse, risk is essentially being equated with danger. This is important, because 'When "risk" enters as a concept in political debate, it becomes a menacing thing, like a flood, an earthquake, or a thrown brick. But it is not a thing, *it is a way of thinking, and a highly artificial contrivance at that'* (Douglas 1994b: 46, emphasis added).

It is risk, translated as danger, which drives the repetitive cycle of contemporary media representations of the young. Youth (not real young people, but the discursive space into which we pour them) come part and parcel with global warming, terror attacks, heart attacks and credit card fraud in the list of risks (dangers) to be contemplated in the everyday diet of mediated representation. This is not to say of course that anti-social behaviour or 'yobbishness' is presented as a danger on the same scale as the potential terror attacks about which the present government in the UK sees fit to pour precautionary leaflets through peoples' doors; but the driving principle is the same: a way of thinking that derives not from our ability to actuarially calculate the probability of something, but from the more generalized pains of late modernity, from which mediated public representation draws its resonance and its drama. In the rest of this section we shall consider just some of the latest examples at the time of writing; by the time this book comes to press you will be able to add many more of your own!

Gangstas guns and drugs: x-treme panic on the streets

Young people, it seems, are responsible for the tide of gun crime sweeping the UK. Guns are the 'latest fashion accessory' and gang culture is one of the newer foci of political and media attention. As is typical, the 'issue' came to particular national prominence when 'real' victims became a possibility: in this case Charlene Ellis and Letisha Shakespear, aged 18 and 17 years, who were killed in a shooting in Aston, Birmingham on 2 January 2003 after a New Year party. 'A trivial dispute, then the girls were caught in a hail of 30 shots' reported the *Telegraph*. The deaths, we are told, 'shook the mainly black community in Aston, Birmingham, where the victims were described as inseparable, happy, church-going girls. Charlene had recently overcome leukaemia' (www.telegraph.co.uk/news/main.html). The shooting, between rival local gangs, led almost immediately to massive coverage of the dangers of young men with guns, and the dangers of black music forms such as gangsta rap and hip-hop.

The national media had a ripping few days reporting the more peculiar statements of ministers, police chiefs and assorted 'commentators' as the picture emerged of Britain's streets under siege from inadequate posses of posturing, machismo-driven black young males sporting their guns as fashion accessories and massacring the innocent at, it seems, the slightest provocation. What is most perplexing about these accounts is not that they should reach such prominence: in what might be described as a traditionally 'non-gun' street culture such as the UK, violent death by gunfire is, descriptively, shocking. Rather it is the immediate and unproblematic attribution of 'gun culture' to the young that is confusing. How young is young, in this case, became increasingly unclear (and remains unclear!). On 6 January 2003, BBC News reported that 'the Home Office says it is clear that the problem of the possession of handguns lies predominantly with young people' (http://news.bbc.co.uk). The Prime Minister was swift to announce a 'crackdown' on crime involving firearms; meanwhile, Caroline Sullivan in a *Guardian* special report on gun violence in Britain on 6 January declared that hip-hop 'must take its share of the blame for the spread of violence among teenagers'. Remember the Sex Pistols, she warns us, 'what it boils down to is that teenage boys are impressionable and always will be. Just reflect that the Sex Pistols once persuaded fans that spitting at each other was fantastically cool' (http://www.guardian.co.uk/gun/Story). In the end an extraordinarily diverse range of 'black' music ended up being implicated in the rampage of 'youth' gun crime, making no distinction between genres, so that one is left with the impression that any music involving black young people is clearly to blame, and Culture Minister Kim Howells declared that the deaths of the two young women in Birmingham were 'symptomatic' of developments in 'rap and garage' music. Of course, the idea that most of these kinds of pronouncement were made by politicians and journalists who were undoubtedly either too white, or too old, or both, to recognize the 'music' they were allegedly talking about went fairly much unnoticed in this maelstrom of accusation. Despite the claims for gun crime as the trademark of 'youth' moreover, and the frequent citing of official statistics on increases in gun crime in the UK, none of these figures differentiated by gender, age *or* race. Yet gun crime is indubitably a new problem of (black) youth!

Perhaps, whilst the 1990s saw the scandals of ever *younger* young people committing murder and mayhem, the boundaries of 'youth' are now being stretched upwards. On 7 May 2004, the *Guardian* reported that five men *aged between 19 and 25* accused of shooting dead Charlene Ellis and Letisha Shakespear had been remanded in custody; indeed, the original reports on the shooting speculated that one of the gangs involved had been operating in the area for 'over a decade', and the shooting took place on turf that 'traditionally' belonged to another gang (http://www.telegraph.co.uk/news/main.jhtml). In another case, Tony Thompson reported in the *Observer* on 'guns, gangs and slaughter' in the West Midlands. The shooting occurred at the barbecue birthday party of a 32-year-old man, and 'the attack came amid a spate of shootings on the increasingly lawless streets of the West Midlands' (http://observer.guardian.co.uk/uk_news/). According to this 'investigative' piece, the shootings were related to the gang culture of the city, notably a 31-year-old drug baron in a war with other factions – including the two gangs said to be involved in the Ellis-Shakespear shootings – who had allegedly been operating in the city since the mid-1980s when they were formed 'as vigilante organizations to protect the local community against growing threats from the far right'. Then again, it emerges from Thompson's article that Charlene Ellis was related to gang members, one in each of the two main opposing gangs. Two girls had been arrested days before the deaths of Ellis and Shakespear, charged with shooting a gang member, implying a possible revenge killing . . . and so it goes on. Quite how rap, garage, or hip-hop are supposed to have caused over 20 years of gang warfare, then, must be a question, as must the notion that gun crime is a new phenomenon of the lost youth of Britain. Even the slightest acquaintance with early sociological literatures will bring one up against Patrick's *A Glasgow Gang Observed* (Patrick 1973) and of course a history of gang and gun cultures is endemic to cities such as Glasgow, Belfast and Cardiff, and bears very little relation to 'youth' *per se*. Thus the whole edifice of the media and politicians' packaging of young people as responsible for a gun/drug culture running amok on the streets, in some parody of an (equally parodic) notion of US boy gangstas, crumbles. The identified 'danger' (growth of gun crime to unprecedented levels) and its identified causes (young predominantly black males) sit uneasily with even a cursory glance at the events identified as indicative of such dangers (gang-related shootings). The logic, such as it is, is fuzzy. History is ignored. Rhetoric abounds. That is to say, all the usual indications of demonization are present. Our final example concerns a piece of journalism that seamlessly stitches together different events, ignores material facts and makes a nonsense of its own assertions. It is a perfect example of Douglas' risk as 'a way of thinking'.

'Assassination city' . . . 'gun-crazy culture' . . . 'drug dealing is rife, guns are bought and sold as casually as cars'. Assassination city is not in the USA, but in the UK. It is not even in London, or Glasgow, or Manchester (although the latter of course has the most colourful reputation in this direction). It is in the shires of the United Kingdom. It is Nottingham. The description above was provided for us by the *Sunday Times* ('Focus', 15 August 2004). This piece is particularly interesting, not only because it reflects one of the current 'repetitive' fads in apocalyptic envisioning in the media, but because of its configuration. In a full-page spread, it is claimed that Nottingham is a city where 'almost half the killings are now deliberate executions'. It later transpires in the piece itself that the figure given in a Chief Constable's report was 40 per cent and related to a very small and specific area of the city. Nevertheless, gang culture is swallowing the city; and with gangs, guns. Needless to say, the 'gangs' are of young men. The danger, however, is diffuse. On the one hand it seems, the 'gangs' only target each other. Then again, the culture of violence cuts across the whole social spectrum of Nottingham, 'including the innocent out to enjoy Nottingham's nightlife'. Even more intriguing is the example with which the article opens its case for the apocalypse of Nottingham:

> When some young men had their mobile phones stolen by a gang in a takeaway restaurant a while ago, they did not turn to the police for help. They turned to the gun instead . . . They were members of a gang from the St Ann's area of the city and, vowing to win back some 'respect', they armed themselves, went in search of the perpetrators and opened fire. When the smoke cleared, a man named Gerald Smith lay dying in the street.

At this point some salient facts should be stated. First, the incident in question (theft of mobile phones) took place in a fried chicken takeaway in Sheffield, not Nottingham. Secondly, the rival gang who took the phones came from Birmingham. Following this incident, the men (not especially 'young' incidentally, depending upon how you classify the age of 27 for instance) returned to Nottingham and then later returned to Sheffield. The murdered man happened to be in the doorway of the chicken shop when the men from Nottingham returned and had nothing to do with the original incident earlier in the day. All of this information came out in the trial of the nine men (convicted of the murder of Smith) in Sheffield Crown Court in 2004 (Brown 2004).

Guns and gangs, then, are about danger, and the powers of danger are to be attributed to the 'machismic' body of the black teenage male rapper figure, swaggering around the streets of Birmingham, or Manchester, or Nottingham, dealing in drugs and driving flash cars. It is more redolent of the 1991 film *New Jack City*, directed by Doug McHenry and George Jackson, with Ice-T and Wesley Snipes respectively running and seeking to break the crack kitchens of Manhattan, than of the UK's city turf economies. Whilst some research shows detectives' accounts to confirm the presence of conflict over drug 'turf', of firearms use, and even of the direct influence of Jamaican 'yardie' culture in UK cities (Brown 2004), it is hard to see how this can be subsumed under some kind of generic 'youth' issue. Existing in complex juxtaposition with more traditional gang cultures and turf wars in UK cities, the 'new' influences link to drug economies that in even the most basic analysis must be seen as everything to do with global narcotics and very little to do with the vulnerable propensities of 'kids' listening to music.

Constantly seeking the crime kids: yobs, townies and anti-social behaviour

Perhaps the apotheosis of all this has been reached: 'we' are constantly seeking crime kids, and we seek them everywhere. Young people are to blame for drugs, guns, muggings, riots and music (!), and they are also costing the UK economy billions of pounds. As the *Guardian* tells us, 'juvenile crime is now estimated by the Audit Commission to cost the economy more than £10bn a year and accounts for nearly a fifth of the total annual cost of crime' (5 January 2004). Such bizarre actuarialism in the face of the haphazard way in which the notion of 'risk' in relation to young people is treated itself reveals the irrationality of the processes by which media representations engage the popular imagination. 'Youth' have been placed alternately at the wheel of the juggernaut of late modernity, as the yobs and the gun-toters who are ruining our lives, and under its wheels. Thus Amelia Hill, reporting in the *Observer* on 30 November 2003 first laments 'a lost generation trapped on our forgotten estates' and 'the spiralling crisis in Britain's inner cities, where jobless youngsters are locked into a cycle of deprivation and drug abuse'. She then curdles our blood with the 'local gang of 20 boys who blow up cars with firecrackers', terrorizing other residents. In Sheffield, she writes, 'in the last two weeks a milkman has been murdered and the vicar of the local church has been mugged by a gang of 11-year-old boys' (for the confused, these were entirely separate incidents and the former did not involve 11-year-old boys but a jealous lover, a fact which eludes Hill). And of course, when not driving or being run over by the juggernaut, the youngsters are riding it, high on ecstacy and music and vodka jellies. Recently (as we shall see in Chapter 6), girls have become a problem because they are acting like boys, 'ladette' nights out resulting in far too much binge drinking; they too are along for the ride.

Finally of course, young people are packaged as being problematic just for being there. This is probably a foreseeable conclusion given the building up of distaste for youthful autonomy since modernity first made it a possibility. 'Anti-social behaviour', or the criminalization of the state of youth itself, will be considered in policy terms in Chapter 4. The media adore it. The *Sun* newspaper launched its 'Shop a Yob' campaign with relish in 2002, including printing posters of young people made the subject of Anti-Social Behaviour Orders. The Anti-Social Behaviour Act 2003 gives police the powers to disperse groups of two or more people from any public place should a police officer consider them likely to either commit an offence or cause 'alarm or distress' to a member of the public (Taylor 2003). In theory of course, given the anxieties of the adult world in regard to young people, this would apply almost constantly. Hence Taylor's apposite question: 'the gangs of new labour: yobs or just youth?' (2003: 10). The significance of the notion of anti-social behaviour and its enshrinement in statutory provision is thus that it opens up whole possibilities for the demonization of ordinary young people, widening the discursive category of 'yob' until it is virtually infinite in its possibilities. Moreover, since automatic reporting restrictions on youth courts have been lifted, the press may 'name and shame' any young person subject to an anti-social behaviour order (ASBO), widening ever more the public profile of the 'yob'. It is almost as if one might ask, 'where have all the normal children gone to?' Williamson (2004) reports attending a debate hosted by the Royal Society for the Encouragement of the Arts, Manufactures and Commerce on the subject of young people and the media: 'it was Martin Townsend, the editor of the *Sunday Express*, who raised the issue of the "ordinary kids". He admitted to not having a clue who they were. They were not newsworthy.'

A totalizing discourse of panic?

These 'stories' of end-of-millennium panics raise some unnerving possibilities in the history of 'repackaging problem youth'. Firstly, that the 'discrete' panics surrounding relatively small groups of young people and youth culture have been replaced by a total panic surrounding children and young people. Secondly, that beyond this, we are seeing the birth of a totalizing discourse of panic: a societal anxiety that the last bastions of innocence, purity and hope in society are under siege. If children are not immune, then the implication is that nothing is sacred, and all is corrupted, profaned, in a global web of mass viewing, video nasties, the internet and popular music. Thirdly, that only a return to ever stronger authoritarianism, censorship and regulation can save the world 'as we have known it'.

All concern with facts, with balanced debate, is lost in the terror of 'world as horror movie'. In the perception of an inevitable and never ending implosion of morality, the promise of modernity as the harbinger of a better world is submerged under its supposedly self-destructing tendencies. Liberalism is revealed as an illusion, a false promise which is leading to the downfall of civilization.

Anthropological work suggests that strong blaming systems emerge in the face of fragile constitutions (Douglas 1994b); 'the media' is not a monolith, as Thornton (1995) correctly points out in her critique of 'moral panic' theory. Newsworthiness, however, as we discussed at the beginning of this chapter, depends upon certain conventions. In the twenty-first century it becomes necessary to broaden out from Chibnall's original 'rules of relevancy'. The media are no longer just concerned with the visible and the spectacular, the deviant and the violent, but precisely with the demonization and spectacularization of the mundane, the everyday. This is the logic of reality TV, and it is the logic of the ever more totalizing panic over 'youth'. The everyday becomes drama, even to the extent of *House of Grime*, a TV reality programme about peoples' dirty houses! Set against the context of a 'risk society', a fragile constitution, the woeful state of media representation of young people can be comprehended as part of the condemnatory urges within a culture beset by self-doubt.

Despite all this 'reality', young people's voices rarely find their way into mainstream media discourse. That young people find their own spaces and their own media is unquestionable, notably through the internet, as we shall see in Chapter 7. When this happens the space becomes contested, questionable. But, in the most visible, adult controlled mediascapes of the tabloids, of the television, young peoples' real lives remain relatively undiscussed (except insofar as they constitute a problem to adults, as in reality shows about controlling wayward and hyperactive children). Were the 'media' a disembedded or dislocated formation, this may not matter, but as we have seen, it is not. To a large extent the media *is* everyday life; refracting it and constituting it. Moreover, as we shall see in the following chapter, media representations become ever more closely allied in late modernity with the processes of policy development, with potentially serious consequences for young people's experiences of punitiveness, repression and exclusion.

Further reading

Cohen's original *Folk Devils and Moral Panics* (1973) has to be a starting point. Hall *et al.* (1978) should also be looked at. Pearson (1983) again, is interesting and useful. Muncie and McLaughlin (1996: Ch. 1) provide a useful and up-to-date summary of many of the issues touched upon. Barker and Petley (1997), in their edited volume, provide some interesting insights into more recent media panics. Kidd-Hewitt and Osborne (1995) is also of general relevance. Critcher (2003) provides an accessible up-to-date summary of a range of issues and literatures.

chapter four

In whose interests?
Politics, policy and UK youth justice

Thus far we have dwelt at length on the processes by which youth and crime is constructed through media, political and academic discourses. Equally important, however, is the question of how policy legislation frames the 'youth crime question' through its *responses* to perceived problems.

In this chapter, we shall examine in detail policy developments in the UK between the 1960s and the 2000s, emphasizing that, despite many changes, about-turns and resurrections of old policies under new names, there are underlying themes which dominate the period. We shall see that contemporary policies and practices cannot be understood without a broader historical comprehension of the concerns of commentators, policy-makers and legislators, which in turn relate to the debates and constructions charted in other chapters.

The languages of youth justice

'Youth justice', as a diverse and contradictory policy domain, may be conceptualized at one level as a constellation of languages in which to communicate priorities and practices through which the governance and control of young people is to be achieved. It is important to examine carefully what is being 'said' through policy. This is not a simple matter of semantics, but rather a recognition that all of the words used in framing youth justice carry an array of overt and covert meanings which construct youth and crime in particular ways and which have crucial implications for the lives of young people and the way in which they are positioned within social relations.

Whatever our sources of information – official reports, policy documents, political debate, legislation, the writing of academic commentators or professional practitioners – we find that the discourse surrounding how society should respond to youth crime has been dominated variously by a focus on 'welfare' and/or 'justice', 'care' and/or 'control', 'treatment' and/or 'punishment', and latterly, a return to 'justice' through new languages of intensive intervention, surveillance and campaigns against 'anti-social behaviour' and/or 'community safety' and 'crime and disorder reduction partnerships'. At one level these words provide a useful, if oversimplified, shorthand description of developments which have taken place in youth justice. Thus England and Wales moved in some three decades from a system based on welfare, care and treatment culminating in the Children and Young Persons Act (CYPA) 1969 to a system based on justice, control and punishment following the Criminal Justice Act 1991; and then, driven by the rise to power of a New Labour government, to what has been dubbed a 'new youth justice' (Goldson 2000) based on both increased intervention and surveillance and a 'get tough' punishment regime following the 1997 White Paper *No More Excuses: A New Approach to Tackling Youth Crime in England and Wales* (Home Office 1997).

We must include the caveat, however, that these meanings are problematic and not necessarily shared by legislators, policy-makers and professional practitioners. We must therefore approach them critically in terms of both what they 'appear' to say and what they may actually mean. For example, it should be noted that often the concepts are discussed as if they are in opposition: treatment *versus* punishment, welfare *versus* justice (Morris *et al.* 1980). Yet it may also be argued that it is not so much opposition which characterizes these apparently contrasting approaches as the linkages. Hence it may also be claimed that care goes with control (Davies 1986: 69–70), or that 'just welfare' is a viable option (Harris 1985), or that the punishment involved in the deprivation of liberty may be needed for treatment to be effective. In addition to this, although we tackle developments chronologically, it must be recognized that youth justice is a composite, and tends to be accumulative: the 'old' approaches and institutional bases are not relinquished but remain within an ever expanding system of 'initiatives' and rationales as 'new' elements are added (Garland 2001).

The advance of welfare: the 1960s

Firstly, then, we examine the development of the language of 'welfare' in youth justice, culminating in the Children and Young Persons Act (CYPA) of 1969. How was youth justice framed within the concept of welfare, and what were the implications of such terminology?

There is general agreement that the development of a welfare-based juvenile justice policy culminating in the Children and Young Persons Act (CYPA) 1969 was based on a consensus: the political parties, while they might have differed about the means, accepted the provision of a comprehensive system of state social welfare. We shall not engage in a detailed examination of the legislation prior to 1969 but should note some key developments leading up to the watershed represented by the Children and Young Persons Act (CYPA) (see Parsloe 1978; Bailey 1987; Harris and Webb 1987; Morris and Giller 1987 for more detailed historical discussion).

There are two important aspects of legislation from the nineteenth century through to the precursor to the 1969 Act: firstly, the development of a range of social control mechanisms specific to young people and, secondly, the widening of the net of social control which affected increasing numbers of working-class youth.

Legislative changes in the last half of the nineteenth century extended the scope of summary trial for juveniles under 16, beginning with the Juvenile Offenders Act 1847 (Radzinowicz and Hood 1974: 621–2). The effect of these extensions was 'not simply to transfer to the Petty Sessions those larcenies which had previously been tried at Quarter Sessions . . . but also to increase by a vast extent the number of such larcenies which were tried at all' (Phillips 1977 in Pearson 1983: 216).

Penal developments – Parkhurst as a juvenile prison (1838), the establishment of Reform Schools (1854) and Industrial Schools (1857) – 'saved' children from the adult prison system. At the same time, by separating them, it enabled the authorities to address not just their delinquencies but to seek to reform their characters and lifestyles within an institutional setting in which rigorous discipline was imposed and which replicated the harsh conditions of industrial employment.

Equally important during this period were the philanthropic and educational initiatives which, while they were directed at 'saving' and 'protecting' children, kept young people off the streets and subjected them to less formal surveillance and controls (see also Chapter 1). As Morris and Giller (1987: 31–2) argue, these nineteenth-century reforms, which began the separation of juvenile from adult offenders, were essentially 'authoritarian conservative'. They sought to reaffirm traditional middle-class values of family life, parental authority, order and discipline.

The Children Act 1908 represented a major step in the development of the belief that children were a special category of problem. By establishing

Juvenile Courts which were criminal courts in terms of their procedures and giving them jurisdiction over 'care' and 'protection' issues as well as criminal cases, social control was consolidated and extended. In essence the Juvenile Courts became 'family law courts' dispensing family justice (Donzelot 1980: 100). For the first time the courts and the state could intervene directly in working-class family life when children were deemed immoral or unruly (Alcock and Harris 1982: 84–5). The conditions which were regarded as indicative of neglect were wide-ranging – including being beyond control, truanting, begging, and associating with thieves and prostitutes. Thus the boundaries were blurred between the criminal and the neglected child (Harris and Webb 1987).

In theory, this could have changed in 1927, when the Molony Committee considered substituting civil proceedings for criminal proceedings in the Juvenile Court. Rather than criminalizing neglect, this would have recognized crime as a symptom of neglect, through *decriminalization*. The Committee rejected this option. It was argued that delinquents do commit serious offences, and the public interest requires that they are held responsible for their actions if they are to learn respect for the law (Home Office 1927: 19). However, the Committee also recognized the importance of the welfare of young people who could be the victims of social and psychological conditions and who require individualized 'treatment'. In this respect the Committee felt there was little to distinguish the delinquent from the neglected child. If the offender was to be reformed, full information about his or her home circumstances and schooling was necessary.

The recommendations of the Molony Committee formed the basis of the Children and Young Persons Act (CYPA) 1933. This Act is important because it placed a duty on magistrates to consider the welfare of the young person and brought closer together the provisions for the treatment of the delinquent and the neglected. The Act laid down a general principle that, when dealing with offenders and non-offenders, the court 'shall have regard to the welfare of the child or young person and shall in a proper case take steps for removing him from undesirable surroundings and for seeing that proper provision is made for his education and training' (CYPA 1933 Section 44(1)).

The stress on welfare in the CYPA 1933 had two important consequences. Firstly, 'in effect the court became a site for adjudicating on matters of family socialization and parental behaviour even when no "crime" as such had been committed. When families were "at fault" the court acted "*in loco parentis*" ' (Muncie 1984: 45). Secondly, the Molony Committee sought and achieved a widening of the net of social control: 'When it is realised the courts are especially equipped to help rather than punish young people, we hope that the reluctance to bring such people before them will disappear' (Home Office 1927: 23).

Pearson (1983) notes how this perception that Juvenile Courts were places in which young people received 'help' resulted in the number of boys brought before the courts doubling in the three years after the CYPA was implemented. *The Times* commented in 1937 that it was 'not that children have become more wicked . . . but that the legal machinery has become more efficient' (Pearson 1983: 216).

The decade after 1945 has been described as a period of 'penal optimism' (Hood 1974: 376) during which the value of policies which sought to reform and rehabilitate the young offender through individualized 'treatment' was rarely questioned. In 1946 the Curtis Committee (Home Office 1946) reported on the existing modes of provision for children who were deprived of a 'normal' home life. While deprived children were the focus of the Curtis Report, the Committee noted that the difference between such children and delinquents 'is often merely one of accident'. Both were regarded as the victims of family and environmental circumstances which triggered emotional disturbance. Following the report of the Curtis Committee, the Children Act 1948 set up local authority children's departments to provide, for the first time, a specialized and individualized social work service based on social casework theory to meet the needs of young people. The local authorities '*must* take *into care* any children whose parents did not properly provide for them, or where for some other reason were receiving inadequate care' (Alcock and Harris 1982: 88). The justification for extending the state's right to intervene was the belief that the roots of young people's problems were in the malfunctioning of individuals and their families due to a faulty upbringing.

While the Children Act 1948 addressed welfare issues, seeing young people as victims, the Criminal Justice Act 1948 gave the Juvenile and Magistrates' Court new powers to punish young offenders with the introduction of attendance centres (involving the deprivation of leisure on Saturday afternoons) for those aged 12 to 20 and detention centres (the 'short sharp shock') for those aged 14 to 20. The different approaches adopted in the Children Act and the Criminal Justice Act thus both reflected and strengthened societal ambivalence concerning troublesome youth.

By the 1960s, then, 'welfare' had become the dominant language in relation to juvenile offenders. The Ingleby Committee was set up in 1956 to look into the operation of the Juvenile Court and consider what new powers and duties could be given to local authorities to prevent the neglect of children at home. The Ingleby Report recognized the inherent conflict when 'justice' and 'welfare' were pursued simultaneously in the same setting. It rightly regarded the Juvenile Court as a criminal court which tried offences employing a 'modified form of criminal procedure', but also acknowledged that

> the requirement to have regard to the welfare of the child, and the various ways in which the court may deal with an offender, suggests a jurisdiction which is not criminal. It is not easy to see how the two principles can be reconciled: criminal responsibility is focused on an

allegation about some particular act isolated from the character and needs of the defendant, whereas welfare depends on a complex of personal, family and social considerations.

(Home Office 1960: para. 60)

It is, perhaps, not surprising that a committee largely made up of magistrates, lawyers and administrators but without any social workers, and which accepted the by now commonly held view that the needs of the neglected and the delinquent were the same, with both being a product of family failure, could not resolve this conflict (Bottoms and Stevenson 1992: 34). The solution proposed was to retain the Juvenile Court because the available disposals interfered with a young person's liberty, but to raise the age of criminal responsibility from 8 to 12 (and eventually 14), with care and protection proceedings replacing criminal proceedings. It was thought by maximizing 'welfare' considerations for children under 14 more would be referred to the court. As Morris and Giller (1987: 76–7) note, the Report endorsed a social welfare approach but the reforms addressed only procedural issues.

Bottoms (1974) points out that the Report was received coolly by the Conservative government, which was concerned about the increase in juvenile crime. The age of criminal responsibility was raised by the CYPA 1963 to 10 with little enthusiasm – the House of Lords voted for 12. Although the CYPA 1963 was a limited measure it did give local authorities the duty to engage in preventative work with children and families thought to be 'at risk'. Whereas the Children Act 1948 had given social workers the task of rescuing children by taking them into care, the CYPA 1963 sought to prevent 'trouble' before it developed.

The consequence of this shift from reactive to proactive social work was far-reaching. Child care officers and family caseworkers were given a mandate to search for social problems in poor families, and not surprisingly they found them, 'armed' with their 'bible' – Bowlby's (1951) *Maternal Care and Mental Health*, which purported to show that short- and long-term maternal deprivation led to the development of maladjusted and delinquent personalities. Delinquent children and deprived children were seen as the products of – victims of – undesirable family and social circumstances. Nineteenth-century beliefs about the moral deficiencies of working-class family life, lack of parental care and discipline had, by the middle of the twentieth century, been given a scientific gloss. Thus a strategy designed to reduce the number of children coming into care ended up sucking in a new population of children 'at risk' into the increasingly welfare-oriented juvenile justice system. The problem of delinquency had become synonymous with the 'problem family' (Clarke 1980); but, unlike the nineteenth century, when the immorality of working-class family life was the object of attention, it was now those families who had fallen through the net of postwar reconstruction, the 'residue', or 'residual problem' of delinquency linked to poverty.

Thus, as with our discussion in Chapter 2, we need to appreciate the social and political context of postwar optimism.

The report of the Longford Study Group in 1966 (a private Labour party committee on which professional social work was not represented), whose proposals were embodied in the 1965 White Paper *The Child, the Family, and the Young Offender* (Home Office 1965), regarded minor offending as 'part of the normal process of growing up' (Clarke 1980: 85). Generally, more serious offenders were 'the victims of a deprived and unhappy home' (Harwin 1982). As 'victims' they should not be held criminally responsible for their actions. Thus the 1965 White Paper proposed non-judicial Family Council(s) in place of the Juvenile Courts for young people under 16, staffed by social workers and involving parents in discussions: the welfare needs of the child and the family would become central to the whole process (Harwin 1982). Councils would be able to order the child (parents) to pay compensation, arrange supervision by social workers and utilize local authority residential institutions. The age of criminal responsibility would be raised to 16, and those aged 16–20 would be dealt with in Young Offender Courts, which would be concerned with the welfare of the offender as well as with punishment.

If these proposals had been adopted, juvenile offending would have been effectively decriminalized. However, they were extensively criticized by powerful groups with a vested interest in the juvenile justice system (Bottoms 1974; Harwin 1982). Lawyers objected to the due process of the law being replaced by administrative procedures lacking legal safeguards. Clerks to the justices and magistrates saw their role disappearing, and argued that the proposals would fail to protect the public adequately. The probation service felt threatened by the prospective loss of their responsibility for supervising young offenders at a time when the future of the service was in doubt. It was argued that the authority of the court was necessary to deal with 'difficult or inadequate offenders' (Harwin 1982). Finally, the White Paper was opposed by the Conservatives, and the Labour government had a majority of only three (Bottoms 1974). The Labour party's own Home Secretary, Roy Jenkins, was unsympathetic, as were Home Office civil servants. The proposals foundered on the strength of the opposition.

By contrast, Bottoms (1974) argues that the 1968 White Paper *Children in Trouble* (Home Office 1968) succeeded where the earlier White Paper had failed because it retained the Juvenile Court, and thereby defused the objections (in the short term at least) of lawyers, magistrates and probation workers. At the same time, social work as a profession was gaining in strength, and the emergence in the top echelon of the Home Office of civil servants with a strong child care orientation was significant. The result was the CYPA of 1969, underpinned by a philosophy of treatment which removed any lingering distinction between children who offended and those who needed 'care and protection'. The causes of delinquency and deprivation were seen as the same; both kinds of children suffered from essentially the same problems and had the same 'treatment' needs. Primacy is given to the family and the social circumstances of the deprived and underprivileged whose circumstances caused crime, truancy, lack of control and neglect – but it should be noted that primacy was accorded to individual factors, rather than structural factors such as poverty or poor housing. Thus Morgan (1981: 47) has argued that 'As "need" replaced neglect, the welfare targets of the Act were subtly shifted from differences in people's life chances to the deficiencies in their personalities and the mess they were making in their interpersonal relationships'.

Moreover, because the White Paper claimed that delinquency was 'often' a part of the normal growing-up process, but 'sometimes' a 'symptom of a deviant, damaged, or abnormal personality'; observation, assessment and flexible 'treatment' were required.

The CYPA of 1969 was, then, a watershed in the development of a welfare approach: it represented a culmination of the preceding developments of the twentieth century. However, it is important to recognize that the rationale of the Act was based on care and control. Thus the Home Secretary, James Callaghan, claimed 'there is general agreement that care and control run in harness' (cited in Davies 1986: 70). Hence as Davies comments, care and control are seen as 'mutually supportive, complementary, and even synonomous. Coercive and restrictive forms of containment and restriction were justified as "good for the child" and meeting his or her "needs" ' (Davies 1986: 69).

So, while one may be lulled by the language of welfare into thinking that the shift from 'punishment' to 'welfare' in the Act was progressive, it actually represented a further erosion of children's rights, as it left social workers to determine the 'best interests' of the child or young person. Indeed, the whole language – and practice – of welfare becomes problematic on closer inspection. The meaning of 'care', 'needs', 'best interests' and 'good for the child' cannot be taken at face value. As Allen has argued, 'If the measures result in the compulsory loss of the child's liberty, the involuntary separation of the child from his family, or even the supervision of a child's activities by a probation worker, the impact on the affected individuals is essentially a punitive one. Good intentions and a flexible vocabulary do not alter this reality' (Allen 1964 cited in Morris and McIsaac 1978: 58).

The *reality* of care, then, often does not mean what we would commonly assume from the connotations of the word; it can also mean 'locking up into care', 'taking into care', the granting of legal permission to social workers to remove a child from the home and place him or her into an institution (Cohen 1985: 277) – where, as we shall see in Chapter 5, she or he may be vulnerable to further layers of victimization through physical or sexual abuse.

The CYPA was debated in Parliament at (yet another) time of anxiety about increasing juvenile crime. The debate in fact focused less on the overall 'welfare' objective of the Act than on the means to appease this anxiety. Davies (1986: 74–6) argues that the desirability of 'welfare' measures may have been seen as valid by academics and social work professionals, but that such measures lacked 'deep popular roots'. They were never accepted by organized Labour or working-class voters. The Labour government therefore stressed that it was not 'soft' on punishment, since care and control went together. The government conceded that custodial institutions would need to remain in place for juveniles until 'alternative provision' became available. Meanwhile, the Conservative Party opposed the reduced role of the courts. Politically speaking, one weakness of the Act was that unlike previous reforms, it actually threatened the existing institutions and legal procedures (Bailey 1987). Thus when the Conservative Party won the general election in 1970, they did not implement central clauses of the Act.

The retreat from welfare: the 1970s

Since the language of welfare was ambiguous, since in its purist form it did not have support from powerful sectors, and since in any case it was grafted onto, rather than fundamentally challenging, an existing criminal justice system, it was a simple matter for the Conservative government to undermine it. The police and the magistrates retained many of their powers, the age of criminal responsibility was maintained at 10, and attendance centres, detention centres and borstals for juveniles were to be phased out only if social services developed 'suitable alternatives'. The retreat from welfare had begun before it had arrived. Even those portions of the CYPA (1969) which were retained were soon attacked vociferously by police and magistrates, who argued that it left them powerless to deal adequately with juvenile offenders. Again, it must be remembered that these changes took place within the postwar concern with increasing crime rates in the face of affluence. The police and the magistracy were able to play on the perception that delinquents were increasingly roaming the streets, running wild and offending with impunity.

It is important to note here that such perceptions were largely false. Firstly, Pearson (1983: 217) points out that the apparent 'crime wave' in the 1970s was 'totally fictitious'. It resulted, he argues, almost entirely from a change in police practices. The use of the formal caution (which was recorded) increased, replacing the informal warnings before 1969 (which were not recorded). Superficially, the diversion from the criminal justice system envisaged by the CYPA seemed to have occurred. However, research indicates that any diversion which was achieved was very limited (Ditchfield 1976; Bottomley and Pease 1986: 119–22). In reality, yet again, as following the legislation in 1908, 1933 and 1963, a 'welfare' measure had widened the net of social control to register more children and young people as delinquent. The consequence was an inflation in the level of recorded crime which stimulated yet another moral panic about youth crime. Since despite magistrates' protestations, the only partial implementation of the 1969 Act had left them with direct access to custodial sentencing for juveniles, the use of these sentences and of the attendance centre escalated during the 1970s. In contrast, the use of care orders and supervision orders declined. During the 1970s the courts were using custody more frequently, earlier in young people's criminal 'careers', and for less serious offences (Millham *et al.* 1978).

The persistence of the belief in the 1970's 'crime wave' stemmed partly from the power of the Justice's Clerk's Society, the Magistrates' Association and the Police Federation, with their access to governmental sources; it also continued because the views of these bodies coincided with the Conservative government's expressed doubts about the CYPA within the context of their developing platform of 'fighting crime', restoring social discipline and asserting the ideology of 'individual responsibility' (Pitts 1988: 28).

Meanwhile, there were a range of 'problems' in relation to the social work profession in the 1970s which according to Harwin (1982) combined to call into question the value of social work treatment of delinquents. The Home Office Children's Department (which had drafted the 1969 CYPA) was abolished at the same time that social work was reorganized with the establishment of generic social services departments without adequate resources; few social workers had experience in dealing with 'difficult' young offenders; social work practice was oriented towards casework with individuals and found it hard to come to terms with the unfamiliar controlling demands of their role; social workers themselves failed to develop effective community-based programmes as alternatives to custodial punishment. In such a climate, dramatic events such as the failure of social workers to prevent the battering to death of a child (Maria Colwell, known to be at risk), facilitated further erosion of the credibility of social work. As with the responses to the James Bulger case 20 years later, 'reforms of the system take place not so much because of a careful routine analysis by ministers and civil servants . . . nor even because of a critique or exposé by an outside journalist or pressure group, but because one or more individual incidents occurs, drawing attention to some underlying imperfections of policy in a dramatic way which seems to demand change' (Bottoms and Stevenson 1992: 23).

The tenacity of the magistrates and the Police Federation, and the inability of social workers to respond to concerns about their ability to cope with offenders, meant that when the Labour government elected in October 1974 reviewed the operation of the CYPA, it did not consider that the full implementation of the Act would solve the problems associated with it. The House of Commons Expenditure Committee in 1975 concluded that 'The major failing of the Act is that it is not wholly effective in differentiating between children who need care, welfare, better education and more support, from the small minority who need strict control and an element of punishment' (1975: para. 167).

The Committee's view reflected the changed nature of the debate about how to deal with juvenile offenders. 'Ordinary' delinquents were not an issue; concern focused on the 'hard core of criminals for the future who required stronger punitive measures' (Scotland Yard statement 1 July 1974 in the *Guardian* 2 July 1974). The Expenditure Committee's solution was a twin-track, 'bifurcatory' approach which distinguished the less serious occasional offenders from the more serious persistent offenders. Morris and Giller's interpretation was that the Committee was influenced more by 'an image of a physically mature, often economically independent, adolescent who was a threat to the established order' than by 'an image of the juvenile in trouble or need of care' (1987: 109). It is this perceived 'hard core' of serious and/or persistent offenders which continued to excite politicians, policy-makers and practitioners through the 1980s to the present time. Whereas the 1969 CYPA had been predicated on the similarities of care and control cases, in the 1970s the differences were being highlighted.

Although a White Paper in 1976 on the CYPA reaffirmed the philosophy of the 1969 Act (Home Office 1976) in accepting the value of non-residential care or supervision and intermediate treatment (IT) for the majority of 'soft end' offenders, it supported firmer measures for 'hard end' offenders through the use of attendance centres and detention centres (Morris and Giller 1987: 111). In addition, financial assistance was to be provided to local authorities to expand residential accommodation and places in youth treatment centres for the most 'disturbed' young offenders. As Harwin (1982) points out, the government did not seek to alter the balance of power in the courts between the magistrates and social workers, but sought instead to give added 'control' responsibilities to social workers for persistent offenders by banning the courts from remanding 14-year-olds into custody and encouraging the building of secure accommodation. Concurrently came an increased emphasis on the use of more intensive forms of intermediate treatment (IT) concentrating on behaviour modification rather than a needs-based model, which had been the intention of the original IT (Pitts 1988: 37–9).

These changes occurred in a wider context of general disillusionment with 'treatment' among academics and civil liberties organizations. The 'collapse of the rehabilitative ideal' (Cavadino and Dignan 1997) was imminent. Reviews of the literature on attempts to rehabilitate and treat offenders inside and outside institutions suggested 'nothing works' (see e.g. Lipton *et al.* 1975 and Brody 1976). The dominant 'medical model' was accused of being 'theoretically faulty'; more specifically, social workers were criticized for the subjectivity of their judgements, for the seemingly discriminatory way in which they exercised their discretion, and for their willingness to use institutional care and recommend custody in their reports to the courts. Young people were being deprived of their liberty and parents of their 'rights' without adequate legal controls (Bean 1976; Taylor *et al.* 1979; Morris *et al.* 1980; Thorpe *et al.* 1980).

Politicizing criminal justice: the 1980s

By 1979 Britain was in the throes of an economic crisis, the 'mugging' scare had commandeered the headlines (see Chapter 3) and industrial unrest was out of control. Anxiety was rampant. The Conservative election campaign 'made more of law and order, in a more strident and populist way, than hitherto' (Windlesham 1993: 144).

King (1991) sees the crime problem at this time as constructed to fit the particular ideological vision of society held by the political party in power, so that the 'identification of causes' and the solutions adopted became a 'political rather than a rational scientific exercise' (King 1991: 87). During the 1980s the government consistently emphasized the importance of individual responsibility, initiative and self-discipline within the context of a free market economy as the only way of achieving the 'good life' (p. 94). As Brake and Hale (1992: 2–3) argue, 'The conservative government was setting its agenda around law and order, welfare, shiftlessness, and immorality. It intended to move social responsibility back to the individual and morality back to the family.'

Any link between social conditions and crime had to be rejected because such a link would have implied increased public expenditure involving welfare benefits, which the government was pledged to reduce.

Law and order rhetoric portrayed offenders as 'evil people', as fundamentally different from law-abiding citizens. King (1991: 91) notes some of the epithets used to describe youth offenders by Tory politicians and the tabloid press: louts, thugs, brutes, hooligans and monsters all surfaced or resurfaced. Delinquents were no longer social casualties, they were deliberate lawbreakers who must be held responsible for their actions – in other words, they were young criminals. In so far as offending had a cause, its roots lay in a decline in discipline and a growth in permissiveness in families and schools. This produced a lack of respect for adults, authority and the law. Crime could only be controlled if it was punished more severely by tougher custodial and non-custodial sentences. The police needed to be strengthened and the courts given increased powers. Thus the attendance centre order was promoted and the provision expanded as 'a disciplinary method of invading the leisure time of hooligans and vandals', and the regime of the detention centres was modelled on army 'glass houses' 'as a short sharp shock to violent young thugs' (Windlesham 1993: 152). Windlesham (pp. 157–60) makes clear that the changes in the detention centre regimes were implemented against Home Office advice and despite the opposition of the prison service and penal reform groups.

In developing criminal justice and youth policies consistent with their political philosophy, the Conservative government immediately axed the non-political Advisory Council on the Penal System which had been used by previous Labour and Conservative governments as an aid to policy formulation. It disappeared not because it was ineffective but because 'of the Government's distaste for independent advice', according to Louis Blom-Cooper in a letter to *The Times* (29 August 1981 cited in Windlesham 1993: 150).

In 1980, a White Paper on 'young offenders' (Home Office 1980) was published which indicated clearly government thinking in dealing with offenders under the age of 21. It shifted the emphasis from the 'child in need' to the 'juvenile criminal' (Morris and Giller 1987: 119). The approach proposed was to be refined and developed through the 1980s, culminating in the Criminal Justice Act (CJA) 1991. The 1980 White Paper advocated diversion from the court through the expansion of cautioning for minor offenders, which it claimed would reduce reoffending (Home Office 1980: para. 38); but also proposed tougher penalties for serious offenders, including more demanding forms of non-custodial supervision.

The CJA 1982, which incorporated most of the proposals in the White Paper, 'represented a move away from treatment and lack of personal responsibility to notions of punishment and individual and parental responsibility' (Gelsthorpe and Morris 1994: 972). While allowing individual 'treatment' to be pursued in relation to the supervision order and the probation order, the Home Secretary stressed the retributive model of making the punishment fit the crime (Windlesham 1993: 165).

The CJA 1982 was important because it accorded magistrates increased powers to determine the form and content of Juvenile Court disposals through the attachment of conditions to supervision orders and the extension of community service orders to juveniles, thus demonstrating a further rejection of social work; it simultaneously required social workers to exercise more control and discipline when supervising juvenile offenders. For the first time, however, courts were restricted in their use of custody for offenders below the age of 21. These restrictions were not part of the original CJA, but resulted from amendments proposed by members of the Parliamentary All Party Penal Affairs Group which were actually opposed by the government (Windlesham 1993: 167–9).

Morris and Giller (1987: 132–3) see the policy changes introduced by the CJA 1982 as largely political and ideological in that the measures introduced were not based on research. For the government they had symbolic value in that 'they provided the appearance of a strong government willing to take tough measures against crime' (p. 133). This interpretation is supported in the history of the detention centre. In 1985, Home Secretary Leon Brittan extended the 'experiment' of short sharp shock regimes in some detention centres to all such institutions (Home Office 1984). Hence 'it is hard to avoid the conclusion that sound penal administration had been made to serve the needs of a defective icon of political ideology' (Windlesham 1993: 161).

Despite the government's belief in the value of the punitive detention centre, pragmatism triumphed over symbolism, and their actual use by magistrates declined. This, however, was compensated for by an increased use of youth custody, rooted partly in the magisterial belief that this offered 'training' and was therefore more constructive. Consequently the 1988 CJA replaced the separate detention centre and youth custody sentences with a single sentence of detention in a young offender institution. This Act also allowed courts to attach a new condition to supervision orders that the offender comply with local authority education requirements; this in effect criminalized non-school attendance.

It should be noted here that the 1980s saw a sharp fall in the use of custodial sentences for juveniles, due mainly to the restrictions on custody included in the CJAs of 1982 and 1988. However, an increased use of 'punitive' community measures occurred in this period, particularly intensive intermediate treatment (IIT) orders. Fifteen million pounds were made available following the 1982 Act to voluntary organizations for the development of IIT schemes. These were to be offence-focused as alternatives to custody, and were supported by the government ideologically in so far as they would control and discipline young offenders. The money was not offered to social services departments, thus completing the refashioning of intermediate treatment (IT) in a 'law and order' image (Cohen 1985: 139–55; Davies 1986: 83–4). The projects were managed on an inter-agency basis, including social workers but also probation services, voluntary organizations, the police and Juvenile Court magistrates, further linking them into a criminal justice structure.

In 1981, the Parliamentary All Party Penal Affairs Group had proposed statutory criteria to restrict the use of custody and care, and had recommended the increased use of non-custodial sentences and the extension of cautioning. Successive Home Office Circulars in 1985 (14/1995) and 1990 (59/1990) used increasingly strong language to encourage the use of the formal caution with prosecution as a last resort, and advocating the use of post-cautioning 'support services' when 'problems' or 'needs' were identified. The result was a massive increase in cautioning. The growth of inter-agency panels and juvenile liaison bureaux required police and social services to work together, thus shifting the police into 'areas of social intervention previously guided by social workers' assessment of the needs of the child and the family' (King 1991: 103). Conversely, the social work agencies were shifted into an area of decision making previously reserved for the police – the decision to prosecute.

This discussion of legislative and policy developments in juvenile justice in the 1980s has shown an increase in the proportion of juveniles cautioned and a decrease in the numbers sentenced to custody. How does this fit with the ideology of a government apparently committed to a more authoritarian solution to social problems (Hall *et al.* 1978) and a more repressive juvenile justice system (Clarke 1985)? Pratt (1990), in his analysis of the form and nature of social control, draws attention to the pragmatic approach adopted by the Conservative government and their concern with efficiency and cost effectiveness in the management of recalcitrant youth. This involves dealing differently with the minor/occasional offender and the serious/persistent offender: a policy of bifurcation. Prosecution is costly and the juvenile justice system unpredictable. Magistrates may decide on a discharge but they may opt, unnecessarily, for some form of supervision. If many young people do not reoffend after a formal caution, why prosecute them? If they can be persuaded to accept some form of voluntary supervision, activity or reparation, then they can be brought under control and subjected to surveillance more cheaply and efficiently than by processing them through the courts. Custody is extremely costly and reconviction rates are very high, so that the pragmatic logic would be to restrict the use of custody to a minority of 'hard core' offenders requiring punishment. Most non-custodial sentences can be 'strengthened' to provide control and discipline at less cost. The ideological focus by the government on law and order must be balanced against its ideological commitment to anti-welfarism and decreased public spending, thus helping to explain the apparently perplexing juxtaposition of the 'darkest hour' for juvenile justice with some of the greatest successes in reducing custodial sentencing through 'systems management', developed by juvenile justice agencies working together at the local level and not directly seeking to change government policy (Cavadino and Dignan 1997).

Also, the changes in juvenile justice needs to be placed in the context of wider economic, social and policy developments which have increased significantly the state's surveillance and regulation of youth. Davies (1986: 81–2) draws attention to the inner-city riots of 1981 and 1985, incidents of violence at football matches and the miners' strike of 1985. These events strongly influenced ministers and were taken as evidence both of a breakdown in social discipline and the need to combat lawless behaviour, if not particularly youth lawlessness. The Police and Criminal Evidence Act 1984 strengthened police powers of stop and search, and the Public Order Act 1985 gave the police considerable discretion in dealing with disorderly behaviour; both heightened the climate of intolerance and could be used in practice to increase the surveillance and control of the young even if that had not been their original intention.

Most IT in the late 1970s and early 1980s was preventative in that it involved those perceived to be at risk of offending – non-school attenders, disruptive pupils, unemployed youth. Pratt (1983) sees this form of social intervention as a means of regulating and 'normalizing' unattached and potentially threatening youth. Similarly, Bottoms and Pratt (1989) suggest that developments in IT for girls in the 1980s seemed designed to produce 'normal' girls. Furthermore, ministers, the Home Office and the police promoted an expansion of the 'preventative' role of the police in schools and youth work, including organizing sporting and leisure activities for disadvantaged young people (King 1991: 103–4). These activities gave the police a more direct involvement in young people's lives and moved them into the field of social work.

Carlen shows how welfare policies in the 1980s shifted from what she describes as 'facilitative disciplinary welfare' to 'repressive disciplinary welfare' (1996: 29–30): 'the overall outcome of welfare, housing, educational, training, and employment policies during the 1980s resulted in a much strengthened disciplining of pauperised and redundant youth *independent of the criminal justice and/or penal system*' (pp. 45–6, original emphasis).

These policies treated youth as a 'dangerous class' to be denied adult status and the rights and duties of citizenship. The government refused to recognize that young people had 'needs' independently of their families and sought to 'enforce their continuing dependence on adults, especially parents' (Davies 1986: 127) as a means of controlling them.

Just deserts, false starts: the Criminal Justice Act 1991

The years 1987 to 1991 were to prove a period of intense activity and significant changes in the field of criminal justice policy. It was a brief interlude during which policy-making was characterized more by principle than by an ad hoc response to the political and pragmatic exigencies of the moment. This brief flowering of relative rationality, probably engineered through an alliance between Douglas Hurd (Home Secretary 1985–9) and David Faulkner (Under Secretary of State in charge of the Home Office Research and Statistics Division 1982–90), arose from a cautious and reasoned approach to policy-making rarely seen in criminal justice (Windlesham 1993 and Rutherford 1996 comment in more detail on this alliance).

Hurd articulated a consistent message based on 'just deserts'. He envisaged a 'wider and tougher range of community based sentences' in his speech to the Conservative Party Conference in 1989 (Rutherford 1996: 104) which, he argued, would be potentially more effective 'than the often pointless, and sometimes corrupting, experience of imprisonment' (Windlesham 1993: 462). Again, of course, reductions in public expenditure (particularly the soaring costs of prison building) may be seen by the cynical as an issue here.

Between 1987 and the publication of the White Paper *Crime, Justice, and Protecting the Public* (Home Office 1990), considerable efforts were made by the Home Office and ministers to gain the support of the criminal justice agencies for the proposed reforms. A major political problem even at this stage was that the eventual triumph of the law and order ideologies of the post–1979 period had fostered expectations of harsher punishment and damaged the credibility of non-custodial penalties. The Conservative Party needed to be won over to an ideologically unpalatable change in policy, the judiciary to sentencing reforms which would limit sentencers' discretion and the probation service to punishment in the community (Windlesham 1993). Windlesham (p. 245) describes the White Paper as 'a classic statement of public policy'. It sought to establish the objectives of the criminal justice system and provide a framework for sentencing offenders of all ages. Sentencing should be 'based on the seriousness of the offence or just deserts' (para. 2.3), and be 'in proportion to the seriousness of the crime' (para. 2.2), although 'depending upon the offence and the offender, the sentence may also aim to achieve public protection, reparation, and reform of the offender, preferably in the community' (para. 2.9). Deterrence was rejected because 'it is unrealistic to construct sentencing arrangements on the assumption that most offenders will weigh up the possibilities in advance and base their conduct on rational calculation. Often they do not' (para. 2.8).

The White Paper adopted a 'twin track' or 'bifurcatory' approach to sentencing which distinguished between property offenders (excluding domestic burglary) and those convicted of violent or sexual offences. The former were envisaged as being normally dealt with in the community, or by shortened prison sentences. The latter were seen as requiring custody and longer sentences. Punishment should be based on the restriction of liberty 'applied either in the community or through custodial penalties' (para. 2.11), but 'nobody now regards imprisonment, in itself, as an effective means of reform for most prisoners . . . it can be an expensive way of making bad people worse' (para. 2.7), and 'more offenders should be punished in the community' (para. 4.1).

There are serious flaws with a 'just deserts' philosophy. It oversimplifies the relationship between crime and its punishment. By making the criminal act the criterion for punishment it rules out of consideration the 'material realities' of offenders' lives (Davies 1986: 87), creating a structure of punishment but saying nothing of the causes of crime. Despite the coercive and covertly punitive potential of the 'welfare' approach discussed earlier in this chapter, it did involve a concern for the needs of the deprived and disadvantaged. The White Paper further distanced itself from such an approach in its specific provisions for young people, replacing the Juvenile Court by the 'Youth Court' dealing with a wider age range of 10–17 years and emphasizing that young people aged 16 and 17 'should be dealt with as near adults' (para. 8.16). Since 'care' cases had already been removed from the Juvenile Court under the 1989 Children Act, 'welfare' was by now on the distant horizon. The focus on the family as the 'site' of youth crime was retained as central, but with an eye to parental discipline and control rather than deprivation, making provision for courts to require the attendance of parents, to order parents to pay financial penalties or to bind over parents of young people convicted of criminal offences (paras. 8.7 and 8.8). Moreover, offence-focused pre-sentence reports (PSRs) replaced the welfare-focused social inquiry reports (SIRs). Although report writers were still required to address 'welfare' issues, this would seem to be little more than a gesture (given the strong emphasis on the seriousness of the offence); in practice this would probably amount more to a mitigation plea than a true consideration of 'needs'.

Despite the focus on just deserts and the distantiation from 'welfare', the proposals had already run into trouble by the time the Criminal Justice Bill was published (nine months after the White Paper). The most punitive aspects of the legislation were being emphasized. The new Home Secretary, David Waddington, argued that the Bill was not designed to reduce the prison population, thus contradicting the White Paper; he also emphasized lengthy imprisonment for violent and sexual offenders, and toughened-up community punishments. This, unsurprisingly, has been related to political fears that conservative opinion might turn against the Bill, seeing the more controlled use of custody and the emphasis on community punishment as 'soft options'. Meanwhile, the changes proposed by the Criminal Justice Act 1991 necessitated extensive preparation and training of criminal justice personnel, and implementation was delayed until October 1992. The intervening period was to assure the demise of the rational aspects of the White Paper.

Howard's way

By 1991 'crime pressure' (Radzinowicz, cited in Rutherford 1996: 14) had mounted and the stage was once more set for a return to 'short cut solutions', the hallmark of 'authoritarian systems of government' (p. 14). After the brief respite of policy at least based on reasoned argument, a new era of authoritarian and punitive penal populism was born in the 'form of campaigns against "bail bandits" and "joyriding" ' (Newburn 1995: 121), which were the subject of intense media attention. The police responded by 'cracking down' on public displays of joyriding, and there were serious confrontations with young men which led to disturbances on housing estates in the form of the 1990s 'riots' (see Chapter 3). The government responded by speedily enacting a new offence of aggravated vehicle taking with a maximum penalty of five years imprisonment. The courts responded by treating this offence as on a par with domestic burglary and 'deserving' a custodial sentence. At the same time, Kenneth Baker, now Home Secretary, blamed the parents and sought to establish a 'clear relationship between problem families, delinquent youth, and the (re)production of a criminal underclass' (McLaughlin and Muncie 1993: 155).

When Kenneth Clarke became Home Secretary in April 1992 after the general election, he gave the impression that he was 'unhappy not only with the CJA 1991 but with the generally liberal course that had been pursued in the latter part of the eighties' (Rutherford 1996: 127). Rutherford also argues that Clarke had an eye to the danger of Tony Blair stealing 'his party's law and order mantle' (pp. 127–8), with his rhetoric of 'tough on crime, tough on the causes of crime'. The Criminal Justice Act 1991 was undermined within a few months of its implementation in October 1992. It was criticized as restrictive by the Lord Chief Justice and the Magistrates' Association, and government response was swift. The Criminal Justice Act 1993 'amended' the 1991 Act, most notably loosening the criteria governing custodial sentences. Custody had returned to the forefront of the political agenda in a political climate eloquently expressed by John Major, the Prime Minister: 'society needs to condemn a little more and understand a little less' (*Mail on Sunday* 21 February 1993).

Meanwhile, during 1991 the police had initiated a 'sophisticated campaign ... converted into a moral panic by the media' (Rutherford 1996: 127) which focused on a small number of persistent offenders. The offenders were said to be responsible for a disproportionate amount of crime in the areas in which they lived, and neither the police nor the courts had the powers to deal with them (Hagell and Newburn 1994: 19–22). Early in 1993 when the House of Commons Home Affairs Commission examined the issue it was presented with conflicting evidence – of a rise in juvenile crime (Association of Chief Police Officers) and a reduction in juvenile crime (Home Office) – which it was unable to resolve. Indeed, the Justices' Clerks' Society questioned the 'concept of the persistent offender' and the 'danger of emotive reactions ... resulting in "sentence by label" ' (Gibson *et al.* 1994).

Kenneth Clarke had already indicated his willingness to introduce secure training orders for 12- to 14-year-olds to combat the 'problem'. By the time Michael Howard became Home Secretary in 1993, the 'folk devilling of children and young people' (Carlen 1996: 48), escalating since 1991, had gathered force as 'the Bulger case' provided a window into the worst imagined excesses of youth crime (see Chapters 1 and 3). At the Conservative Party Conference in October 1993 Howard outlined a wide range of 'tough' policies to cut crime which would increase the use of custodial sentences and which he justified by claiming 'prison works'.

Some aspects of the role of the tabloid press in this context have been explored in Chapter 3; suffice it to note that Jonathan Steele, writing in the *Guardian* (7 March 1997), commented:

> Howard's appointment as Home Secretary coincided with a surge of interest in the tabloid and the Murdoch press. Lord Windlesham, a former Tory Home Office Minister who made a study of crime stories, found *The Times* running 10 a day in August 1993, while the *Sun* ran a 'campaign for justice', highlighting violent crime. 'Howard's strategy could not have been more different from his predecessor's', says Windlesham. 'He [Howard] was generally dismissive of professional expertise, including at times advice from his own officials. Before long a consistent pattern could be detected of conforming to perceived public opinion, taking particular notice of the coverage of crime and editorial comment in the press'.

Thus it seems that advice, unless it was the media's 'advice', was to be ignored. What seemed rhetoric was to become policy.

A good example of 'Howard's way' is provided by the events leading up to the Home Office Circular 18/1994 on the cautioning of offenders. During 1993, when the moral panic about juvenile crime was at one of its heights, stories and commentaries appeared in the broadsheets and tabloids critical of the extent to which cautioning had developed for young offenders. On the BBC *Public Eye* programme *Cautionary Tales* (22 October 1993), a young offender talked of a caution meaning 'nothing'; police officers spoke of rising crime as linked to rising cautions and of offenders laughing at the law; magistrates told of offenders not brought to justice ... Actually, there was a case to be made that juvenile recorded crime had fallen, and multiple cautions were extremely rare, as were cautions for the more serious offences. Howard reacted by overriding the advice of his Home Office professional advisers, and reversed the policy developed since 1979. The outcome was Home Office Circular 18/1994, which established that offenders should normally only be cautioned once, except under special conditions. In spite of the evidence that cautioning did not lead to an increase in offending, Howard had decided 'your first chance should be your last chance' (Gibson 1995).

The pursuit of a policy of waging war on offenders in which justice equals revenge was to draw extensively on developments in the USA where punitiveness had developed apace. The custodial 'screw' was tightened in relation to youth offenders. The Criminal Justice and Public Order Act (CJPOA) 1994 represents a significant step in reversing the non-custodial policies of the Criminal Justice Act 1991. The Act introduced secure training orders for juveniles aged 12 to 14 of up to two years, with five centres being planned to take 200 offenders. This was despite evidence to the effect that targeting persistent young offenders in this way would have negligible results (Hagell and Newburn 1994).

The CJPOA 1994 also gave powers to Crown Courts to order the long-term detention of 10- to 13-year-olds convicted of an offence which, had an adult committed it, could be punishable by a maximum of 14 years imprisonment (this provision had previously only applied to 14- to 17-year-olds). Further provisions included increasing the maximum sentences for detention of 15- to 17-year-olds, tightening of the law with regard to the granting of bail and the relaxation of requirements on the provision of PSRs prior to passing a custodial sentence. The detail here is important, for one must note the overall effect of the provisions was to make it easier for courts to lock up more young offenders for longer.

By 1994 Howard had visited Texas and returned with a proposal that US-style military 'boot camps' should be introduced in Britain to 'knock the criminal spirit out of young offenders' (*Guardian* 2 June 1994). Reporting in the *Guardian* the same day on the initiative in the USA, Martin Walker headlined with 'Effectiveness of strict regimes unproven but volunteer schemes catch public imagination'. Despite the manifest failure of the 'short sharp shock' experiment under William Whitelaw in the 1980s (Penal Affairs Consortium 1995), the thirst for 'revenge justice' (Rose 1995) remained unabated. By 1995 Mr Howard was attempting to persuade a reluctant Ministry of Defence to accept young offenders into the Army Corrective Training Centre in Colchester (*The Times* 24 August 1995).

Nor did Mr Howard neglect punishment in the community: he sought to 'toughen' community sentences ('strengthening punishment in the community', Home Office 1995a), revise national standards for the supervision of offenders to tighten enforcement by supervising officers (Home Office 1995a) and to increase the element of discipline in community sentencing by making the 'activities' more demanding and challenging. Howard argued that 'offenders should be punished not rewarded for their crimes' (*Guardian* 10 March 1995). The requirement for probation officers to qualify via a diploma in social work was abandoned in 1996. Mr Howard considered that former armed forces personnel had the 'relevant skills and experience to offer' and that they should not be disadvantaged by lack of a social work qualification. He called for 'punishment with a purpose' and argued that retired army officers 'understand the need for discipline and they won't stand any nonsense. That's exactly what young offenders need' (*Guardian* 1 April 1995).

The last half of 1996 saw calls for a moral crusade around family values aimed at children and their parents. However, notably absent from the extensive discussion of moral and family values was any recognition that 'morality does not exist independently of social and economic relations' (*Observer* editorial 27 October 1997).

Then came zero tolerance: the ultimate policing solution. In an ironic turn of events, the original 'zero tolerance' campaign (a public awareness campaign aimed at heightening public sensitivity to the abuse of women and children) was forgotten in another favourite US import: zero tolerance policing. A form of proactive aggressive policing, this was introduced in selected parts of England based on the belief that if the police act on 'quality of life' offences, such as noise, rowdyism, criminal damage, drinking in public, swearing, dropping litter and so on, then the streets will be reclaimed for respectable citizens (Gibbons 1996; Johnston 1997). Young people, for obvious reasons (and see Chapter 5 in this volume) are often the target of such policies. In one version, employed in Hartlepool, the policy at the time of writing was to 'hit' youths – whether committing offences or not – on the streets, on the grounds that 'all crime begins on street corners' (Detective Chief Inspector Mallon, *Daily Mail* 1 August 1996).

It is clear how the repressive policies and practices of the 1990s in particular constructed young people as outsiders. As Vivien Stern pointed out, while other European countries tend to favour the reintegration of offenders into the community, Home Office press releases and government ministers 'use the language of conflict, contempt, and hatred' where 'doing good is a term of derision' and seeking to help offenders means that you 'do not care about the pain and suffering of victims' (*Guardian* 2 May 1996).

Should one want a rational and utilitarian scale against which to measure the policy developments outlined here, it would be advisable to glance at the 1996 Audit Commission review of young people, crime and criminal justice. The Audit Commission has a government brief to make recommendations on the economy, effectiveness and efficiency of public sector agencies. The Commission found the youth justice system to be costly, inefficient and ineffective, and as failing both young people and their victims. The report draws attention to the need to develop preventative services for those at risk of offending. In dealing with youth crime the emphasis is on providing help and support for parents and families who find it difficult to cope. An array of unmet needs are identified in relation to housing, employment and training, leisure provision, and drug and alcohol problems. Cautioning was found to work well for first offenders and could be more widely used for second- and third-time offenders if more use was made of cautioning support schemes. The Commission estimated that the number of young offenders prosecuted could be effectively reduced by 20 per cent. In respect of programmes for persistent young offenders the report noted the value of intensive behaviour-based and need-based programmes.

The government's response to the report was swift: the Home Office Minister, David McLean, dismissed it as 'pathologically defeatist' and announced the government's intention to change the law to extend the electronic monitoring of offenders to juveniles.

Millennial miseries: New Labour, new punitiveness?

On 1 May 1997 the Conservative Party were defeated in a Labour landslide general election victory. Was there really any reason to expect a change in youth justice policy, as had happened under 'old Labour' governments? Even before the general election, as we have seen, New Labour was competing gamely for the law and order high ground. The then shadow Home Secretary, Jack Straw, jousted with Michael Howard in 'tough talk' about youth crime. The Labour Party's support for many of Howard's contentious proposals facilitated the passage of the Crime (Sentences) Act 1997 through Parliament. In this last piece of legislation before the election, the courts were given powers to 'name and shame' juvenile offenders and allowed the electronic monitoring of juveniles to enforce curfews.

Before and after the election, Jack Straw pursued the tactic of demonizing young people. On becoming Home Secretary, he indicated his priority was a 'root and branch' overhaul of the youth justice system. Drawing selectively on the 1996 Audit Commission report, he pointed to a 35 per cent increase in youth crime over the past decade and equated this with a 35 per cent fall in the numbers dealt with in court: unfortunately the implied connection (that crime increases when offenders are diverted rather than brought to court and punished) is invalid since the crime figures were drawn from the British Crime Survey whereas those relating to the courts were drawn from the Home Office criminal statistics. The new government's Crime and Disorder Bill suggested parental responsibility orders; child protection orders to impose curfews on under-10s; community safety orders to 'restrain the anti-social behaviour of named individuals'; the abolition of *doli incapax*, thereby holding 10- to 13-year-olds fully responsible for their acts; a single 'warning' to replace the formal caution which would 'trigger' referral to multi-agency young offender teams; setting limits to the court's use of the discharge (i.e. to prevent them 'over'using it); 'reparation orders'; the development of more intensive community sentences; and the transfer of 17-year-olds from the youth court back to the adult court, thus reversing the provision of the 1991 Act (*Guardian* 15 May 1997). More broadly, the inexorable focus of ministerial attention centred on the problem of juvenile behaviour, under-age drinking (including claims that youthful alcohol consumption was linked closely to a career in offending – in which case around a quarter of juveniles would become career offenders, whereas the actual proportion is probably more like 3 per cent – see e.g. Brown 1994a), and the establishment of a Task Force on Youth Justice to 'overhaul' a system which Mr Straw announced 'mimicked the behaviour of a bad parent – indulgent one minute, overly harsh the next' (*Guardian* 22 May 1997).

The most insidious shift in thinking was thus from a focus on crime to an expansion of the purview of the criminal justice system toward 'crime and disorder', 'incivilities' and the now infamous 'anti-social behaviour'. Along with this came a series of measures providing for earlier and more intensive intervention in the lives of children and young people, and an extension of criminalization of what had formerly been regarded as 'civil' matters (Muncie 2001; Newburn 2002). Commentators are united in seeing the Crime and Disorder Act 1998 as the key to New Labour's approach to youth justice and as the most definitive change in youth justice policy of recent decades (Goldson 2000, 2004; Pitts 2001; Newburn 2002), heralding the 'new youth justice' (Goldson 2000).

In a new unifying theme, S37(1) of the Act gave the aim of the youth justice system as a whole as *preventing* offending. Following the Audit Commission's recommendations in its report on the youth justice system in 1996, a number of important changes were made by the Act. At its heart lay the managerialist mode of governance operated by New Labour in general. This entailed both a centralizing of control and a dispersal of responsibilities under the rubric of 'joined up thinking', and an increasingly interventionist stance. Under the Act the Youth Justice Board was created. Newburn (2002) argues, following Bottoms (1995), that the Board's role exhibits the four chief characteristics of systems managerialism: 'an overall strategic plan; the construction of key performance indicators; the active monitoring of aggregate information; and inter-agency co-operation in order to fulfil the overall goals of the system' (p. 456). The introduction of the Youth Justice Board has in particular been criticized for imposing centralized discipline whilst appearing to be devolving power to local 'partnerships', notably through the creation of new 'Youth Offending Teams'

(YOTs) with representation from the police, probation service, education authority, social services and health services. The function of YOTs, unlike the multi-agency diversionary panels of the 1980s, is explicitly to intervene: to assess referrals on the basis of their measurable 'risk factors' under the rhetoric of prevention. Thus a concern with the causes of offending had at least been re-established, but in a form which was primarily concerned with its amenability to measurement and outcomes. A youth offending plan was required of each YOT, which in turn was to be subject to auditing from the Youth Justice Board. Meanwhile, local authorities and police authorities as 'joint stakeholders' were also required by law to develop community safety partnerships with the voluntary sector (Pitts 2001). Thus were born mandatory community safety 'strategies', crime audits and public 'consultation' exercises, with requirements for target-setting and timescales for intervention. A drive toward rationalization, efficiency, governance and strategy on the one hand thus embedded the delivery of services for children and young people in a morass of abstract 'strategy talk' on the other. 'Delivery' grew less and less about listening to youth, and more and more about devising and meeting 'targets'. This is not to say that the new approach lacked populism: far from it. However, the 'populism' was to be based in a strategem familiar to analysts of Conservative Party politics in former decades: the appeal to popular authoritarianism based on a frequently overt hostility to young people. This time however, it was to be combined with earlier and more intensive intervention into the lives and morals of children and young people.

Accordingly, a raft of interventionist orders were produced under the 1998 Act that both criminalized what were formerly non-criminal matters and yet also were 'responsibilization' strategies of governance (Garland 2001). The most notable (and notorious) of these was the anti-social behaviour order (ASBO), although other important features were reparation orders, parenting orders, action plan orders and child safety orders. Whilst the ASBO is a civil measure, a court order applied for by local authorities and/or the police, non-compliance with an ASBO is a criminal offence carrying a maximum sentence of five years' imprisonment. Yet as Newburn (2002: 563) notes, since ASBOs are formally civil, they only require a civil burden of proof.

The ASBO is, both politically and theoretically, a deceptively complex measure. It appeals to popular sensibility and to media sensationalization, since the categorization of 'youth' as constantly prone to anti-social behaviour makes capital out of fear of, and hostility toward, young people. It is perfectly suited to supplement and exaggerate discourses of 'yobbishness', binge drinking by young people (especially girls), and the vulnerability of the elderly: a gift, in other words, for the popular media and for moral entrepreneurs such as ITV1's Trevor McDonald (who has hosted numerous 'investigative' shows on such issues). Hence numerous 'name and shame' campaigns by tabloid newspapers and even local police forces identifying young people subject to the orders have taken place. In terms of local crime and disorder partnerships, 'anti-social behaviour (by young people of course) is also a perfect vehicle for appearing to consult with 'the community'. As an alternative to a flat out zero tolerance campaign, which sits uneasily against New Labour's avowed commitment to fighting social exclusion, it is a palatable way to extend intervention into the lives of young people and to extend the reach of punitive law. It is very difficult to argue with adult residents of public housing estates, who appear in the media or populate the local community consultation forum, declaring that they are 'terrorized' by gangs of young thugs. Social exclusion in the form of poverty and homelessness among young people then is easily and cosmetically separated from such behaviour. The 2003 White Paper, *Respect and Responsibility – Taking a Stand Against Anti-social Behaviour* (Home Office 2003) drew for its rationale on the British Crime Survey 2002 (Home Office 2004). Crimereduction.gov.uk (http://www. crimereduction.gov.uk/) – 'the no.1 online information resource for the crime reduction community' stated that the British Crime Survey 2002 'highlighted the need for tough measures to tackle anti-social behaviour. A third of people cited anti-social behaviour problems such as rubbish, vandalism and "teenagers hanging around" as a very or fairly big problem.' This can hardly be surprising given firstly the enduring propensity of Britain's adults to resent young people being in public space, 'hanging around' (Brown 1994b); secondly, the enduring propensity of the media to fan the flames of this hostility through a constant focus on young people (see earlier discussion in this volume); and third, the extensive publicity generated around 'anti-social behaviour' and 'yobbishness' since the 1998 Act. In other words, having defined the 'problem', legislated for it, and its social construction having become firmly entrenched in the popular imagination, it is now defined as a problem! Which, of course, calls for more legislation, in terms of the 2003 White Paper, to deal with all of its ramifications:

> Anti-social behaviour means different things to different people – noisy neighbours who ruin the lives of those around them, 'crack houses' run by drug dealers, drunken 'yobs' taking over town centres, people begging by cash points, abandoned cars, litter and graffiti, young people using airguns to threaten and intimidate . . .

> Anti-social behaviour creates an environment in which more serious crimes can take hold. It can occur anywhere – in peoples' homes and gardens, in town centres or shopping parades and in urban and rural areas. It blights people's lives, undermines the fabric of society and holds back regeneration.

> This White paper is a response to these problems. It outlines the need for a cultural shift where too many people are living with the consequences of anti-social behaviour, to a society where we respect each other, our property and our shared public spaces.

> (Home Office 2003: 7)

This shameless adoption of tabloid journalese refers to a package of punitive and even quasi-vigilantist measures that, among other things, include ending the right of 'neighbours from hell' (a direct quote from the government website) to buy their council houses; consulting on powers to introduce benefit sanctions; giving the police 'powers to designate areas, in consultation with local authorities' where they can 'disperse intimidating gangs of youths and take home children out late at night' (i.e. create arbitrary curfews and no-go areas for young people without recourse to the courts); dealing with parents who fail to control their 'disorderly children' by forcing them to attend parenting classes; taking their children away from them ('intensive fostering'); and issuing fixed penalty notices. Begging becomes a 'serious crime', since measures also include 'tackling aggressive beggars . . . begging, already a criminal offence, will become a recordable offence, helping to tackle serious crime' (presumably it will also increase the 'crime problem' since the criminal statistics will increasingly be inflated by crimes of begging due simply to this change). Removing automatic newspaper reporting restrictions on young people subject to ASBOs will apparently 'send a clear message that anti-social behaviour will not be tolerated and . . . enable local people to identify breaches' (in other words, a thinly disguised condonation of vigilante justice on the part of the media and the public).

By suspending the seductively 'common sense' language used in defence of these policies, and substituting a more transparent discourse of punishment, we are able to see what the ASBO is really doing. The ASBO exercises 'punitive responsibilization' by punishing parents for failing to control their children (in extension of the 1998 Act, S38 (18–29)); it devolves moral condemnation by handing over 'offenders' to public shaming, using the media as a contemporary stocks; it neatly avoids use of the criminal justice system proper – and due process – by 'devolving' powers to the police 'in consultation with' local authorities, giving housing departments more power than the courts to punish people by making them homeless; it provides for the imposition of draconian financial punishments on people by definition already living in poverty (who presumably would have to turn to the 'serious crime' of begging to stay alive), also bypassing due process, by cutting off their income ('benefits'). It thus involves powers to make vagabonds of the socially excluded and to further alienate them from any connectivity with sociality by rendering them public outlaws. As an exercise in intolerance and incitement to public hatred of the poor, especially the young, the 2003 White Paper cannot be bettered in post-Victorian Britain.

Moreover, since 'prevention' will undoubtedly prove ever more impossible to demonstrate despite the rhetoric of the 1998 Act – since as we have long known, more control produces more (visible) crime (Box 1981) – 'performance' is increasingly measured in terms of deliverables: deliverables not being overarching successes such as real reductions in harmful behaviour, but rather measurable target-output achievement. This is an actuarial goal related to the justification of public spending. It now has almost two decades of history in 'regeneration' and 'partnership' service delivery but is increasingly enveloping criminal justice. Its clearest manifestations are in the activities of the Audit Commission in assessing the efficiency of the criminal justice system and in the 'devolvement' of 'crime reduction and crime and disorder' issues to local 'partnership' mechanisms, thereby making them subject to the same practices of actuarial accountability as, say, the funding of community businesses or sports facilities under the aegis of regional development plans and strategies. What this means in practice is that managerialist measures – measures of throughput (e.g. how fast a young person can be brought to court and sentenced), technical 'evaluation' of projects (e.g. how many young people through a project, how many complete the full programme, how many inter-agency strategy targets are met, within what timescale, how many young people are diverted from other parts of the system and what monetary savings are thereby made, and so on), how much 'capacity building' has been achieved – become the *raison d'être* of policies and programmes. Often such targets of achievement may simply be achieving a certain degree of involvement with other agencies so that the system efficiency is measured by how many contacts each component initiates with another component (or put cynically, how many expensively serviced inter-agency meetings and community forums are attended by how many officials of each of the respective partners and stakeholders etc.). The whole, as Pitts (2001: 39) correctly notes, represents a strategy of penal populism that requires that 'both policy ends and policy means must accord with the dictates of an invariably retributive "common sense" ', whilst in terms of delivery, 'the evaluative tail appears to be wagging the rehabilitative dog' (p. 40), and in terms of principles of justice and the treatment of young people, we see a further erosion of the former and a further deterioration in the latter. Nor is populist satisfaction necessarily increasing: the Audit Commission's own recent review of the youth justice system (Audit Commission 2003) found that 'public concern about youth crime remains high and public confidence in the youth justice system is low'(Renshaw 2003: 8), more minor offences are reaching court, reconviction rates for offenders subject to more serious community penalties have not fallen, and intensive supervision and surveillance programmes (intended as an alternative to custody) have not impacted on custody rates so by implication have increased intervention and punitiveness overall (Renshaw 2003: 8). A number of further issues were the focus of a recent 'Youth and Crime' edition of *Criminal Justice Matters* (Centre for Crime and Justice Studies 2003). These included an observation by Rod Morgan, HM Chief Inspector of Probation for England and Wales, that the sentencing 'drift' of recent years has been towards more punitiveness, and that 'more offenders are getting mired in the penal system for doing less and less' (Morgan 2003: 44); an indictment of the scandal of young offenders committing suicide in prison service institutions (relating to the overuse of custody and the lack of local authority secure provision) from the Chief Executive of NACRO (Cavadino 2003: 26); and an explanation of how the

Howard League for Penal Reform has come to see it as necessary to set up the first law department inside a charity 'specifically to pursue its charitable objectives', so that the League is in a stronger position to litigate against breaches of human rights. Frances Crook, Director of the Howard League, notes particularly here that following proposals by the government for commercially run children's prisons in 1995, it had felt itself faced with a choice between using traditional campaigning methods or using the courts to bring about changes in prison law and prison policy, and decided that the latter was necessary, especially since the establishment of the Youth Justice Board failed to end practices that 'in all likelihood breach the fundamental human rights of children' (Crook 2003: 24). In other words, the threat to human rights, and within this to children's rights, had become so severe during the 1990s, even after the establishment of reforms, that litigation against the government became a necessary option.

Perhaps none of this should be surprising. The so-called 'actuarial new penology' retains most of the aspects of the punitive 'old' penology within a framework of governance that is increasingly managerialized and interventionist in its 'centralized decentralization', inherently net-widening in both criminalizing incivilities *and* allocating punitive powers to non-justice based agencies and individuals, and is increasingly distanced from any notion of rights or social justice for young people in its aggressive promotion of a somewhat barbaric populism. Indeed, the 1998 Act included a provision whereby the age of criminal responsibility was lowered to 10 by the abolition of *doli incapax* and Jack Straw uncompromisingly asserted in a speech to the Blackburn Magistrates' Association that a presumption that 10-year-olds might not fully know the difference between right and wrong 'flies in the face of common sense and is long overdue for reform' (cited in Goldson 2004: 456).

Before we are swept along by this tide of 'common sense' it might be worth noting that as well as the concerns expressed by senior figures in the UK's own non-governmental organizations and professional criminal justice bodies, the United Nations Committee on the Rights of the Child regard UK policies with little short of alarm and has registered a formal protest and requirement for the UK to correct breaches of international rights as a signatory of the *Convention on the Rights of the Child* (CRC). Thus in 2002 the UN Committee made its 'concluding observations of the rights of the child' in the UK, Northern Ireland and dependent territories (United Nations 2002) following a detailed study of UK policy. Some findings of this report are discussed in Chapter 5 but the conclusions in relation to the UK criminal justice system are worth considering here in terms of their strong use of language as well as points of detail. On the 'administration of juvenile justice', the observations include:

> 151. The Committee . . . notes with serious concern that the situation of children in conflict with the law has worsened since the consideration of the initial report [in 1995]. The Committee is particularly

concerned [that] the age at which children enter the criminal justice system is low with the age of criminal responsibility still set at 8 years in Scotland and at 10 years in the rest of the State party and the abolition of *doli incapax* . . . The Committee is particularly concerned that since the States party's initial report, children between 12 and 14 years of age are now being deprived of their liberty . . . the Committee is deeply concerned at the increasing number of children who are being detained in custody at earlier ages for lesser offences and for longer sentences imposed as a result of the recently increased court powers to issue detention and restraining orders. The Committee is therefore concerned that deprivation of liberty is being used not as a measure of last resort and for the shortest appropriate period of time, in violation of article 37(b) of the Convention.

153. In line with its previous recommendations . . . the Committee recommends that the State party establish a system of juvenile justice that fully integrates into its legislation and policies and practices the provisions and principles of the Convention . . . and other relevant international standards in this area . . .

(United Nations 2002)

Is there a counter to this pessimistic conclusion in the era of New Labour? Certainly an opportunity for a real break from escalating punitiveness has been seen by some to lie firstly in the potential for restorative justice and reparation contained in recent policy, and secondly in the explicit concern of the 1998 Act with the prevention of crime, and the associated emphasis of YOTs on risk assessment and intervention.

However, Pitts argues that 'the implicit aetiology underpinning the Crime and Disorder Act 1998 is derived from "developmental" theories of criminality, whilst most of the preventive and punitive measures available under the Act involve interventions aimed at getting the offender to "think straight" ' (Pitts 2001: 75). In other words, the New Labour approach is ostensibly based on 'developmental criminology and risk-focused prevention' (Farrington 2002). Developmental criminology 'is concerned with three main issues: the development of offending and anti-social behaviour; risk factors at different ages; and the effects of life events on the course of development' (Farrington 2002: 658). This is not the place for an extensive review of such propositions, but a number of key points are immediately relevant. Firstly, many thousands of factors may place young people 'at risk' of offending, including, at different ages, 'biological, individual, family, peer, school, neighbourhood, and situational factors' (p. 659). It should be noted here that a risk factor is some specific characteristic displayed by a person or their circumstances that bears some statistically significant correlative position in relation to their behaviour. Predictors of 'delinquency' are said to include impulsivity, attention problems, low school attendance, low family income, large family size, broken families, lack of self-control, poor parental supervision, poor school performance and so on. It is of course hard to tell which of these 'risk factors' are in the event outcomes and not causal factors (Pitts 2001); moreover a further problem arises because many children who are technically 'at risk' lead 'successful lives', requiring a further equally over-populated theory of protective factors which may in various combinations militate against risk factors. Unsurprisingly, this leads to 'a great deal of interest in cumulative, interactive, and sequential effects of risk factors' (Farrington 2002: 659).

Using the approach applied to tackle cancer and heart disease, the application of risk factor theory was imported into criminology in the 1990s. Farrington alone has generated a whole industry out of the 'scientific' identification of risk factors and 'modifiable risk' factors (i.e. those amenable to intervention through behavioural programmes aimed at generating change in the offender). Perhaps the most unnerving aspect of the whole approach is that as Farrington comments, 'prevention requires change within individuals' (p. 661). Since the vast majority of 'risk factors' appear to be beyond the individual's control (low family income, family breakdown, single parenthood, low IQ etc.) this is puzzling. Presumably the idea is to change an individual's *response* to their life circumstances, not the life circumstances themselves. In other words, offending is conveniently individuated and is not a matter for social justice or social inclusion. All of this is really little more than traditional positivism of course, 'sexed up' with a contemporary gloss of 'on message' managerialism. Unsurprisingly, the 'implications' of the research are more jobs for the industry, for despite the 'commendable' (Farrington 2002: 691) UK crime prevention initiatives in recent years, much more is needed, including earlier and earlier intervention, and

> Consideration should be given to implementing a multiple component risk-focused prevention programme such as *Communities that Care* more widely throughout Britian. This integrated programme could be implemented by existing crime and disorder partnerhsips. However, they would need resources and technical assistance to measure risk and protective factors, to choose effective intervention methods, and to carry out high quality evaluations of the effectiveness of programmes in reducing crime and disorder . . . a national agency should be established with a primary mandate of fostering and funding the prevention of crime.
>
> (Farrington 2002: 691–2)

In Farrington's frighteningly totalitarian world, it seems, socio-legal studies, the sub-discipline that has painstakingly revealed the relative, cultural, economic and political basis of the creation of law, has never existed; nor has symbolic interactionism, showing meaning to be culturally and historically constructed and dependent; nor has social history, showing crime to be variable over time; nor has any of the philosophy of knowledge that regards even 'science' as developed in relation to primarily social and economic interests; nor has any of the post-1960s critical criminology.

Like the history of the application of eugenics in the service of racial purification or ethnic cleansing, this is a case of asserting an obvious continuity between technoscience and policy with utter disregard for matters of social justice or human rights discourses. All of which could not be defended even if the 'science' of risk factors *had* proved itself an effective basis for 'crime prevention'. But, of course, we will not know if this could be the case unless we adopt Farrington's suggestions for policy. For, as he notes, programmes directed at working with actual offenders, such as those dealt with by YOTs, are only the tip of the iceberg. We need to weed out all those who have risk factors and might possibly at some point in their lives become offenders, or become anti-social, and intervene in *their* lives. What risk analysis studies more plausibly suggest is that 'risk factors' reflect the complex interaction of individuals within a series of interconnected experiences of social exclusion, experiences that have both psychological and behavioural consequences for individuals, and cultural, social and economic consequences for social groups; and that this situation in turn results in the imbrication of such individuals and groups within a penal-welfare complex; and that all of this renders them both more likely to become 'statistically' criminal *and* statistically criminalized (e.g. Box 1981; Carlen 1996; Young 1999). Pease (2002), in a far less chilling account of 'crime reduction' than Farrington's, defends some of the technicist, interventionist agenda, but also makes some important and distinctive points that restore balance to the question of 'reducing crime' and 'appropriate policy'. Whilst in general accepting the importance of developmental criminology and the notion of risk factors, Pease also acknowledges the importance of 'secondary' and 'structural' factors and 'distributive justice'. Moreover, he suggests, 'the aspiration must be to develop a crime reduction agenda which is ethically grounded' (2002: 964). In other words,

> Secondary and structural crime prevention does not require a crime reduction justification, just notions of fairness in the initial distribution of resources. People should not be raised in appalling communities, not because such communities may swamp family efforts to bring up children to 'fly straight', but because existence there is wretched. People should not be at the mercy of abusive or indifferent parents, not because that represents a risk factor for delinquency, but because it makes for misery. In short, the kind of enhancements to quality of life, which could be done in the name of crime reduction, could also be done in the name of fairness and humanity.
>
> (Pease 2002: 960)

Pease correctly identifies that whatever current policy may say and do, crime reduction is not a technical matter, but ultimately a moral one. Thus the irony of a policy approach, as in New Labour, which allegedly seeks to rejuvenate social responsibility, becomes apparent. For, 'with the technicist infrastructure of crime reduction – audit processes, target-setting, and the other apparatus of managerialism – may come intolerance of diversity ... by-passing the debate about tolerance of diversity in relation to the affirmation of central values' (Pease 2002: 971). Making *social* policy a matter of *crime* policy, and making *moral* decisions matters of *technical* management, is quite simply, ominous for notions of liberal democracy. One's critical assessment of youth crime policy in the era of New Labour rather depends therefore on one's normative orientation to the sociopolitical formation.

Politics, policy talk and problem youth

In addition to the critique offered in the previous section of an academic 'science' forming a resource for penal policy, any explanation of the changes which have taken place in the youth justice system must give primacy to the influence of political beliefs and ideology. Hood (1974: 417) writes that 'the belief that expert advice based on criminological and penological research is the foundation for penal change is only a screen behind which ideological and political factors, perhaps inevitably, shape those attitudes which imbue legislation'.

While the influence of criminology has been marginal on the ways in which society views and responds to youth crime, an appeal to penological theory and research has proved useful when it offers support to political objectives and ideological imperatives. This occurred during the 1960s when the Labour government sought to promote a welfare-based response to juvenile crime. Conversely, criminological knowledge and research can be readily discounted or ignored when it appears to conflict with political objectives and ideological imperatives. This occurred when the Conservative government sought to promote a punishment-based response to juvenile crime in the 1980s. An emphasis on political beliefs and ideologies does not mean that legislative change is necessarily characterized by conflict. It is generally accepted that the development of a welfare-based juvenile justice system between 1908 and 1969 was largely consensual, in that the political parties, although differing about the speed of change and the means to achieve change, accepted the overall objective of the state provision of a comprehensive system of social welfare. Even during the 1970s, when cracks began to appear in the consensus, and the role of the state in the provision of social welfare began to be debated, the questioning did not lead to a fundamental reappraisal of the welfare-based Children and Young Persons Act (CYPA) 1969. The election of a Conservative government in 1979 inaugurated the beginning of a long period during which political ideology has become increasingly the dominant force in determining criminal justice and youth justice policies. While Windlesham (1993: 106) argues that there are 'few restraints on a Home Secretary's freedom of action', he recognizes that governments have always been especially sensitive to the views of the judiciary, the magistracy and the police. In addition, governments pay close attention to the 'tabloid and middle market press' (p. 19) as indicators of public opinion. In the 1990s, as the public's fear of crime and the politicians' fear of being seen as 'soft on crime' increased, so did the influence of the tabloid press increase. At the time of writing there are few signs that the fixation with punishment has run its course. For nearly 27 years, scant attention has been paid to the possibility that crime might have social causes and there are no signs that New Labour is about to become 'tough on the causes of crime'.

Through the twists and turns of youth justice policy, we see a recurring and ongoing preoccupation with the perceived threat to social stability posed by unregulated, undisciplined and disorderly youth outside adult control. Youthful misbehaviour has come to be regarded as symbolizing all that is wrong with adult society: family failure, inadequate parenting, all these perceptions influenced policy proposals and legislative changes throughout the twentieth century.

Even though the ' "normal" family has now narrowed to the structure of the nuclear unit' (Griffin 1993: 101), neither the diagnosis of the problem (the deficiencies of working-class family life) nor the solutions (state intervention in various guises) changed during the twentieth century. Both major political parties ignore the 'structural factors (housing, health, employment, education) that condition criminality' (Johnston 1997). Perhaps the 'political and cultural enterprise' (Hendrick 1990: 56) of the late twentieth century was the same as in the late nineteenth century. However, the modes of representation and response became ever more sophisticated and less tolerant: 'If we don't check yobbish behaviour, we create a licence to commit other crimes. Young people seem to feel they can do what they want and nobody's restraining them. We're saying there are limits to what society tolerates. If we deal with minor crime, it reinforces the idea of how to behave' (Barry Shaw, Cleveland Constabulary Chief Constable in Gibbons 1996).

From the nineteenth century through to the present day, youth and youth justice policies have been rooted in the adult world, have reflected adult concerns with the threat of youth and have been constructed to allay adult fears.

For many adults 'crime is seen as young people, and vice versa' (Brown 1995: 32). Perhaps it is understandable that 'crime' and 'young people' are bracketed together given the way media and politicians have fanned the flames of popular anxieties. However, whether the youth justice policies developed have been based on care or control, welfare or justice, treatment or punishment, they have reflected adult society's view of what is in the best interests of young people. The perception that young people are immature and are (or should be) dependent upon their 'carers' has underpinned legislation and policy-making. The consequences of such beliefs can be seen in the way in which society reacts to young people as victims. Despite the virulent punishment culture surrounding youth crime, the question of adult crime against children and young people is barely raised. And, in the policy era of 'joined-up thinking', the number of short circuits that are appearing suggest a severe wiring problem between the realms of criminal justice and crime reduction in relation to young people, and the allegedly interrelated area of combating social exclusion.

Further reading

Most of the references provided within the text of this chapter would form appropriate further reading on the specific issues. On the 1960s, see Harris and Webb (1987), Morris and Giller (1987) and Parsloe (1978). The former two texts are rather more theoretical and analytical; the latter is a historical survey. Millham *et al.* (1978), Harwin (1982) and Pitts (1988) provide various insights into the 1970s. For the transition from the 1970s to the 1980s, see Morris *et al.* (1980), Thorpe *et al.* (1980) and Morris and Giller (1987). On the 1980s, King (1991), Windlesham (1993) and Rutherford (1996) are useful contextualized accounts of developments up to the 1990s. Pitts (2001) provides an acerbic and readable critique of developments under New Labour.

chapter five

'Punishing youth': victims or villains?

In Chapter 3 we charted the processes of successive media 'demonizations' of young people under modernity and suggested that these particular ways of 'repackaging reality' reflected and reinforced a long history of excluding and silencing the young which militates against 'youth' being seen as anything other than society's 'villain'.

In this chapter we take up these themes in the context of a dualism we have termed 'victims and villains'. We aim to explore the ways in which authoritarianism operates at the level of politics, media commentary and popular opinion. We shall suggest that this both reflects and perpetuates a conceptualization of youth and crime which masks alternative realities and silences alternative voices. In particular we look at the relatively scant attention paid to the victimization of children and young people, despite studies which suggest that the young are, indeed, 'more sinned against than sinning' (Hartless *et al.* 1995). The comparative lack of research – and lack of interest – in young victims goes hand in hand with the massive pre-occupation with young people as offenders: all are seemingly inextricable from a general culture of punishment towards young people, that further compounds their invisibility as victims. We shall examine the ways in which the high visibility accorded to *some* young victims under *some* circumstances operates within a discourse of 'acceptable' victimhood which, rather than serving to challenge the systemic vulnerability of children and young people to adult crimes, makes *causes célèbres* out of certain cases and so diverts attention from the underlying aetiology of serious crimes against children and young people. Discourses of 'penal populism' (Goodey 2005: 28) exacerbate this situation further and encourage unhelpful responses such as vigilantism against individuals and ad hoc policymaking that, in the long run, is unlikely to prove helpful to children and young people.

In attempting to understand some of the key ways in which this situation is produced and maintained, we shall frame our discussion within the problematics of citizenship for young people, and within the overlapping institutions and ideologies of the state and the family as modes of governance. Finally, we shall consider the implications of these analyses for our understanding of youth and crime.

Throwing away the key: punishment, politics, press and the public

John Redwood, speaking as the Conservative government's Welsh Secretary in 1993, called for a 'crusade for commonsense' in the fight against crime: 'Home truths that once seemed banal do need to be reasserted . . . People are keener than ever to return to some bedrock of commonsense and certainty . . . Reasserting traditional values is not some antiquarian nicety, nor some new political initiative here today and forgotten tomorrow. Traditions cannot be manufactured by press release. They are in the blood' (*Guardian* 13 November 1993).

Redwood was providing support for the then Prime Minister John Major's call for a return to 'back to basics' decencies. In particular, he continued, 'children should be instilled with the fear of punishment for wrong-doing'. His assertions were an intriguing blend of political expediency, wishful thinking and accuracy – if 'accuracy' is taken as the extent to which his sentiments mirrored the values promulgated by the press and their relationship to the prevalent 'structures of feeling' (Pearson 1983, 1985) in 1990s Britain. For this may not be regarded simply as an attempt by the Conservative Party to hold onto the 'law and order' high ground which helped gain them the 1979 election and a subsequent nearly 18 years in government. Throughout the 1990s and into the twenty-first century the press and the public's voracious appetite for punishing the young has remained constant, making the past decade one of the historically buoyant eras for punitiveness (Carlen 1996; Cavadino and Dignan 1997).

As we have shown in Chapter 4, this can be demonstrated by the successive stream of proposed initiatives and legislation to curb young criminals, most particularly since the abduction and murder of James Bulger (see Chapter 3) provided a window into the worst imagined excesses of 'youth crime'. The Criminal Justice and Public Order Bill, published on 17 December 1993, proffered a 'three pronged' increase in the severity of sentences for juvenile offenders (*Independent* 18 December 1993). The *Independent* commented, 'The measures ... are seen by the Government as a response to widespread concerns over juvenile offending. Michael Howard, the Home Secretary, said 'Many communities suffer terribly from the activities of a handful of young hooligans who offend time and time again. They are a menace to their communities' (18 December 1993).

Ironically, the controversy surrounding the Bill, as Ben Adler pointed out, tended to emphasize the regulation of popular music and the 'right to rave', so that

> The proposals for young offenders have gone largely unnoticed, despite opposition from all groups concerned with young offenders ... The Bill ... introduces a new sentencing measure, the secure training order, to deal with persistent young offenders ... Five of these privately run centres (whose primary concern will be security and confinement) will be created, with places for 200 young people between the ages of 12 and 14 years.
>
> (*Guardian* 26 August 1994)

Despite a setback to Mr Howard's crusade in 1996 when both Appeal Court judges and the European Court of Human Rights found him to be unlawful in increasing the Lord Chief Justice's recommended sentence for Venables and Thompson from 10 to 15 years, the Home Secretary remained unabashed in his pursuance of the scourge of child criminals: in 1997, with an election pending, a Green Paper was unveiled proposing curfews for under-10s. Proposed parental control orders would empower magistrates to order parents to control children under 10 who were deemed 'at risk' of becoming persistent offenders. Conditions would include night curfews, accompanying children to and from school or even staying at home to impose the curfew.

From 1 May 1997, the Labour government continued in the same spirit, showing that punitiveness toward young people is a much broader and deeper issue than one of party politics. As noted in Chapter 4, the 1998 Crime and Disorder Act represented a significant extension in the criminalization of the everyday activities of young people. The emphasis on 'antisocial behaviour', 'early intervention' and 'crime prevention' serves to reinforce a hegemonic discourse of young people as a problem – indeed, the *defining* problem – of civil society. It is not the specific proposals for juvenile and youth punishment which concern us here, but the framing of criminalization and punishment as the predominant mode of governmental and popular response to young people. De Haan (1990: 112) points out that the concept of punishment was originally a feudal one which meant being 'treated like a slave'. It is quite distinct from the concept of sanctions. Punishment, argues de Haan (following Nils Christie 1985), 'intends inflicting pain, suffering or loss and so excludes other sanctions from consideration' (1990: 112). The philosophies and languages of penalty form a large and complex area which is beyond the scope of this book (see e.g. Duff and Garland 1994; Hudson 1996). For present purposes we are concerned with two 'levels' of the punitive response to the young: firstly, the insistent emphasis on the need to control youth crime through punishment in the penal sense (Hudson 1996) and, secondly, the notion of punishment as a broader cultural response to young people inside and outside the formal institutions of the state. The two facets of punitive culture, of course, reflect and reinforce each other.

It is quite clear that the framing of provisions for responding to youth crime, along with most public discourse on the subject, takes place within a language of punishment. The predominance of 'punishment' as a cultural response (in Britain particularly) means that young people are mostly seen as criminals deserving of punishment, rather than as citizens entitled to justice. As Carlen argues, 'questions of the democratic state's right to punish are necessarily bound up with issues of citizenship ... a moral reciprocity is set up: the state is to satisfy the minimum needs of citizens and protect their lives and property from attack; citizens are to obey the law and to carry out other civic responsibilities laid upon them by virtue of their citizenship' (1996: 2). The delineating feature of the punishment culture is that by sleight of hand it proclaims from the rooftops the need to punish young people, to inflict pain, as a legitimate response to their wrongdoings against the citizenship of others (i.e. adults), while simultaneously denying or suppressing the reality that young people themselves are barely accorded citizenship rights. Just as the 1990s saw an escalation in punitiveness, it also saw a corresponding diminution in the already scanty citizenship 'rights' accorded to the young. This is neatly captured in Carlen's 'political criminology' of youth homelessness. The young homeless – penalized, stigmatized and criminalized – are responded to as a 'problem population' of outsiders, a particularly vilified sector of the already vilified youth population. The punitive social culture almost completely ignores the fact that many of their 'careers' into homelessness, and the resultant survivalism (Carlen 1996) which can bring them into conflict with the law, began with criminal victimization *of them* (such as sexual and physical assault within the familial home), and was compounded by the successive failure of the state to deliver minimum levels of protection or provision. Hence,

> During the 1980s the British state failed to meet the minimum standards of increasing numbers of young citizens at the same time targeting them for receipt of tighter disciplinary controls, and, in the 1990s, even harsher punishments. During the same period it was revealed that while young persons suffer criminal victimization on a large scale, the crimes committed against them are seldom redressed ... Instead of a moral reciprocity of citizen rights, there is an asymmetry of citizenship, with young people being punished for not fulfilling

> their citizenship obligations even though the state fails to fulfil its
> duties of nurturance and protection towards them.
>
> (Carlen 1996: 2)

Since the election of the Labour government in 1997 there has been an escalation in political discourse over young people as citizens, and the notion of 'giving a voice' to young people has been launched as rhetoric on a number of fronts. There have been some cosmetic initiatives, some less so, involving schools and youth councils, and proposals to lower the voting age, as well as the ingenious idea of having young people sentence other young people. Despite these limited gains, we should focus on the hard reality that *in fact* children and young peoples' rights have not improved in the past decade, and *in fact*, despite sweeping reforms in the child protection system, it is hard to see how the criminal victimization of young people and children has been significantly addressed at all in comparison to the increasing penal hostility toward youth and the degree of concern expressed by the United Nations over the UK youth justice system.

A major issue within this is the resistance within the punitive culture to the notion of 'rights' for children and young people. The question of children's rights is discussed in Chapter 4 and in detail in Chapter 8 and it will suffice to reiterate a few important points here. In 1989 the General Assembly of the United Nations adopted the Convention treaty on the Rights of the Child (UNCRC). The UK government ratified the treaty in 1991, meaning that the government is committed to 'ensure that the minimum standards set out in the Convention are met' (Save the Children, no date given; see also Roche 1997). These include the right to freedom of thought (Article 14), the right to freedom of association (Article 15), the right of children to be listened to in matters which affect them – including court proceedings and other official proceedings (Article 12) – and that in all actions concerning a child, the child's 'best interests' should be a primary consideration (Article 3) (United Nations 1990). In January 1995 (preceding several of the legislative measures discussed above), a UN monitoring committee produced an eight-page report listing numerous UK policies and social conditions which were incompatible with the 54 articles of the Convention. These included (in a list 39 paragraphs long) the continuing legal status accorded to the smacking of children, proposals for secure training orders for 12- to 14-year-olds, the retention of the age of criminal responsibility at 10 (with the exception of Scotland, the lowest in Europe), and the extent of homelessness and poverty among Britain's children. The UN recommended an independent body be set up in the UK to monitor the implementation of the Convention, and the establishment of a children's ombudsman. The report also recommended that children's rights should form part of the school curriculum, and part of the training of the police, judges, social workers, health care workers, and staff in care and detention institutions (*Guardian* 28 January 1995).

The scepticism, and indeed outrage, with which these criticisms were received in the UK by the press and politicians demonstrates clearly enough the contemptuous dismissal with which attempts to broaden citizenship for the young are greeted. As has been noted in Chapter 4, the 2002 report from the United Nations (United Nations 2002) expressed 'serious concern' that the situation of children 'in conflict with the law' in the UK had *worsened* since the critical 1995 report. It must be acknowledged that despite this rather dismal picture, some extension of children's rights was potentially achieved through the 1989 Children Act. These, however, were narrow gains which relate principally to specific issues of the management of child welfare cases (see Roche 1997: 50–1 for a summary). Dramatic and horrific cases of child abuse, as with the Victoria Climbie example discussed further below, produce inquiries and proposals for reform in the management of child protection systems which, whilst welcome, do little to address the social structural origins of violence against children and young people. Neither do they address the culture that supports such violence – not least through the continuing obsession with criminalization and punishment. Ultimately the problem is one of cultural hositility to youth, and a deep-seated reluctance to accept that in many cases the institution of the family is a place of danger and not safety for the young. Overall, the punitive culture surges on unabated.

It is the broader cultural resonance of punitiveness in the UK which encourages and enables politicians to define 'youth' as a problem to adult society rather than as citizens, so that children and young people are legislatively placed outside 'society' proper in so far as any notion of social contract or citizenship is involved. Through an unholy alliance, the popular media generally operate in tandem with this 'moral' climate. 'Boot camps' may never have been practicable, but as a symbolic and rhetorical device for channelling adult fears they gained great popular currency, and it seems likely that equivalent languages and preoccupations will live on. The following sections explore some of the more complex and detailed elements in the maintenance of punitive desire. This necessitates locating the victimization of children and young people within, on the one hand, the domains of the family and the welfare state and on the other within the domains of public space and policing.

Young people as victims I: 'behind closed doors' and wilful ignorance

'Historically children appeared as victims for only a very short period of time alongside the appearance of childhood as a separate and protected stage in the life cycle. During the twentieth century this way of viewing children largely became entangled in viewing them as offenders ...' (Walklate 1989: 58).

In this section we consider some of the victimization experiences of children and young people which form a familiar part of our media diet, emphasizing how they are framed in such a way as to prevent them being seen as part of the legitimate concerns of criminology or victimology, thus in turn preventing them from affecting the dominant conception of youth as offenders.

Child victimization within the family

Firstly, there are the areas of victimization commonly characterized as child 'abuse' (physical or sexual) within familial settings (Walklate 1989: Ch. 3). For many young people, the family is a 'place of danger' (Muncie and McLaughlin 1996).

Despite a wealth of academic research in this area and recurrent media attention, such research, and such attention, has typically avoided conceptualizing child abuse as crime: indeed, 'a good deal of the research which has been conducted on child abuse has been concerned with issues of practice ... and the management of abuse cases' (Walklate 1989: 58). Child victimization in familial settings is fenced off as a 'special' case which is treated more as the concern of social work, medicine or psychiatry than the criminal justice system or criminology. This has occurred in a number of ways.

Child sexual abuse within the family in particular is treated within a vocabulary of 'dubiousness' or 'difficulty'. It is assumed that children are unreliable witnesses; the burden of proof may be placed on 'conflicting' scientific evidence; or, where the evidence is gathered from adults, 'false memory syndrome' may be invoked: for the criminal justice system 'deals with evidence and views retraction as evidence of telling lies. This obviously works against the interests of the child if the system fails to recognize the processes involved in normal adaptation to abuse. The image of the malevolent child appears again' (Walklate 1989: 75). This in turn relates to a broader social conception of children as liars or untrustworthy raconteurs (we shall return to this issue below).

The Cleveland Child Abuse cases of 1987 raised further central issues regarding judicial and societal evasion of child victimization. After the introduction in Cleveland of a medical diagnostic technique known as 'reflex anal relaxation and dilation', confirmed cases of child sexual abuse rose from 2 in the year for 1986 to 104 between March and July 1987, with 90 referrals occurring in May and June (Walklate 1989: 65). Of 121 children examined by the two doctors carrying out the diagnoses, 70 per cent were removed from the home by place of safety orders.

Within months, public attention was being focused by the media on the abrogation of the rights of parents, on supposed 'conspiracy' campaigns between the two doctors, on the incompetencies of social workers (Campbell 1988). Stuart Bell, a local MP, fashioned himself as a one-man campaigner for the rights of parents, and particularly the rights of fathers, and launched a high level and highly personalized campaign against the doctors and social workers involved in the diagnoses and removal of children.

The continuation of the saga of the Cleveland child abuse case (dubbed the 'backlash backlash' in a 1997 three-part television programme, *The Death of Childhood* on Channel 4) revealed that much original evidence against parents used in the Butler Sloss Inquiry into the affair was then not allowed to be submitted in the criminal prosecutions, so that in many cases children were returned to the homes of known abusers. Gerrard (*Observer Review* 25 May 1997) noted that, 'Ten years ago, 121 children in Cleveland were taken from their parents. The doctor who suspected sexual abuse was vilified and 96 were sent home. But to what? Second opinions have since confirmed 75 per cent of her diagnoses.'

This is testimony to the willingness on the part of politicians, the media and the public to embrace thankfully any suggestion that the scale of abuse is exaggerated. We are apparently unable to face the factual evidence to suggest that 'the happy family is a consoling myth . . . no matter what we discover about marital breakdown, infidelity, domestic violence and sexual abuse, still we cling to it' (Gerrard in *Observer Review* 25 May 1997).

This evident climate of denial and invisibility make it extremely difficult to estimate the extent of child abuse. In a report for the National Society for the Prevention of Cruelty to Children (NSPCC) using only official registrations, Creighton and Noyes (1989, cited in Muncie and McLaughlin 1996: 194) found that over the period 1983 to 1987 the 'sexual abuse rate increased from 0.08 to 0.65 per thousand children'. In 1989, 23,000 new cases of child sexual abuse were registered; in 1993, 26,000 (p. 194).

A more recent 'child abuse' scandal is the case of Victoria Climbie, who was originally from the Ivory Coast and arrived in the UK in 1999 with her aunt. They subsequently moved in with the aunt's boyfriend. Victoria was 8 years old. An escalating cycle of violence ensued against Victoria between July 1999 and February 2000, perpetrated it seems principally by this man but also by the aunt. Victoria died on 25 February 2000. She had been admitted to hospital suffering from malnutrition and hypothermia, but the examining pathologist found 128 separate injuries and scars on her body, many of them cigarette burns. It later emerged in trial evidence that other abuses had taken place, included forcing Victoria to sleep in a garbage bin liner in the bath, scalding and injuries with various utensils. Both the aunt and the boyfriend were subsequently convicted of murder.

Despite all of this, the predominant focus was not upon the horrific crime and its aetiology, nor was there a huge public outcry against child murder, as one might expect – as would happen if Victoria had been murdered by strangers. Nor was the case followed by a massive denouncement of the state of Britain's adults, in the way the James Bulger murder produced endless pronouncements about the state of childhood. Instead, the focus as always was upon the state of Britain's welfare systems and their repeated failures to intervene as Victoria entered the system at several points with injuries.

Of course, a public inquiry was a responsible and necessary response, since Victoria and other children's deaths might have been prevented through a more effective child protection system. The Victoria Climbie inquiry report, published on 28 January 2003 (http://www.victoria-climbie-inquiry.org.uk/News_Update/news_update.htm) revealed that Victoria had come into contact with numerous agencies, all of whom had failed to intervene. Lord Laming, chairman of the inquiry, concluded that 'the legislative framework is fundamentally sound. The gap is in its implementation . . . the greatest failure lay with the senior managers and members of the organizations concerned.' So, ultimately, this murder, as with many others like it, is placed firmly within a discourse of the failure of welfare agencies to deliver effectively; within a discourse of child abuse and child protection.

Meanwhile, Creighton and Tissier, for the Research Department and Media Office respectively of the NSPCC, reported in January 2003 – the month before Victoria's death – that 'there has been a spate of national newspaper reports which claim that the number of child homicides in England and Wales has halved since the 1970's . . . these claims . . . contradict statements put out by the NSPCC, most recently as part of the Child Abuse Deaths initiative, that the number of child killings in England and Wales has remained constant for almost 30 years' (Creighton and Tissier 2003: 1). Creighton and Tissier go on to say that 'the Home Office also provides unpublished figures on the relationship between the child victims of homicide in any one year and the principal suspect. Latest figures for 2000/2001 show that the parents were the principal suspect in 78% of child homicides' (p. 2). They conclude on the basis of research into published and unpublished statistics that 'there is therefore no basis for media reports that Britain has the second largest reduction in baby and infant intentional killings [in Europe] in the last 25 years' (p. 4).

The questions in the face of the available evidence must be ones of why the media appears to be in denial; why public discourse continues to speak of such murders as 'abuse'; and why there is so *little* 'moral panic' about killings of children.

Firstly and most obviously, abuses within the family are largely hidden victimizations. Moreover, the power to resist intervention into the 'privacy' of family life still remains a paramount social value in Britain, as was amply demonstrated throughout the Cleveland cases. The 'policing of families' (Donzelot 1980), although extending the network of the social surveillance and regulation of the poor, has not primarily concerned itself with the victimization of young people, but has rather been a history of strategies of the state to effect 'government through the family' (Donzelot 1980: this is discussed in more detail in Chapter 4 of this volume). Although the late nineteenth century saw some recognition of the concept of 'cruelty' to children, the difficulties which this was seen to pose to the preservation of the 'sanctity' of family life were never to be surmounted: 'A wall of denial . . . faces those who seemingly exposed the possible extent of this abuse; in other words when the dominant ideology of the patriarchal family structure is challenged. Within this ideology, children do not have rights. The accused parents were seen to have rights insofar as they were championed in their claims of innocence. Their potential as voters, at least was recognized' (Walklate 1989: 68 citing Campbell 1988).

The history of attempts to legislate against child victimization within the family has never approached the constant stream of law and order legislation for youth crime (see an excellent summary of these issues in Muncie and McLaughlin 1996: Ch. 5). As writers in this field have often noted, the national concern over cruelty to animals has been stronger than that over children (Walklate 1989).

The 1969 Children and Young Persons Act (CYPA), in its focus on the 'problem family', conflated the deprived and the depraved, treating 'children in need' and offending behaviour as virtually synonymous, the latter being a symptom of the former (Walklate 1989 and Chapter 4 in this volume). The 1989 Children Act, although approaching child welfare from a more rights-oriented perspective (as noted above), was vociferously challenged as a 'Trojan Horse whereby the integrity and sanctity of family life are undermined' (Roche 1997: 53), and was received with fears that 'the law has gone so far in advancing rights for children that family life itself is under threat' (p. 53).

Thus ambivalence towards 'child protection' remains the predominant feature of the debate over child abuse. The framing of 'child abuse' as a 'family matter', with an emphasis on the welfare rather than the criminal justice system, as Morgan and Zedner note, 'may well obscure the fact that a criminal offence has been committed. The tendency to marginalize children as victims of crime is reinforced by the use of the term "abuse" rather than "assault" ' (1992: 20).

Thus any attempt to understand the 'fencing off' of child victimization in the family goes to the heart of the relationship between the family and the state, and the predominant cultural framing of the place of the child within the family. These complex issues are summarized nicely by Walklate (1989: Chapter 3) and Muncie and McLaughlin (1996: Chapter 5).

Victimization in care

The growth of social work intervention has also brought with it an escalating problem of victimization in care institutions. The assumption that a child is being removed from a dangerous family setting to a 'place of safety' has its own difficulties. Care institutions, in their role as 'substitute' family settings, are largely invisible bureaucratic sites for the control of troubled and troublesome children and young people. They are, by definition, controlling institutions operating on the basis of 'professional judgement' within legal parameters; the potential for abuses of power is therefore incipient within them.

It has been estimated that there are approximately 8000 children and young people living in residential settings administered by social services and education departments (Corby 1997: 210). As with familial settings, the common term for victimization in residential care is 'abuse' or alternatively 'mistreatment' (Corby 1997: 211). Again, the framing of, and responses to, serious criminal victimization of children and young people has tended to be denied, subsumed under the discourse of the independent 'inquiry', or in some cases deliberately concealed from public view. Despite spates of criminal prosecutions, the victimization of children and young people in care has not been responded to in the state or public domains as a 'crime problem'; rather, the problem has been conceptualized as either a 'bad apple' syndrome where 'bad or wicked individuals in authority are seen to take advantage of relatively powerless young people' (Corby 1997: 211), or as the unfortunate result of situations in which 'a policy goal approved by an institution is later judged to be abusive' (p. 211). These characterizations of victimization in care are revealed as highly inadequate, and indeed the readiness with which they are accepted (despite the identification of institutional abuse as a significant problem involving substantial numbers of children; see Westcott cited in Corby 1997: 211) by the media and the public is once more indicative of much deeper problems in framing the youth crime problem. This may be seen in relation to a number of cases emerging in the last decade.

During the 1990s, media depictions of child abuse cases focused on projecting the 'evil' onto perversion rather than ordinariness (e.g. *Guardian* 27 May 1992, 14 July 1992, 15 July 1992, 6 April 1996, *Observer* 21 April 1996). 'Paedophilia', rather than victimization arising out of the everyday relationships between children and adults or the nature of institutional cultures, becomes the favoured discourse. Even here, much of the coverage warns against taking the issue 'too far', as in Barry Hugill's *Observer* coverage of a court case that 'cleared eight defendants but closed a children's home run by Quakers': 'ABUSE CASE PUT HUGGING ON TRIAL' ran the headline (21 April 1996). One might be forgiven for thinking that no occurrence of child abuse in the home had taken place. Yet the piece further reveals that children in the home had been kept in solitary confinement; that in April 1992 police officers had intercepted child pornography posted to a child care expert and consultant to the school, Peter Righton, who was living with the principal of the school, Richard Alston; that Alan Stewart, a member of staff, was charged in April 1993 with sexually assaulting three girls under 14 and subsequently jailed for four years. But, claims Hugill: 'At issue was the right of residential care workers to hug and hold children. It posed questions of discipline, affection, and punishment, illustrating the fear of paedophilia that haunts police and social workers ... the school was run on democratic principles ... It housed children rejected by other homes, many so disturbed that they were a danger to themselves and others ...' Hugill details the 'good work' done by the school and implies that its closure was part of a dangerous tendency to make a moral panic out of the occasional 'bad apple'.

Even a casual reading of the reports of other such episodes suggests a far more complex picture. The 1990s saw a wave of child abuse scandals in care homes suggesting a scale and an invisibility of abuse which implies both widespread institutional complicity and even organized 'paedophile rings'. Discussing the case of the official inquiry into care homes in Cheshire, Roger Dobson writes: 'Detectives have explored the idea that the perpetrators of these crimes belonged to organized paedophile networks, but they have been hampered by the refusal of all the convicted abusers to talk . . . There have to be some links (said one Officer) – everyone networks at some stage – but no one has ever said anything' (*Independent on Sunday* 9 June 1996).

The most prominent case of the decade has been that of child abuse in North Wales' Clwyd care homes. Eventually the subject of a three-year, £13m tribunal of inquiry chaired by Sir Ronald Waterhouse (HMSO 2000), it was revealed that hundreds of children had been physically, sexually or emotionally abused in care homes in North Wales between 1974 and 1990. The inquiry itself heard from 240 victims spanning 40 homes, but hundreds more victims are estimated to exist. Twelve victims have committed suicide. The report mentioned 200 people who were abusers, alleged abusers, or who had failed to protect children from abuse (*Guardian* Online 29 June 2000). In particular, two senior officers, Peter Howarth and Stephen Norris, sexually assaulted – including anally penetrating – boys over a ten-year period, but in addition wide evidence of sexual abuse by other perpetrators was found across a range of care homes, and foster homes, as well as a finding of physical abuse, unnacceptable use of force and a 'heavy atmosphere of fear' in the homes (*Guardian* Online 16 February 2000). Prior to this a series of 14 separate inquiries had been held over allegations in Clwyd before the Waterhouse Inquiry was finally established in 1997, but the results were withheld from the public.

In 1996, the *Independent* reported on another interesting aspect of the Clwyd case: a leading insurance company had tried to prevent the Jillings Inquiry (an earlier independent inquiry commissioned into the affair) taking place, claiming that it would be a 'hostage to fortune' and a 'dress rehearsal to claimants' (*Independent* 6 April 1996). Councillors had appointed the independent inquiry team 'in response to fears that a paedophile ring had taken hold in a children's home over a twenty-year period of abuse', but we are told that the insurer's response was to threaten the council with an invalidation of cover. They also allegedly prevented councillors from seeing a full report of an earlier investigation, sought to control claims to the Criminal Injuries Compensation Board and 'blocked the routine practice of placing public notices in newspapers seeking information from former residents and staff'. The company, it seems, feared legal claims from victims. Meanwhile, 'the Welsh Social Services Inspectorate did not inspect a single home. The Inspectorate is quoted as saying in 1992 that "There is no evidence to suggest that this problem [child sex abuse] occurs frequently" ' (*Independent* 6 April 1996).

At issue, again, is the assumption that young people in care are essentially *offenders*. Little distinction is made between categories of residential incarceration, so that in the public imagination at least, there is little to choose between a secure unit housing young offenders and a care home housing young people who may well have ended up there because they were initially victims of criminal offences. The question of the rights of children in homes is viewed dimly; control regimes bordering on or including criminal victimization are legitimated because of the supposed 'nastiness' of the 'inmates', and clear cases of institutional complicity and hints of organized crime are passed over.

Eventually, following the Clwyd case, *Lost in Care*, the report of the Waterhouse tribunal of inquiry (HMSO 2000), concluded that between 1974 and 1984 the Bryn Estyn home, near Wrexham, became the worst centre of child abuse in North Wales over a period of ten years, 'undetected by outsiders'. As well as the principal perpetrators of the 'abuse', and Clwyd social services, the report criticized central government because for more than half the period under review children's services were given insufficient priority. However, the clear implications of an organized paedophile ring, which had surfaced repeatedly during a previous and this inquiry, could not be upheld due to lack of 'documentary evidence'. At the same time the report conceded that a paedophile ring did exist in the Wrexham and Chester areas.

In the end, among the 72 recommendations made in the report was the setting up of an independent Children's Commissioner for Wales, which the Labour government subsequently acted upon, and in 2001 a Commissioner was appointed. Perhaps the most positive step ever made in the history of the UK 'care' system, the idea was welcomed by children's charities such as the NSPCC and Barnardo's. Based on a Scandinavian model, the principal role of the Commissioners is to respond to complaints from children and to oversee effective complaints procedures, as well as having various duties relating to the overall monitoring of children's services. The Commissioner's role, in other words, is precisely to 'listen to youth', and thereby provide some independent protection from flaws in the 'protection' system itself.

It remains the case however, that all of this is about 'the system', and none of it is about the fundamental social dynamics that render children, in foster families and in institutional settings, so vulnerable to criminal victimization of a violent and sexual nature from adults; and it remains the case that the clearly systematic nature of assault in the Clwyd case has been ignored (as has the obvious implication, and some evidence, that it is not in any sense 'unique'). The avoidance of this core question of the crime itself is seen nowhere more clearly than in the culminative official response to the Victoria Climbie Inquiry, ironically enveloped in a 2003 Green Paper entitled *Every Child Matters*.

The sequel: Every Child Matters

The culmination of the Victoria Climbie Inquiry, indeed of the state of the 'child protection' system in general, was to be the Green Paper *Every Child Matters*, published in September 2003 (DfES 2003). This essentially systems management set of proposals was interesting in the particular way in which it framed discourses of care and control. Described by Prime Minister Tony Blair as 'the most far-reaching reform of children's services for 30 years', it was, he announced, 'founded on the principle of the equal worth of each child' (http://www.number-10.gov.uk). 'Our goals', according to Mr Blair, 'are summed up in three words. Security. Opportunity. Responsibility'.

Apart from setting up a Children's Commissioner for England, the bulk of the Green Paper deals with proposals for 'rolling out' a service delivery plan, principally through umbrella partnerships called 'Children's Trusts'. The proposals for the Trusts were somewhat vague (and at the time of writing are still in their infancy), but broadly appear to involve a managerialized (and franchised) structure including drawing care/control organizations (social services, health services, education) and punitive agencies (YOTs, the police) together in a loose alliance. According to the Department for Education and Skills, Children's Trusts 'are a key organizational vehicle in the drive to achieve the five main outcomes for children identified in the recent Green Paper *Every Child Matters* – being healthy, staying safe, enjoying and achieving, making a positive contribution and economic well-being' (http://www.dfes.gov.uk/childrenstrusts/). The actual question of children's victimization and its causes and effects recedes further into the distance as the preoccupation with 'service delivery' expands. Unable to deal with the crimes of adults against children, and reflecting the trend toward governance and managerialism in general in the welfare and criminal justice systems, policy-makers ensure that managing risk and protecting systems from accusations of failure take precedence.

Moreover, we should not forget that 'for children who become involved in crime and anti-social behaviour, we will continue our youth justice reforms with the introduction of intensive fostering for the under-10s, a simplified menu of community sentences for juveniles, and rolling out the toughest community penalty, with greater use of electronic tagging' (http://www.number-10.gov.uk/output/Page4426.asp).

In sum, the Children's Commissioners aside, it seems that the principal response in UK political and policy culture to the widespread criminal victimization of children and young people in families and 'care' institutions is to be a systems management one. Whilst children and young people are to be held increasingly accountable for their criminal – and indeed 'anti-social' – behaviour through a barrage of punitive and increasingly interventionist measures, adults are accountable only to 'systems'. Individual adults are of course prosecuted and sentenced for some crimes, particularly homicides, but in many other cases the perpetrators are never brought to justice because, as Mr Blair proclaimed in his speech on the Green Paper, 'Government should not seek to influence the way parents choose to bring up their children – it is a very private choice'. Discourses of abuse and 'protection management' therefore ignore the sheer weight of violent criminality enacted upon youth, and we refuse to acknowedge the glaringly obvious fact that adults systematically abuse their power, resulting, according to Creighton and Tissier (2003: 2), in 79 child homicides a year in the UK – in which, to reiterate, the parents are the principal suspects in 78 per cent of cases.

Young people as victims II: the other side of the youth crime coin

As we have previously argued, children and young people in western modernity have generally been accorded legitimate 'victim' status within very narrow parameters. This has been either at the extremes of 'private' violence – child cruelty and latterly child sexual abuse in the family – or as 'innocent' victims of psychotic or sexual stranger violence. Responses to these forms of victimization will be discussed in the next section of this chapter. In this section we wish to examine what, if possible, is an even more controversial issue: the notion of children as 'normal' victims of 'normal' crimes. Until the 1990s, a growing interest in victim studies in the UK had largely ignored children (but see Mawby 1979 for an exception). As Goodey comments: 'Children under sixteen years of age are often disqualified from participation in much of social science research ... Too often children's role within criminological studies is seen as "offender" while in the eyes of the media the child is regarded as victim, for example, of a sex attack or incest' (Goodey 1994: 195).

Victimization surveys are particularly significant here because, unlike the police crime statistics, they go some way to uncovering the 'dark figure' of unreported or unrecorded crime (Coleman and Moynihan 1996). Although adopting differing methodologies, such surveys typically take a representative sample from a general population and use structured interviews to gather information on individuals' experiences of a wide range of victimization over a given period of time. Despite several valid criticisms of the technique (Zedner 1994; Coleman and Moynihan 1996), victim surveys have provided extremely interesting insights into the nature and extent of everyday victimization, particularly among the most powerless or fearful sections of the population, who are unlikely to report. National victim surveys were adopted by the Home Office with the first sweep of the British Crime Survey in 1981 and subsequently in 1982, 1984, 1988, 1992, 1994 and 1996. Only in 1992 did the Home Office begin to include younger people aged 12–15, largely due to the innovative work carried out in the late 1980s by a research team based at Edinburgh University (Anderson *et al.* 1994; Home Office 1995b). Up until this point, child victimization in the general rather than the 'special' or 'sexualized' sense had not been considered an issue in the British context (Morgan and Zedner 1992). Intrigued by the emergent findings of the Edinburgh survey (discussed further below), researchers in Glasgow in 1990 (Hartless *et al.* 1995) and in Teesside in 1992 (Brown 1994a, 1995) undertook verificational studies with 11- to 15-year-olds. All three surveys produced startlingly similar results. With sample sizes of 1150 (Edinburgh), 208 (Glasgow, research carried out in the same sample areas in Edinburgh as Anderson *et al.*) and 1000 (Teesside), in different regions – indeed, different countries – analysed independently using varied questionnaires and by different research teams, the consistency of the results underscores a number of key issues in youth victimization generally.

All three surveys found high levels of harassment of young people by adults, defined as staring, following on foot, following by car, 'asking' things, shouting or threatening and even higher levels of victimization of young people by other young people. Significant levels of victimization for more serious offences, including physical assault and theft from the person, were also revealed in all the studies. In Brown's study for example, nearly half the sample had been the victim of harassment from other young people in the year preceding the survey; nearly one quarter had been physically attacked by another young person; and 1 in 12 had been a victim of theft from the person (Brown 1995: 36). As regards victimization of young people by adults, over half had experienced harassment, 7 per cent had been physically attacked and 5 per cent had experienced theft from the person (p. 37). Again, these figures are commensurate with the Scottish surveys, and become even more startling when reanalysed by age category and gender. In all three studies, the relatively low levels of reporting to the police (compared with adult surveys) and the relatively high levels of fear engendered by victimization suggest that the experience was far from trivial in many instances. Brown, who also conducted a victimization study with adults over the same period, found considerably lower levels of victimization of adults, and concluded that young people endured levels of victimization which would not be tolerated by adults. Similarly, Hartless *et al.* (1995) categorically refuted the notion that victimization of young people was 'child's play'.

The British Crime Survey findings produced lower, but still substantial, levels of victimization of 12- to 15-year-olds, using an instrument based to some extent on Anderson *et al.* (Home Office 1995b). This is probably due in part to methodological differences: for example, the Edinburgh and Teesside studies were carried out in schools but without teachers present, thus enhancing confidentiality, whereas the British Crime Survey was carried out at the family home; the Edinburgh and Teesside questions on some items were phrased more loosely, and the Crime Survey included victimization at school and home, whereas the Edinburgh and Teesside studies focused only on public places (see Home Office 1995b). Nevertheless, despite such disparities, the British Crime Survey study conceded that the patterns of victimization in its study and the Edinburgh study were similar (Home Office 1995b).

These findings show conclusively that, despite young people's undoubted widespread involvement in petty offending (a fact which none of the cited studies attempts to dispute), their role in serious offending is minor (Anderson *et al.* 1994; Brown 1994a) and is far outweighed by their vulnerability as victims. Yet adults, whether as politicians, journalists and programme-makers, or as the general public, are far more concerned with the 'lack' of secure units, the 'terrorizing' of estates by young 'thugs' and the lack of 'discipline' in modern society. This is also despite consistent findings from numerous surveys which demonstrate that young people's attitudes on a number of measures of social attachment, such as law and order, education, the environment and the family, show them to be, if anything, *more* socially concerned than adults (e.g. Furnham and Gunter 1989; Brown 1994a; *Guardian*/ICM 1996). We are not concerned here to engage with the debate which may be summarized as 'but what do we do about the hard core of persistent young offenders who wreak havoc'; for this is in itself part of the sleight of hand which repeatedly shows an adult population in denial. The question should rather be one of *why*, despite a mass of carefully gathered empirical evidence suggesting the need for a whole range of policies which support community safety for young people, the prominent discourse is, quite literally, 'victim blaming' (Griffin 1993).

True victims? children and the effects of 'exceptional evil'

Even worse, as we have noted, there are certain types of 'acceptable' or 'true' child or youth victim. That is to say, not that their victimization is acceptable, but rather that they are accepted as 'real' or 'true' victims. Some child victims 'appeal' to the media, the politicians and the sensibilities of the adult public because they relate in some idealized to way to notions of 'innocent childhood'. 'Acceptable' victims are either victims of strangers or victims of extreme 'child abuse'. They tend to be babies or infants, or pre-teen and female – although pretty female teenagers are also frequently constructed as 'acceptable' victims. These qualities are typically stressed in the media reports, alongside photographs of them in life, smiling out at the camera from a school photograph or family holiday; or through the use (increasingly and with a ghoulish voyeurism) of home camcorder footage. James Bulger was an 'acceptable' victim. More recently, so were Sarah Payne, Amanda Dowler, Holly Wells and Jessica Chapman, and Victoria Climbie.

This is not to denigrate these children's suffering, nor to disrespect that of their families. The fact remains that in the massive media coverage and construction of a particular *type* of public grief and mourning, negative effects are produced with real consequences for other victims. Firstly, attention is deflected away from the realistic appraisal of the nature and characteristics of the majority of young victims of crime. The 'wicked step-parent' or 'dangerous stranger' stereotype is reinforced and it is repeatedly forgotten that young people are systematically victimized both in their own families and on the streets by familiar faces, or in care homes by their carers, and that these are by far the most common occurrences. Secondly, the massive public outcry and outpouring over the lament of 'lost inno-cence' dictates that 'acceptable' victims shall conform to nostalgic images of childhood. Victims who do not conform (such as offenders, or asylum seekers, or even just unattractive children) are somehow 'less' victims. The implications are always clear – 'she was just a lovely, normal, happy girl, very popular . . .' – with the subtext *and therefore a genuine victim.*

Two contrasting cases illustrate this trend. The first is the case of Holly Wells and Jessica Chapman. Following the massive national coverage of the case, and the enormous venting of emotion accompanying it, the bodies of the young girls were found on 18 August 2002. On Monday 19 August 2002, the *Guardian* reported 'the whole town is weeping', and 'yesterday, as people in the tiny market town struggled with a reality they had refused to countenance, they began to appreciate that life would never be the same. Like Lockerbie, Dunblane and Hungerford, Soham will now be synono-mous with tragedy.' Some 500 people gathered for a 9.30 a.m. church service, and 'communion took 25 minutes, as young and old, communi-cants and non-communicants, surged forward in a fervent desire to be blessed'. Speaking outside the church, the vicar stated that 'there is, I would say, evil at work when two *delightful, charming, 10-year-old girls* are abducted and not seen for a fortnight. Now we are faced with the prospect that their bodies have been found' (*Guardian* Online 19 August 2002, emphasis added). The second case is that of Johnny Delaney. Johnny, aged 15, was savagely beaten to death in the middle of a playing field in Ellesmere Port, Cheshire. He was found lying next to a Ribena bottle and a packet of spicy Monster Munch, his favourite snack. Johnny was from a traveller family and had been subject to hate harrassment. Two boys aged 15 and 16 were charged with his murder, and three other chil-dren were released without charge. Beyond some immediate coverage in the national press (these details are taken from the *Guardian* of 10 June 2003), no public outcry accompanied his death. There were no mass, out-raged appeals to end racism against travellers, or to name and shame those convicted of attacks against travellers. There were no books of condolence, just a small shrine erected on the playing field; Johnny Delaney was 'just a gypsy'.

The high-profile cases of 'acceptable victimhood' by contrast, precipitate a penal populism (Goodey 2005) that has led to dramatic and sometimes hysterical calls for everything from tougher sentences to the publication of the sex offenders register, vigilantism and death threats. The end result of the release from custody in 2001 of Robbie Thompson and Jon Venables, James' Bulger's killers, included death threats, an alleged proclamation by James' mother that they would never sleep safely in their beds, and postings of the released young men's identities on the internet (Brown 2003). After Sarah Payne, aged 8, was abducted and murdered by a known sex offender, the concept of 'naming and shaming' campaigns was born, and with it the boom of vigilantism in the UK. That this has since extended to young people made the subject of ASBOs should give us serious pause for thought. After the Sarah Payne debacle, instigated by the *News of the World*, known and *suspected* (often wrongly) paedophiles were hounded and attacked by public mobs of both men and women. After the deaths of Holly Wells and Jessica Chapman at the hands of a man who, it transpired, had previous allegations of rape and sexual assault made against him, more uproar came. Yet, in all of this dangerous and ugly trend for media-fuelled popular emotion to dictate criminal justice policy, the realities of the majority of young victims are further obscured. Far from discouraging this, the government tolerates it, and appeases it through piecemeal legislation and increased surveillance and 'vetting' to weed out 'sex offenders'; yet fails to publicize or attempt to tackle the realities of youth victimization.

The murky waters of golden pasts: accounting for collective myopia

The accounts of victimization discussed above, then, sit very uneasily with the tenacious adherence to a punishment culture which appears to be central to contemporary British societal attitudes. The overwhelming evidence is that society barely recognizes young people's vulnerability to crime, refuses to acknowledge the status of adults as overwhelmingly the perpetrators of crime and refuses to loosen its attachment to the framing of 'youth' as the villain. There are a number of ways in which it may be possible to account for the persistence of the punishment culture and the denial of youth victimization, all of which have some degree of plausibility.

The first possibility is that punitiveness towards the young is an essentially understandable, if not exactly rational, response by the adult world to the actual problem of youth crime. Such a position would be compatible with 'radical realism' in criminology (Matthews and Young 1992; Young and Matthews 1992; Young 1994). Young has claimed that a crisis has arisen in criminology partly from a refusal by criminologists to take crime seriously: that is, by playing down the importance of discovering the causes of crime, and by failing to recognize the real effects of crime on everyday life. Later on in this section, we shall be deploying this argument in relation to young people as victims of crime; here, however, we wish to examine the implications of radical realism for understanding adult punitiveness towards young people. Despite all that has been said in this book about the 'scapegoating' of young people, it remains true that young people are also commonly offenders. As we have pointed out, none of the studies of young people and crime which have stressed the victimization of young people has attempted to wave away the picture suggested by the official statistics – that there is a powerful association between youth and offending behaviour (Braithwaite 1989). Indeed, the studies cited in the earlier part of this chapter, particularly that of Anderson *et al.* (1994), may themselves be loosely located within the realist perspective, in that they also studied young people as offenders and witnesses of crime. Thus, just as Home Office criminal statistics repeatedly show peak ages of known offenders to be between 15 and 18 years of age (Coleman and Moynihan 1996), the self-report questions in Anderson *et al.* (1994) and Brown (1994a) show that petty offending among 11- to 15-year-olds is so common as to be almost 'normal'. Anderson *et al.* comment that official statistics of youthful offending cannot be taken seriously because they 'are a ridiculous *understatement*' (1994: 88).

Can the admittedly wide extent of petty offending among teenagers be used to help explain the persistence of the punishment culture? One application of the realist argument would suggest that the answer to this is 'yes'. To understand this, we must return to the studies of adult victims carried out by radical realists before youth victimology was raised. The initial implementation of the British Crime Survey provoked a realist critique in taking a national sample and the Survey had the impact of disguising not only specific localized pockets of victimization within certain areas but also particular subsections of the (adult) population. Hence local victim studies of adult populations in areas such as Islington, Merseyside, Teesside and Edinburgh (Kinsey 1985; Jones *et al.* 1986; Brown 1992; Anderson *et al.* 1994) showed that in deprived inner-city areas, the effects of crime, even 'petty' crime, could have highly deleterious effects on vulnerable sections of the population. Victimization was found to be disproportionately distributed in already deprived areas, so that contrary to a once-common wisdom, it was the economically disadvantaged resident in public housing (for example), or the socially discriminated-against groups, such as ethnic minorities and women, who were more likely to be victims of crime than the socially and economically powerful. Moreover, the effects of victimization were also disproportionately felt by those who were vulnerable, whether economically, physically or psychologically (poor people, women, ethnic minorities, elderly people, people with disabilities). The reasons for this are fairly obvious: a lack of economic resources and social power rendered such groups less able to protect themselves against victimization (e.g. the protection to property afforded by expensive security systems, the personal protection afforded by being able to travel in private rather than public transport, or by physical strength). The same disadvantages also increased the effects of crime (e.g. the economic impact of property crime on people already in poverty, the psychological impact on the frail or elderly). The Merseyside study in particular (Kinsey 1985) also highlighted the importance of differential access to effective policing. Put simply, among populations where the quality of life was already low, crime was highest and had the greatest effect.

If we apply these findings to the phenomenon of young people as offenders, most of whose offences consisted of incivilities, criminal damage, theft and offences concerning motor vehicles (Anderson *et al.* 1994; Brown 1994a), then it becomes easier to see why the apparently 'minor' crimes of the young become anything but minor in their effects on adults. It is true that it is very often the young who perpetrate precisely those quality of life offences which form the proverbial last straw for people who already have nothing. Qualitative research captures the flavour of this problem in a way which shows how patronizing the categorization of offences as 'petty' can be. For example, in one study, 'The first time I planted vegetables, and they took those. Then I put some flowers and shrubs in – they waited until they just got established and they took those. I've grown this Christmas tree and I'm taking it in before it's ready or they'll take that. The garden is the only thing I've got, it's my only outlet, but I'll just give up now and grow a few plants indoors' (single parent, victim of local young people, in Brown 1992: 42). Or again, 'They wrecked the furniture but [child] needs it . . . he suffers from Cerebral Palsy . . . they wrote "spacca" all over the walls . . . that's what hurts the most' (single parent, victim of local young people, in Brown 1992: 37).

Numerous repeated incidents of damage to gardens, fences and cars, and even incivilities such as calling 'coffin dodgers' after elderly people (p. 37) or being sworn at by children, are draining and depressing to people who are already finding living a struggle. Moreover, young people are highly *visible*: much of their offending behaviour occurs in groups and in public, a fact which in itself increases adult anxiety. As Young (1992: 49–50) comments, 'what can be more central to the quality of life than the ability to walk down the street at night without fear, to feel safe in one's own home, to be free from harassment and incivilities in the day-to-day experience of urban life?'

For a number of reasons, however, these arguments are insufficient. Firstly, they do not sufficiently recognize the damage done by the crimes which are entirely or predominantly those of adults: environmental crimes, serious burglaries, rape, murder, pension fraud and so on. In constructing the 'effects' literature in the way it does, realism is far from 'true to the nature of crime' (Young 1992). The effect and visibility of youthful offending in itself is not enough to explain the persistence of the punishment culture. We must also consider the parallel question of why the victimization of young people is so effectively downplayed, resulting in a failure to challenge the punitive frame and retaining this obsession with youth crime.

Here, indeed, realism can be turned around upon itself. It is no accident that youth victimization studies arose in part from radical realists themselves (Anderson *et al.* 1994). Most of the points made above in relation to victimization of adults could equally – if not with more justification – be applied to the young. Yet youth victimization is rarely taken seriously

(Morgan and Zedner 1992). Young people, as we have demonstrated, are a disadvantaged group; their fear of crime is commensurate with their actual experiences as victims of it; they are relatively powerless (including economic marginality, lack of citizenship status or 'personhood', non-enfranchisement). This is in *addition* to the disadvantages of power – divisions of gender, ethnicity, disability and poverty – experienced by adults. Young people's vulnerability is actually *exacerbated* by the ways in which childhood and youth have been constructed. They are not only highly likely to become victims of crime, but their relationship to the adult world renders them less able to protect themselves against crime, renders them more susceptible to its effects and renders them less likely to be accorded a legitimate voice and therefore to receive adequate support or protection. In relation to policing in particular, their complicated social positioning as offenders, witnesses *and* victims makes their access to effective adult protection problematic. This has been represented by Anderson *et al.* (1994: 158) as a 'vicious circle of young people and crime' whereby adults are indifferent to the victimization of young people and the police do not take it seriously, with the consequence that young people develop their own strategies for coping with crime, some of which may involve them in offending, such as carrying weapons for protection, and others which reinforce their invisibility, such as 'not grassing' – and the whole cycle of indifference/invisibility both reinforces their vulnerability and makes it more likely that they will primarily be characterized as offenders. This characterization then feeds the notion that we must take (youth) crime seriously, leading to a further preoccupation with the aetiology of youthful offending, to a further criminological and policy preoccupation with 'youth as problem' and 'youth-as-other' . . . and so the cycle is reinforced. Thus although the punitive culture is partly explicable in terms of the *real* effects of youth crime, mediated through inequalities of power experienced by its victims, we must also acknowledge the complex processes whereby youth crime is constructed as the 'predominant' problem precisely through the processes of rendering invisible the victimization of the young; this then becomes a crucial factor in the maintenance of punitiveness.

We have noted above some of the ways in which this process happens in the context of the everyday, public acts of victimization. However, as we have touched upon in the preceding section, public acts of victimization are only one side of the story. The welfare and the criminal justice systems both operate to reinforce particular conceptions of the 'victim' and the 'villain', so that child victims are not considered in a comparable way to adult victims. For all the increased concentration of victims of crime in recent years, 'The victimization of children is seen solely in terms of child abuse . . . In the criminal justice system allegations of child abuse are treated in a different way from other types of allegation . . . as a result, interest and concern about child victimization has developed largely outside a criminological framework' (Morgan and Zedner 1992: 6).

This is why measures such as the ASBO – and indeed, the tone of the

Criminal Justice and Public Order Act 1998 itself – are so invidious. As a 'vote catcher' the ASBO appeals to the distorted perceptions of adults that they are substantially and constantly at risk from young people; it reinforces in the strongest manner possible the notion that young people represent a criminal nuisance. By highlighting and trumpeting the need for early intervention, current policy reinforces the public perception that ever younger children are a public threat. By making legislative provision to prevent gatherings of 'more than two', current policy undermines young people's main source of protection when out in public: the presence of other young people. Fostering hostility to young people in public space (impose curfews, send them home) ignores the extent to which the home is an isolating, pyschologically distressing and sometimes downright dangerous place for many young people. Adult society, to put it bluntly, is riddled with hypocrisy. Children and young people have to *earn* their status as victims, whereas they are eagerly *ascribed* their status as offenders.

More broadly, the punitive culture towards young people must be seen as rooted in a long history in which the 'chastisement' of children is the legitimate province of the family as a primary institution of socialization and control. 'Discipline' by parents (or rather the lack of it) has so consistently been placed at the forefront of debates about the crime problem that we must consider whether there is a longstanding and deeply ingrained punitiveness towards children and young people which precedes, and frames, our societal insistence upon seeing young people as a problem population who must first and foremost be contained through punishment.

Further reading

On child victimization in familial settings see Campbell (1988), Walklate (1989) and Muncie and McLaughlin (1996: Ch. 5). On the victimization of young people in public space, see Anderson *et al.* (1994), Brown (1995) and Home Office (1995). Morgan and Zedner (1992) provide an interesting critique of the academic treatment of child victimization. Goodey (2005) provides a comprehensive and analytical introduction to victims and victimology including many references to children and young people.

Youth and crime: beyond the boy zone

At the heart of the youth crime nexus is the 'boy zone'. In criminological research and theory 'youth and crime' has been largely defined by an over-riding concern with the young male offender. This has both reflected and fuelled popular and policy debates, notwithstanding the emergence of more recent critiques.

Returning for a moment to Chapter 2, it cannot have gone unnoticed that all of the formative studies discussed focused virtually exclusively on boys as 'offenders' or 'delinquents'. Constituting the hub of youth criminology in Britain, both in terms of the production of theory and the choice of the discipline's subject-matter, all subsequent studies have then either unquestioningly accepted, or had to take critical issue with, this body of 'standard' knowledge. Latour (1986) would characterize this as an 'obligatory passage point': one is virtually forced to go through it in order to get anywhere else. In this way, *one* crime problem has become *the* crime problem in so far as young people are concerned (Coleman and Moynihan 1996: 111): that of male youthful offending.

Whether in the person of the bespectacled and besuited pre-war 'man of science' academic, or the 1970s eager young leather-jacketed radical academic, or the 1980s football-fan-gone-native academic, most criminology has been written by men, about boys and young men. This tendency is not particularly difficult to understand. An explanation may be found within the wider context of the construction of adolescence and the 'marginal male' (see Chapter 1); in the composition of the criminological fraternity (*sic*) in the formative decades (Chapter 2); in the spectacle-value of young male crime (Chapter 3); and in the obsessions of youth crime policy, which although making provisions for both sexes, have always been ordered around the assumption that the 'normal offender' is the boy or young man (Chapter 4). The interlinking of these histories produced a situation where young males were assured a place as the focus of much criminology (for more detailed accounts of 'malestream' criminology see e.g. Smart 1976; Morris 1987).

Here we must deal with the common sense and the obvious: as we discussed in Chapter 5, it *is* the typical crimes of boys which have most impact on everyday perceptions of victimization and fear – or rather anxiety – about crime. In a consideration of a wide range of official data sources and criminological surveys, Coleman and Moynihan (1996: Chapter 5) conclude that 'we can state, with varying degrees of confidence, that known offenders are disproportionately likely to be young, male and lower class' (p. 110). From the 'realist' perspective (Young 1992), it is both logical and important to concentrate criminological attention in this way. However, there are a number of problems with this enterprise, some of which have begun to be addressed and some of which have not.

In this chapter we shall examine the contributions which studies of girls/women and crime, and masculinities and crime, have made in taking us beyond the boy zone; we conclude by looking at some of the absences which still exist in youth criminology.

Girls and crime: speaking into the silence

The virtual absence of girls and women in the history of criminology is now well documented (Smart 1976; Leonard 1982; Morris 1987; Heidensohn 1994). It is not that girls and women were entirely ignored, but that female criminality was '*relatively* neglected and was treated in certain very specific ways' (Heidensohn 1994: 999).

Thus early commentators on the gender dimension in criminogenesis tended to focus on the 'peculiar' characteristics of women which rendered them less crime prone or their criminal acts less discoverable – a tired history of biologism and sexism. (Box 1983: Ch. 5; Messerschmidt 1993: Ch. 1; and Heidensohn 1994 give readable accounts of the work of early criminologists on female crime.) In general, the assumptions running throughout these diverse works were either that if women did commit crime, then by definition their lack of femininity must be explained since it was not within the true nature of femininity to do so (Lombroso and Ferrero 1895); or, that femininity was productive of specific kinds of crime involving in particular a facility for deceitfulness which rendered these crimes relatively invisible (Pollak 1950). As criminology developed in empirical scope and theoretical sophistication, the study of female criminality was bypassed:

'The consequence of this was a scenario reminiscent of *Sleeping Beauty*. Whereas the rest of the criminological world moved on from positivism, embracing in particular a series of sociological theories of crime and deviance, female crime was cut off from most of this development as though by thickets of thorn . . .' (Heidensohn 1994: 1000).

It was not until the late 1960s that questions began to be raised in any serious sense about female criminality (Heidensohn 1968), nor until the 1970s that the publication of Smart's (1976) *Women, Crime and Criminology* made an attempt at a comprehensive treatment of women and crime. The subsequent decades have seen a massive expansion in research and theoretical work in the field. While the diversity of these contributions cannot be covered adequately here, there have been certain key ways of framing questions about 'women and crime' which it is important to explore.

One orientation has been to problematize control and conformity (Heidensohn 1996). Here, the question posed is based on the importance of understanding the relative conformity of women compared with men. Developing from the work of Hirschi (1969), control theory reverses the question of why people deviate by posing the question of why people conform. In this original formulation, control theory identified four crucial factors in securing conformity: attachment (to parents, schools, peers), commitment (to conventional behaviour patterns), involvement (in conventional behaviour patterns, and belief (in conventional values). Although Hirschi's work did not engage with girls (indeed, the female component of his sample was subsequently dropped 'remarkably and without explanation': Messerschmidt 1993: 3), the problematic of conformity was taken up in later studies with a specific gender focus.

Hagan (1989) utilized this approach by locating conformity as differentially secured within family structures in western societies. The family, as the primary site for the reproduction of gender roles and identities, is seen by Hagan as tending toward one of two types: the 'patriarchal' and the 'egalitarian'. The 'type' of family is in turn defined by its relationship to the paid employment sector. Hence the 'patriarchal' family in its ideal type would have a male father/husband figure working outside the home, and a mother/wife figure in the home (i.e. not in paid employment); conversely in the 'egalitarian' type both would work in paid employment outside the home. Within the family structure of whatever type, daughters tend to be more controlled by their mothers and tend to greater degrees of conformity. In 'egalitarian' families, however, girls are encouraged more to become risk-takers, orienting them toward a future role in the paid production sphere, and the gender differences in socialization diminish. Since risk-taking is in turn related positively to the propensity to become involved in crime, so do gender differences in delinquency diminish in 'egalitarian' families. Girls' conformity in patriarchal families is more readily secured because of the greater controls upon them (Hagan 1989; Messerschmidt 1993: 11–12).

Despite numerous subsequent criticisms for its sexism ('mother's liberation causes daughter's crime', Chesney-Lind 1989: 20 cited in in Messerschmidt 1993: 12), Hagan's work does raise the question of female conformity as an important strand in explaining the gendered character of youth crime.

A directly feminist position is adopted by Heidensohn. Arguing that a feminist approach was 'necessary' to free female crime from its 'invisible state', she comments that 'paradoxically, an examination of female criminality and unofficial deviance suggests that we need to move away from studying infractions and look at conformity instead, because the most striking thing about female behaviour on the basis of all the evidence considered here is how notably conformist to social mores women are' (Heidensohn 1996: 11). Heidensohn approaches the question of women and control in two general senses, not in themselves incompatible with Hagan's analysis, but treated quite differently. She characterizes these as 'women in control' and 'the control of women'.

Firstly, the sexual division of labour (the gendered apportioning of social roles and tasks in the spheres of familial and paid production) locates women as primary 'controllers'. Through their role in the family – and despite the increasing participation of women in the paid labour market – 'the tasks women are required to carry out to ensure stability in civil society are awesome' (p. 166). In particular,

> While rearing the next generation, women must maintain high (indeed increasingly high) standards of domestic order so that their husbands and children have clean, comfortable refuges to return to from the toil of the day . . . It is also assumed that marriage to a 'good woman' will limit the delinquent proclivities of young men and that, once settled into a situation where he is cared for and occupied a young criminal will mature out of his misdeeds.
>
> (Heidensohn 1996: 166)

When women do not comply with the ideology of control, they are blamed for increases in public disorder: absent mothers, inadequate mothers, single mothers, working mothers have all been variously accused of being responsible for the (male) youth crime rate (Heidensohn 1996: 167). Because of the weight of these societal expectations, Heidensohn argues that women's investment in societal stability is 'clearly enormous'. In other senses, too, women play a significant role in the maintenance of social order. In their roles in the control professions (e.g. social work and criminal justice occupations) they occupy the position of the 'patriarchal feminine': they have 'been assimilated into the existing patriarchal system as professional handmaidens . . . women are interposed between the state and people, strategically softening the sternness of its power' (p. 173). Women are not typically in positions of high authority in the police force, the prison service, the legal profession or the social work professions, but they control for the controllers.

Women thus have a high stake in conformity due to their responsibilities as controllers; but more, argues Heidensohn, 'this pales beside the complex but enormously limiting forces which operate *upon* women' (p. 174). Women are constrained at home through domestic responsibilities (the famous truism that it is more difficult to commit armed robbery when pushing a baby buggy), through discipline and domination, whether physically and psychologically through domestic violence, or through other forms of subordinating ideologies which frame women as the peacekeepers and the home-makers rather than the breadwinners and the risk-takers. The public nature of much conventional criminality by default means that women, who even today live far more within the 'private sphere' of home and family than do men, are less likely to participate in 'normal crimes' (Hagan *et al.* 1979; Box 1983). This in turn may be linked to notions of opportunity and differential association (Box 1983), since the sexual division of labour and the ideology of femininity severely limit women's access in particular to more serious forms of crime. Organized crime, for example, 'is not an "equal opportunity employer"; there are glorified Godfathers, but what happened to the Godmothers? They are relegated to subordinate participatory positions' (Box 1983: 182). Similarly, there are so few women in positions of real power within the corporate and financial sectors that they are unlikely to number among the Robert Maxwells of this world (Box 1983; Levi 1994).

Thus the variants of control theory begin to offer possibilities for a broadening of the horizons in youth criminology by highlighting the gendered nature of conformity. A further, related, avenue of inquiry has been to turn attention to the regulation of girls through 'policing'. This term is defined in a much broader sense than that of the police force; rather, it refers to control and containment through the criminal justice system more broadly and through other societal institutions which are implicated in securing conformity among girls and women. As Cain (1989: 1) comments, 'feminist criminologists had begun to point out the continuity between the ways in which women and girls are pressured and schooled to conformity by the criminal justice system and the ways in which they are controlled by a myriad of other institutions and structures in society at large'. The criminal justice system is usually the last domain through which girls are policed because the everyday scrutinies to which they are subjected are far closer than those applied to boys. In this sense feminism *transgresses* criminology because very few girls escape other, 'lower level' forms of control sufficiently to find themselves the object of the scrutiny of the criminal justice system (Hagan *et al.* 1979; Cain 1989). Nevertheless the question remains as to what happens when girls do transcend informal modes of control and become the focus of official attention. Feminist research has suggested that the kinds of concerns – particularly the focus on the sexuality and sexual reputation of girls – which characterize informal controls over them in everyday life (Lees 1989) are reproduced 'writ large' in the criminal justice system. The notion of 'chivalry' suggests that girls are less likely to come to the attention of the courts because of paternalism on the part of police officers, or are treated more leniently when they are brought before the court (see Cavadino and Dignan 1997: 280–3); however, research findings have also suggested that where female offenders are perceived as contravening norms of acceptable feminine behaviour then they may be 'doubly damned': they have broken the formal law, and they have broken the informal rules of femininity. Indeed, in some cases, the very notion of girls having broken the law suggests to the court that (since 'normal' femininity is conformist) there must be something very wrong with these young women. In the latter cases the response of the court is likely to result in greater intervention and more severe sentences than would otherwise be the case (Morris 1987; Heidensohn 1996; Cavadino and Dignan 1997). These are complex issues based on a great deal of often contradictory evidence which it is not the purpose of this chapter to examine in detail; what is of interest is the way in which a focus upon girls as offenders immediately opens up a whole series of new questions which had simply not been considered relevant to traditional criminology.

If girls are offenders, does this mean that there must be something 'special' about them? Why is it not possible to make simple comparisons between the sentencing of boys and girls? The answer to the first question must certainly be that numerically it is unusual for girls to engage in crime to the same extent as boys; whether this must make them qualitatively 'different' (from what?) is another issue. The answer to the second question must tentatively be that certainly the responses of the courts themselves, through the sentencing process, appear to construct female offenders as 'special' and male offenders as 'normal', reinforcing the notion that criminality is a male preserve and that female criminality is a very peculiar phenomenon indeed.

This further highlights the silent spaces in the discipline. What *of* female criminals? Female criminality remains an under-researched area. Studies of female criminals have tended to reflect stereotypes of sex roles by, for example, concentrating on petty female property crime such as shoplifting or prostitution (Morris 1987). This emphasis has been challenged both statistically and theoretically. Morris writes:

> In brief, it is questionable how helpful it is to categorize such offences as predominantly 'masculine' or 'feminine' . . . clearly, women are more commonly labelled prostitutes or criminalized in the interaction, but the actual behaviour objected to requires two persons . . . and the female prostitute services a number of male 'clients' . . . More men than women, therefore, are 'involved' in prostitution. Similarly, shoplifting is not numerically more common amongst women and girls than amongst men and boys . . . The claim that shoplifting is an offence committed mainly by women is a myth, but one which persists.
> (1987: 30)

Morris thus objects to an overemphasis on women's conformity and to the sex role-typing of female criminality. She contends that the tendency to socialize women into a certain role may not speak to their criminality or lack of it at all:

> Explanations for conformity and criminality can be linked: for example, women may be socialized into a certain kind of role – passive, dependent, gentle and so on – which is far removed from the stereotype of criminality; criminal women, therefore, may also be those who are under- or badly socialized, or who reject that socialization . . . But explanations for conformity and criminal behaviour need not be linked. Women can be socialized in a particular way, but nevertheless commit crimes . . . Criminal behaviour is not peculiar to any particular . . . sex; the same explanatory principles should be relevant for each or at least be able to take account of any differences in criminal behaviour.
>
> (pp. 39–40)

On the basis of this, Morris would argue against a 'special' theory for women's criminality, and calls for a reconsideration of the relevance to women of 'general' criminological theories (p. 75). The problem with this, of course, is whether theories which have been constructed on the basis of male researchers studying the experiences of boys and men *can* be deemed to be general theories. Certainly Leonard (1982), Box (1983) and Messerschmidt (1993) show that there are circumstances in which 'general' (that is, 'malestream') criminological theories (as discussed in Chapter 2 of this volume) can plausibly be applied to female crime. But equally, one might contend, there are as many circumstances in which they cannot (Messerschmidt 1993). The problem has been the lack of empirical studies which would make these kinds of argument open to evaluation.

Carlen *et al.*'s *Criminal Women* (1985) was ground-breaking in this respect. Utilizing detailed life histories of criminal women, the authors are able to demonstrate that women who offend express values or objectives which may well be espoused also by male criminals; yet at the same time it is undeniable that their criminal careers are refracted through life experiences which are specifically gendered. Indeed, they are able to use criminal women's accounts (in this case, some of the authors' own) to show that the problem is not so much one of whether crime (or particular crimes) should be conceptualized in terms of 'masculine/feminine', but rather one of the inadvisability of creating any monolithic, monocausal approach to explaining offending:

> The autobiographical accounts demonstrate in fine detail how, under certain material and ideological conditions, either law-breaking and/ or other forms of deviant protest may indeed comprise rational and coherent responses to women's awareness of the social disabilities imposed upon them by discriminatory and exploitative class and

gender relations. Second, that the complexity of the accounts should call into question *all* of the monocausal and global theories of crime.

(1985: 8–9)

The women's accounts in Carlen *et al.*'s study show that criminal women may espouse a desire for fun, independence, success; their criminal acts may be intentional and rational within their particular circumstances; and the nature of their criminal activities certainly do not remain tied to shoplifting or prostitution:

> Although their individual quests for success took entirely different forms, each one of them, at some time in her career, deliberately engaged in lawbreaking as a way of either achieving satisfaction as a person or of resolving some of the contradictions facing her as a woman. Chris . . . saw crime as a way of fulfilling her need for excitement and success; Christina . . . on several occasions saw crime as being the best way of achieving her desire for kicks and high income . . . Jenny, a working class woman with an entrepreneurial flair, saw fraud as being the only method by which she could ever expect to succeed as a business woman in a man's world.
>
> (p. 11)

Carlen's achievement in this and subsequent work (see, e.g. *Women, Crime and Poverty*, 1988) was to show the importance of debunking either an over-reliance on 'grand theory' which denies the complexity of individual experience, or an over-reliance on notions of the 'masculine' and the 'feminine', *without* denying that criminality is undoubtedly engaged in and experienced through life experiences which are differentiated by one's positioning in gendered social relations. As such, this work shifted the ground of debate away from a simple critique of the 'malestream' but retained the need for a recognition of the gendering of the 'crime question'.

What is still lacking, however, is a body of comparable research with girls who offend. While the bulk of criminological research in the 'formative years' concentrated on young male offenders, and the feminist critique at least refocused on women offenders and the gendering of crime, most studies of girls have occurred within a broader ambit of youth studies or cultural studies (McRobbie and Nava 1984; McRobbie 1991). 'Girlhood' has been researched largely within a concern with 'bedroom cultures', the everyday interactions of young female social networks, sexuality or the dynamics of consumption (e.g. of fashion, magazines, music and advertising: Förnas and Bolin 1995). Similarly there are many studies of the ways in which girls are processed by the welfare and criminal justice systems, focusing in particular on the sexualization of their offending (see discussion above and Hudson 1989). A further area has been the feminist contribution to the study of women and girls as victims of crime (see Chapter 5), which while of undisputed importance, still does not address the question of the girl offender. Where studies of girls' criminality have occurred, they have usually focused on issues of drug use, prostitution, or girls' participation in gangs (Campbell 1984; Cain 1989).

Since empirical knowledge of girl offenders is so limited compared to studies of boys, it is very difficult to achieve any finer-grained understanding of the gendering of youthful criminality, and much easier to concentrate on girls' *lack* of criminality on the one hand and boys' crime-*proneness* on the other. The latter are the focus of the latest 'knowledge explosion' occuring within criminology, taking us back to boys through masculinities theories.

Boy-ness and crime: masculinities

The very positioning of boys within criminology as the 'typical' offender has obscured one glaring factor: if it is to be boys who occupy the criminological gaze, then surely their 'boy-ness' ought at least to be an issue? Notwithstanding the references within many of the formative studies (and particularly those of the CCCS) towards masculinity, it has only been recently that masculinity (or, the preferred term, masculin*ities*) has begun to emerge as a growth industry within criminology (Newburn and Stanko 1994). As Messerschmidt (1993: 1) notes,

> There is little doubt that, although traditionally written by men and primarily about men and boys, major theoretical works in criminology are alarmingly gender-blind. That is, while men and boys have been seen as the 'normal subjects,' the gendered content of their legitimate and illegitimate behaviour has been virtually ignored. So remarkable has been the gender-blindness of criminology that whenever the high gender ratio of crime is actually considered, criminology has asked 'why is it that women do not offend'? (rather than 'why do men disproportionately commit crime'?) . . .
>
> (Messerschmidt 1993: 1)

The message to be taken from this is that somehow masculinity is bound up with criminality, and masculinities theory is a necessary precursor to an understanding of how this might be so. We must therefore consider masculinities as an area of study in general before considering how it might be applied to criminological understandings of gender divisions in youth crime. As with feminist theories (and partly stemming from or through engagement with such theories), masculinities theories question fundamentally the innateness of sex-role differences. 'To be a man', as 'to be a woman', is not something which is biologically given, but something which is achieved through social practices. Predicated on a complex analysis of historical developments in the division of labour in society, we can but summarize this briefly here (see Messerschmidt 1993: Ch. 3). As Heidensohn (1996) related female conformity to women's positioning in the structures of the gendered division of labour, so Messerschmidt notes that in western societies, 'labor has been divided by gender for (1) house-work (2) child care (3) unpaid versus paid work, and (4) within the paid labor market and individual workplaces' (1993: 64). This division of labour entails considerable inequalities of power and authority between men and women:

> A manifestation of gender relations of power is the obvious structural fact that men control the economic, religious, political, and military institutions of authority and coercion in society. In addition to such large-scale institutional power, gender power organizes advantage and inequality within smaller social groups and institutions (e.g., the family, peer group, and workplace) . . . in most (but clearly not all) situations, men are able to impose authority, control, and coercion over women.
>
> (Messerschmidt 1993: 71; see also Connell 1987)

Masculinities, however, operate within hierarchies which are not simply based on a male-female dichotomy, but on the notion of hierarchies of power which delineate 'more' and 'less' masculine men. It is important to appreciate that when Messerschmidt talks of 'gender power' he is not characterizing power as a 'thing' which men simply have over women. The whole point about the gender division of labour is that it arranges individuals in relation to other individuals (Messerschmidt 1993: 71). This can include men over men, and also is not dependent upon one source of power such as access to material resources. A woman may have more access to material resources than an unemployed man, but it does not necessarily decrease his interpersonal power in terms of his ability to rape (p. 72). Also, 'power among men is likewise unequally distributed since some groups of men (in terms of class, race and sexual preference, for instance) have greater authority and, therefore, more power than others' (p. 72 citing Connell 1987). Some men, in other words, are more manly than others; some women are more able to resist male subordination than others. The 'ultimate masculinity' reigns both above other men and above other women, in terms of numerous constellations of prowess: cultural dominance, access to material resources, physical force (or the ability to command physical force) and so on.

Unlike (for the most part) early feminist theories of the masculine-feminine relationship, masculinities theories tend to emphasize the notion of hegemonic and subordinated masculinities. This is really to acknowledge the hierarchization of gender/power relations. Referring back to Chapters 2 and 3, this is based on the notion of Gramscian Marxism that hegemony is a dominant conception of reality diffused throughout social life and which 'comprises "the 'spontaneous' consent given by the great masses of the population to the general direction imposed on social life by the dominant fundamental group" ' (Messerschmidt 1993: 81–2 citing Gramsci 1978).

The question is, what does this actually *mean*? Messerschmidt argues that 'simply defined, in any culture, hegemonic masculinity is the idealized form of masculinity in a given historical setting. It is culturally honored, glorified, and extolled' (p. 82 following Connell 1987). Quite who, or what, the 'dominant fundamental group' are may leave one somewhat perplexed, but the general point that a consensus operates in society to sustain notions of idealized masculinity can hardly be misunderstood once the male fantasy figures in sport and popular culture are considered, nor that these notions contain embedded within them connotations of power which may not be easy to articulate or precisely pin down yet are nevertheless strangely tangible. Subordinated masculinities, then, must represent those forms of masculinity which express a different voice, such as male gay culture. This leads to the idea that 'masculinity' (and hence the term masculini*ties*) is a contested ground – to state the obvious! *Men* cannot agree about what masculinity is, but some have more power than others to make their voices heard.

Messerschmidt (1993: 82) argues that hegemonic masculinity is 'defined through work in the paid-labor market, the subordination of women, heterosexism, and the driven and uncontrollable sexuality of men. Refined still further, hegemonic masculinity emphasizes practices toward authority, control, competitive individualism, independence, aggressiveness, and the capacity for violence.'

The qualities of subordinated masculinities receive rather less attention: gay cool? The male victim? The ecological tree-dwelling/tunnel-digging male?

It is further possible (and probably likely) that these rather general sociological treatments of masculinities can go only so far. This is simply because, having stressed that there is a relationship between what is ascribed (hierarchies of material resources, physical power) and what is achieved (the identity of who I am/want to be), masculinities studies hit a central problem: how is masculinity achieved subjectively? Put in its simplest form: if you are a male and you are a football fan, why (Hornby 1992)? Hegemonic masculinity as embodied in football culture denotes not only physical prowess, wealth and sexual power, but also a form of assertion of the desirable way to *be* which locks out femininity by default. No matter how many women watch or even play football, they are ultimately there as spectators to the psychic structure, the 'deep play' in which only masculinity matters (Williams and Taylor 1994: 214).

Jefferson (1994) argues for the need to theorize masculine subjectivity in order to begin to understand how masculinities take expression in culture. Boys and men do not simply assimilate the hegemonic ideal of masculinity unproblematically; some reject it (as through some forms of gay culture) and others adopt an approximation to it, but not without experiencing a good deal of pain along the way. Hegemonic masculinity, indeed, while offering the 'advantages' of power over others, creates a good deal of insecurity for boys and men:

I have argued that the idea of masculinity as an ideal that all men aspire to and which is unproblematically internalised by successive generations of male children ... ignores the obvious difficulties that boys and men often have in either accepting or achieving the ideal, or both. This all but universal experience of failure can lead to an active rejection of the ideal on offer and a positive identification with an alternative, albeit subordinate, masculinity; painful, sometimes frenzied, attempts to drag an unwilling psyche into line with the unwanted social expectations; living a quiet life of desperation; or, perhaps most commonly, a lot of faking it.

(Jefferson 1994: 13)

What then, do these explorations in masculinity imply for the study of youth and crime? Certainly, that if we return to the question of the 'boyness' of crime as a problematic, then it is the relationship between attempts to achieve masculinity, the practices implied by that, and the subjective orientations required for it, which must be placed centre stage in understanding a whole range of male criminal behaviour. It is not too difficult to see how many earlier studies of, for example, boys in gangs or groups show how they become involved in delinquency as a way of 'doing masculinity'. Most of the studies discussed in Chapter 2 can be re-theorized in this way. The 'frustrated aspirations' mode of explanation so often used in early theorizing can be framed as frustrated (masculine) aspirations, as Messerschmidt's (1994) reworking of some of this literature demonstrates. Aggressive normative heterosexuality, power over young women, toughness, smartness, group territorialism, individual competitiveness and other attributes of delinquency in (male) group settings may be understood as ways of aspiring to hegemonic masculinity; if legitimate avenues are unavailable or unattainable then illegitimate ones are usually attainable. Referring back to Willis' 'Lads' and 'Ear'oles' in *Learning to Labour* (1977), Messerschmidt (1994: 92–3) situates the oppositional behaviour of 'the Lads' specifically within masculinity:

> The Lads come to school armed with traditional notions of white, working class masculinity: the idea that 'real men' choose manual, not mental labour ... schooling is deemed irrelevant to their working class future and 'emasculating' to their conception of masculinity ... Constructing masculinity around physical aggression, the Lads – eschewing academic achievement – draw on an available resource that allows them to distance and differentiate themselves from the non-violent 'Ear'oles' ... Such behaviours help transcend the 'sissyish' quality of the school day while simultaneously distancing the Lads from the conformists.

Masculinity, then, will be done differently in different settings and according to the different cultural resources available: sometimes this will fall on the wrong side of the law. Hence Levi, discussing the relationship of masculinity to white-collar crime, argues that the values of deregulated corporate capitalism are themselves highly masculinist, which in turn provides a cultural resource in which fraud becomes a kind of overdrive version of 'normal practice':

> Many [convicted fraudsters] are 'driven' characters for whom, in the words of Gordon Gekko in *Wall Street*, 'lunch is for wimps' and everything is subordinated to the objectives of attaining peer-group respect, of controlling others and avoiding being controlled by them. It may also be that despite the apparent gender-neutrality of 'deceitfulness' that is at the core of fraud, men are prone to adopt an 'aggressive' rather than 'compliant' style of manipulativeness. It may be no accident that mega-salespeople in financial services attract the *soubriquet* 'Big Swinging Dick': I know of no women who have been awarded that honorary title!
>
> (Levi 1994: 250)

Again, Campbell, in a more journalistic account (1993), uses a kind of masculinity theory to account for the activities of young men in episodes of urban unrest. Dispossessed young males in tracts of urban wasteland, deprived of their 'traditional' modes of doing masculinity (the breadwinner, the patriarch, the head of household) instead find alternative resources in the cultures of wrecking and joyriding (see Chapter 3). While the women attempt to deal with the problems of long-term urban decline through communitarian solutions, attempting to 'build up' fragmented structures through credit unions, local self-help schemes and working with the local authorities, the boys concentrate on smashing things up: 'The men and boys arraigned in Cardiff's riot trials would, in the olden days of the Fifties and Sixties, when their parents were their age, have been wrought in the image of what used to be known as "the working man" . . . One generation later the men's relationship to the world of work has changed: instead of being defined by work, it came to be increasingly defined by crime' (Campbell 1993: 196).

For Campbell, this response through crime to a loss of traditional masculinity is not simply rational and material (an income by other means), but ingrained more deeply in 'macho' subjectivity. Hence, for example, her depiction of the joyriding culture:

> The driver was dressed, the car was ready . . . the hooded driver, known as the Don, revved a stolen two-litre Maestro and skated past the police and a watching crowd at 60 mph . . . This master of joyriding did indeed bring great joy to his audience, who savoured the chagrin of the officers doomed to do nothing but watch man tango with machine. Rude and red, the Maestro was a perfect dancing partner for the mystery man . . . 'That was to show that we ain't skinning teeth, we're not fucking around, we're doing what we want!' explained the Don.
>
> (Campbell 1993: 254)

Thus in one sense, writings on masculinities and crime began to attempt what Carlen *et al.* set out to do for 'women and crime' in *Criminal Women* (1985) over a decade before: gender and gendered practices may be seen as a prism through which acts, sometimes criminal, are refracted. Crime is not presented as reducible to masculinity, nor is masculinity seen as a unity; but there, running through much criminal activity, are social practices which frequently are positioned, in various ways, toward the cultural predominance of the hegemonic masculine ideal. Much of this work to date has concerned itself with re-evaluating the mass of previous 'malestream' criminology. But there is a problem here, in that comparatively few studies are as yet available which specifically build masculinities theory into their original conceptualization (*British Journal of Criminology* 1988); and there are many areas yet to be explored, such as the emergent literature on subordinated masculinities: what happens, for example, when boys or men are victims? What of boys' fear of crime? Boys, after all, are not just offenders (Newburn and Stanko 1994; Goodey 1995). The contribution of masculinities theorizing in criminology is very much an unfinished story, albeit one of interest and promise.

Beyond the boy zone?

Clearly the work on gender and crime discussed in this chapter does prise open a little more the vice-like grip which 'youth crime equals male offender' has exerted on the field of youth criminology. It takes us beyond the 'boy zone': but how far?

While many of the recent studies of gender and crime have emphasized the multiple, flexible and achieved nature of gendered practices, thereby rendering gender irreducible to 'crime' or vice versa, perhaps there are difficulties in treating the domain of the 'criminal' as always-already gendered. From a conventional wisdom in early criminology in which gender was virtually ignored, there is a danger in the 'new' gendered criminology of producing a conventional wisdom in which gender *cannot* be ignored, since its importance is so 'obvious'. Is 'gender' always useful in understanding youth criminality, youth victimization or youth justice policy? Does masculinities theory return us too glibly to the boy zone? In beginning to recognize the diversity of both crime (it is not just about the everyday crimes of the young and poor) and gender (it is not just about unitary identities of male and female), criminology may ultimately have to question the relevance of giving either youthfulness or gender too much centrality in understanding crime.

Further reading

Heidensohn (1994) provides an overview of the study of female criminality in criminology, and an application of control theory to gender and crime (1996). Box (1983: Ch. 5) remains a relevant discussion of female powerlessness and crime. Carlen is an unmissable author on gender and criminality (e.g. Carlen *et al.* 1985; Carlen 1988). Leonard (1982) provides a useful early reassessment of 'malestream' criminology, and Messerschmidt (1993) also gives a critique and reassessment of conventional theorizing in the light of 'masculinities'. Newburn and Stanko (1994) provide an interesting edited collection on aspects of masculinities and crime. Jefferson, in the 1997 edition of the *Oxford Handbook of Criminology* (Maguire *et al.* 1997), demonstrates an application of psychoanalytic perspectives to masculinities and crime.

Netdangers: cyberkids and cybercrimes

This chapter will examine the rapid and far-reaching impact of the virtual on our understandings of youth, crime and victimization. We shall begin with an overview of some key theoretical issues in the study of cyberspace and the internet, which have relevance for children and young people's interrelation with information and communication technologies (ICTs), especially in their 'virtual' form.

We shall examine the construction of 'youth' in virtual space, showing how the places and spaces of danger in the offline world have been extended to the global, potentially infinite spaces of the cyber, opening up new challenges for criminologists and policy-makers.

Initially, adult concerns – in the form of policy, academic and popular discourse – will be considered. Oswell (1998) has schematized these as comprising 'the child-in-danger', the 'child-as-victim' and the 'dangerous child'. Adult responses to netdangers will be considered critically in the light of Oswell's observation that 'policy decisions are made, not in response to "real" children, but in relation to their representation and the authority of those who claim to represent them' (Oswell 1998: 271). Finally however, we shall consider positive aspects of virtuality for young people and in particular how virtual space may offer children and young people empowering places in which to exercise their autonomy outside of adult surveillance and control, thereby challenging the passive status that they have been accorded and enabling them to define their own senses of identity and rights, and consequently, strengths. The tension between this argument and the difficulties presented by netdangers, in particular where issues of identity and consent become blurred, needs careful consideration. Echoing dilemmas faced by advocates of children's rights, is there a real possibility that if we refute the ascription of vulnerability to children and young people altogether, then we also collude with those adults who seek to exploit and abuse the less powerful?

There are no clear-cut answers to any of these questions, but this chapter seeks to explore whether cyberspace provides young people with a context within which they can demand that adults 'listen to youth', or whether it is just another 'dangerous space'.

Virtual space, contested space: the nature of the cyber

How may we characterize 'the cyber'? David Bell (2000: 3) writes:

> If we ask the question 'where are we when we are in cyberspace?', we have to move beyond the simple answer that, physically, we are seated in front of a monitor, our fingers at work on the keyboard . . . We are there, to be sure, but we're simultaneously making ourselves over as data, as bits and bytes, as code, relocating ourselves in the space behind the screen, between screens, everywhere and nowhere.

William Gibson, the science fiction writer, is famously credited with 'inventing' the term cyberspace when he defined it in his 1984 novel *Neuromancer* as a 'consensual hallucination'. Since then, the term has been developed and interpreted in many ways. Common to all is the idea that cyberspace is *virtual* space. Although facilitated by hard-wired technologies, it is not *real*; that is to say, it is disembodied and projectively imagined, perhaps a mental geography (Benedikt 2000; Holloway and Valentine 2003). Nevertheless, as we shall see, it is as well to remember that however 'unreal' cyberspace may be in many respects, there is always *connectivity* with the offline world: computers and telephone lines are owned by certain companies and certain people; real people *are* at the end of the keyboard.

Castells argues that in practice the use of the internet, as the main exemplar of cyberspace, is overwhelmingly 'instrumental, and closely connected to the work, family, and everyday life of Internet users. E-mail represents over 85% of internet usage, and most of this e-mail volume is related to work purposes, to specific tasks, and to keep in touch with friends and family in real life' (2001:118). Castells thus cautions us against getting carried away with notions of the social world of virtuality as a special, new, different kind of space that poses particularly new questions. This is a valuable caveat, and one worth remembering when faced with some of the more frantic outpourings about internet crime, netdangers and particularly the notion that young people are either straying into dangerous territory or constituting a danger, in the 'ungovernable' territory of cyberspace. Most children and young people are *not* victims of internet crime, harassment, stalking and the like; similarly most are not regularly busy creating deviant identities, hacking into the White House, learning how to make bombs or even accessing violent pornography. Most are probably doing their homework with a parent somewhere in close proximity, or at 'worst' secretly messaging their friends about the latest game, the hottest babe or the coolest boy at school (e.g. Holloway and Valentine 2003).

Nevertheless, cyberspace *does* pose new questions, and even if their quantitative importance is small, their qualitative importance may not be. Significantly, Castells also concedes that 'the Internet has been appropriated by social practice, in all its diversity . . . this appropriation does have specific effects on social practice itself' (2001: 118), and although 'role-playing and identity-building as the basis of online interaction are a tiny proportion of internet-based sociability . . . this kind of practice *seems to be heavily concentrated among teenagers*' (p. 118 emphasis added).

Certainly cyberspace has been subject to its share of utopians and doomsters, those seeing either fantastic new vistas or apocalyptic disintegration. The problematic of the 'virtual community' compounds all the confusions and contradictions inherent in the notion of good old-fashioned 'modernist' community (what is it, whose interests does it represent?) and also brings with it qualitatively different dilemmas. Reaching back to the mythic structures of modernist insecurity, the utopian vision of virtual community sees cyberspace as a universe where the ideals of community may be fully achieved with the bad bits (coercion, repression), as it were, taken out: for in this scenario cyberspace is conceived of as a fully permissive space which democratizes community, enabling participation by all, freed from the trammels of space, time and their associated embodied identities of nationality, race and gender. The flight from the ontological insecurity of modernity, in this formulation, embraces all, a 'Planet converging . . . virtual community seems a cure-all for isolated people who complain about their isolation. Locked in metal boxes on urban freeways, a population enjoys socializing with fellow humans through computer networks . . . This giant network would surround earth to control the planet's resources and shepherd a world unified by Love' (Heim 1998: 39). As Heim wryly notes (p. 41), this is indeed 'optimism gone ballistic'. Likewise Willson vastly overstates the case. She suggests that the spaces of the cyber offer exciting possibilities which

> Liberate the individual from the constraints of embodied identity and from the restrictions of geographically embodied space; which equalize through the removal of embodied hierarchical structures,

and which promote a sense of connectedness ... among interactive participants ... the multiplicity of self is enhanced and difference proliferates uninhibited by external social structures.

(Willson 2000: 647)

At the other extreme of course, are those who read in cyberspace the end of sociality, the disintegration of community, an isolationalist, unregulable, technically driven world subject to all sorts of repressions and oppressions, the end of privacy and of liberty. From the idea that people will no longer talk to each other any more, to the idea that corporations can track your every move, this is a bleak scenario. It has a directly Orwellian heritage, but finds more prosaic expression in debates over privacy and liberty (Castells 2001). On the one hand, every time you log on, you leave a trail of electronic footprints, unless you are skilled enough to effectively cover them (and the number of people able to do this is surprisingly few, whatever the movies would have us believe). Even without logging on to anything, many transactions in everyday life occur in cyberspace through, for example, electronic finance, so that as Greenleaf ([1998] 2003: 598) points out, 'whether we know or care, large quantities of personal information about each of us will be collected via a pervasive, world-wide network ... the great protectors of privacy of the past such as cost, distance, incompatibility, and undiscoverability are all disappearing in the face of the internet' – and this was originally written in 1998. Governments and corporations now have sufficient access to every aspect of the identity of each individual to make privacy an outmoded concept in developed (wired) societies. From chip 'n' pin shopping to electronic ID cards, let alone personal computer use, the wired denizen is comprehensively digitized and thereby visible. On the flipside of this, the internet also offers many opportunities for imposture – which is another way of seeing freedom from embodied identities. In other words, what is freedom in one context (I can pretend to be someone else on the internet and lose my burdensome earthly self), is deceit in another (I can fool people into trusting me on the basis of someone I am not when offline).

Both the utopian and dystopian versions of cyberspace are 'true'; that is, there are important questions deriving from both extremes. Cyberspace above all is a *contested* space: it does not have any one meaning, but is multi-layered and heterogeneous – as heterogeneous as its users. Its unique characteristic compared with previous generations of media and information systems is that it is interactive; information flows both ways (from user to cyberspace and back the other way), and the user constantly has the option of changing whatever she or he interacts with. Whereas television, for example, has an *audience*, the internet has a *participant*. It is principally from this characteristic that both the 'threats' and the 'opportunities' of cyberspace arise.

Hence in the present context we see one set of 'threats' that relate to the problem of regulating content and behaviour on the internet, and therefore the problem of preventing harm through the proliferation of violent pornography and other images, hate sites, textual violence, stalking, and harassment (Bell and Kennedy 2000; Wall 2003). These might be loosely characterized as 'cyberobscenity' and 'cyberviolence' (Wall 2003). But a second set, of 'opportunities', relate to the emancipatory potential of cyberspace, in particular the ability for individuals or groups to escape embodied identities and to explore new forms of autonomy and identity – either through virtual 'communities' of interest or through the ability to achieve empowerment via access to information (see e.g. Leonard 1998; Wakeford 2000; Holloway and Valentine 2003). Both are crucial to an understanding of how we might approach the question of children and young people in cyberspace.

Back to the future: the 'dangerousness' of computers for the young

'In 2001, 2 in 3 UK households had a computer, and 30% of adults had access to the internet' (Livingstone 2002). 'The number of internet users worldwide has increased from an estimated 37 million in December 1996 to over 407 million in November 2000 . . . there were approximately 9.5 million web hosts in January 1996, whereas by January 2001 an estimated 106 million hosts were online' (Internet Crime Forum http://www. inter netcrimeforum.org.uk/chatwise_streetwise.html). 'About nine in ten Americans aged 5 through 17 use computers, and more than half use the internet' (NCES 2001). And so on. Statistics like this are now familiar, and despite the very real digital divide that exists (NCES 2001; Livingstone 2002), mass market penetration of the internet is here to stay (and is still growing exponentially). As a consequence the discourse of 'dangerousness' surrounding computers, and specifically cyberspace in the form of the internet, has also grown rapidly.

Children are seen as 'in danger' from the internet because it seems that just as adults do not like young people hanging around on street corners, so they do not like them to have unfettered access to the virtual street corners of cyberworlds. Hence we see 'moral panics' surrounding the supposedly deleterious effects of computers on children's development and morals, and the alleged need to control the amount of time children spend on the net, and what they do on it, 'for their own good'. This relates to the further fear that the internet either facilitates or encourages youthful deviance or criminality. We shall question whether adults' concerns over children and young people's safety and the internet is always as altruistic and protective as it might seem, or whether it rather represents yet another extension of adult anxiety that attends upon youthful autonomy. We shall see that there is a need for more research into children and young peoples' actual use of ICTs, and consider some existing research on how ICTs are used within the family home.

Firstly it has to be noted that much of the discourse surrounding the dangerousness of PC-internet use echoes much earlier debates over the supposedly negative effects of television and video games. These have two main components. The first relates to the dangers allegedly inherent in the use of the technology itself. Issues within the latter category range from the complaint that children and young people are encouraged to become isolationist and anti-social, are separated from 'normal' family environments, and so on, to fears of addiction; and they have appeared in every guise from the common sense ('our children spend too much time in their bedrooms'), to the academic ('studies suggest that adverse effects on child development may arise from . . .'), to the simply histrionic ('TV/video games/PC games/internet as addictive as alcohol/cocaine – shock' etc.). The second, and more complex component relates to children and young people's exposure to 'unsuitable' content (typically meaning of a violent or sexual nature) and the harms which, it is feared, will arise from this exposure, such as effects on behaviour (notably delinquency – aggression and 'uncontrollability' – and criminal violence).

In regard to the first of these, Oswell (1999) for example provides a charming account of the introduction of the television to postwar Britain. Considering the question from the perspective of domestic geography, he notes how 'its [TV's] location within the home displaced the centrality of the hearth, which has such a revered place in the history and formation of "Englishness" . . . instead of the warm glow of the flaming fire in the family's faces, there was now the steely grey flicker of the television's radiation' (pp. 67–8). He quotes Monica Dickens (a popular journalist and novelist of the era) as writing in *Woman's Own* magazine in 1950, 'And what might our children become? . . . a generation who couldn't read a book, or play games out of doors, or amuse themselves with carpentry or trains or butterflies' (p. 69). Interestingly, Dickens went on to cite the opinions of 'experts' in America on the matter to support her case – doctors, teachers and sociologists (!) it seems, were all in agreement that television was stultifying to child development and health, and destructive of family life (p. 69). Concerns were expressed over everything from the state of children's eyesight to the possibility of their having misshapen faces from watching television. Because television was clearly 'here to stay' however, discourses of control grew up around it that were of necessity based on dispersed regulation rather than the state – in other words, the now fashionable notion of govern*ance* rather than govern*ment* (Foucault 1991; Rose 2000), so that 'discourse about television . . . mobilizes and constructs particular social actors, and makes visible the child, family and home as sites of governance' (Oswell 1999: 71). Parents were seen as needing to train their children how to avoid 'dangers'. As we shall see, these notions of the threat to 'family life' and child health, and the emphasis on governance, reappear writ large in the case of the internet. A similar point applies to the policy and 'expert' discourse of the era. Psychology, which was growing rapidly in popularity and respectability during the postwar period, 'provided not simply a discourse, but an authority for bringing together a number of actors focused on a common problem: the mental health of the child. Psychology did not offer merely opinion, but truth, a veritable science of the child and a means of correctly governing the domestic' (Oswell 1999: 72). Probably the most well-known of the many psychological studies in the UK was Himmelweit *et al.*'s (1958) study of *Television and the Child*. The research itself generally did not uphold extreme fears about the effects of television, but nevertheless around one third of children were identified as 'addicts', pathologizing television viewing and locating it in relation to family dysfunction and thereby to delinquency. The onus, it was suggested, should however be on parents, teachers and youth club leaders to make best use of television, hence strengthening the tendency toward governmentality, a kind of policing through families and welfare/education (Donzelot 1981). At the same time, the study contained a chapter of suggestions for producers of television, placing emphasis on the self-regulatory obligations of the broadcasters, echoing a broader pressure for the latter to be seen publicly as responsible – indeed in the UK a subsequent Television Act *required* the Independent Television Association (ITA) to establish a Children's Advisory Committee (Livingstone and Bovill 1999).

Thus it was television that was to set the pattern for subsequent public, policy and 'expert' responses to young people and media technologies (as distinct from content). The pathologization, even medicalization, of young people's interaction with ICTs was dependent upon a particular view of children and childhood, a particular ideology of family life and a particular notion of governance, and was often simply repeated in various forms over the ensuing decades as firstly, video games appeared on the scene, then the numerous PC-based variants, and latterly the internet-linked PC. For example, a relatively recent review of research literature on 'the effects of video games on children' (Gunter 1998) contains chapters on addiction and dependency, the effects of playing video games on social behaviour and the health implications of video games. Gunter notes that 'the main worries . . . are that video games take time away from doing homework, general reading, or playing sports. There is the additional suggestion that children who really become hooked on these games tend to play alone and eschew social contact' (p. 126). The video game scare, however, has been more dramatically presented in terms of the content of the games themselves, and will be discussed further below. The next major cry of 'danger!' in the field of ICTs was to be over children and young people and PCs in general, especially internet-connected PCs.

The particular 'problem' with the internet, above and beyond all of the dire consequences predicted from TV, is of course its interactivity. If we consider interactivity more carefully, it is easy to see why adults see it as problematic in relation to the control of children and young people. Livingstone and Bovill (1999, Ch.1: 9) suggest that interactivity incorporates several dimensions which characterise the *changing modes of involvement* with media: the mutuality and exchange of roles in a two-way interaction; the degree of user control and management of content and timing of the interaction; individual and asynchronous rather than shared mass experience . . . Internet communication particularly opens up possibilities for reframing the relation between public and private, for constructing individualized lifestyles, and for challenging traditional knowledge hierarchies through various forms of democratic participation.

In other words, interactivity offers the potential for a good deal of autonomy on the part of the user, in direct conflict with the hegemonic discourses of childhood and youth examined so far in this volume: discourses variously of infantilization, pathology, deviance, exclusion and demonization. Both the efficacy of regulation (of content) and governmentality (of use), the traditional comfort blankets in relation to television, are challenged by the internet because children and young people are theoretically free to roam anywhere in the places and spaces of the cyber. The comment by Donnerstein is typical of the genre of paternalism when he writes:

> Unlike traditional media such as TV, radio, and recorded music, the Internet gives children and adolescents access to just about almost any form of content they can find. For the first time, youth will be able (with some work) to have the ability to view almost any form of sexual behaviour, violent content, or advertisements. Unlike years past, this can be done in the privacy of a child's bedroom with little knowledge of their parents . . . A Time/CNN survey . . . reveals . . . that the Internet was considered more important than fathers.
>
> (Donnerstein 2002: 302–3)

Access to PCs and the internet at home thus poses a range of problems in terms of discourses of control. More 'traditionally' come those of controlling the geography of the home, of regulating children and young people's bodies so that they are in the 'right' place at the 'right' time: at meal time, at bed time, and so on; of regulating patterns of association (who may be 'mixed' with, and when); of regulating the production and consumption of knowledge (what may and may not be seen, heard, said); and in the virtual sense, of regulating behaviour (textual or imagic 'delinquency'). The more recent additions to interactive media such as cheap webcams of course add to these possibilities for subverting regulation (the issue of the 'digital divide' – i.e. the fact that not all young people have equal access to new media – will be dealt with later).

Although the discussion above has focused on the threat to dominant *adult* conceptualizations of childhood and youth in public, policy and popular discourse, the threat is typically reversed. Instead the 'concern', the danger, is framed as being the threat to the *safety of children and young people themselves*: familiarly, as a concern for the welfare of the child or young person. Children and young people are constructed as *endangered*, not as *empowered*.

The response to this danger takes a range of forms, which retain the rhetoric of paternalism and protectionalism characteristic of modern state regulation, but are at the same time re-framed within the rhetorics of governance. Appealing to the 'archaeologies of anxiety' (Murdock 1997) in modernity, risks and dangers are allocated to the cyber, echoing and magnifying the traditional horrors and myths surrounding child victimization, as in the following example:

Menace on the Net
This 13-year-old was brutally murdered by a man she met on the Net. Yet a growing number of British teenagers are posting pictures of themselves on the web in return for gifts from strangers. David Rowan reports on the 'camgirls'.
EVERY PARENT'S WORST NIGHTMARE

(*Observer* 7 July 2002)

Juxtaposed with a videocam image of the murdered girl and a screen extract from camgirlsgonewild.com, we are told that she 'met her killer online'. The rest of the full page article makes only one cursory reference to the murder of this 13-year-old American girl 'believed' to have met her killer online. Yet we are invited to make a clear and unproblematic leap between quite different phenomena. The rest of the article talks about girls in the UK placing images of themselves on websites whilst simultaneously posting a 'wishlist' of gifts they would like to receive; it does not deal with the phenomenon of off-online crossover victimization but merely implies it as an inevitable outcome. 'The Net' is used as a loosely bundled metaphor for all things (virtually) dangerous to 'our young girls'. The notion of 'the Net' itself becomes a metaphor for places of danger. In this case the news-paper purveys a vision of the internet allowing 'men in their thirties and forties, often overseas' willing to send 'expensive gifts to their favourite children' – known as 'camgirls'. The head of Britain's 'National Hi-Tech Crime Unit' interviewed by the newspaper suggested that *the girls were placing themselves* at 'severe risk'.

This narrative raises a number of highly problematic issues for the paternalistic/governance approach to young people and cyberspace. In its embracing of a stereotypic 'stranger danger' approach to the geography of the internet, and the attribution of an 'unwitting innocence' construction to the girls, what the real girls are trying to say is ignored, or rather merely paraded as evidence of their dangerous naïvete. Hence 'Kerry' is a 14-year-old schoolgirl who operates a web business selling images of herself in various forms of undress in return for gifts; and more lucratively, receiving commission on providing links to 'adult' pornographic websites for users. 'I actually plan on making a members' section with my livecam on there . . . I need some money and I would really like to do this for a living. I'm always offered money to go on cam . . . so I might as well take advantage.' 'Kate', meanwhile, an 18-year-old who frequently 'masquerades' as a 15-year-old to please her clientele, recounts of the images, 'I don't count it as "me".

They get their fantasy, I get my profit . . . I'm a normal girl offline, nobody would ever guess that I do this. My boyfriend does know – I always run my pictures past him. He knows that I'm just trying to earn money. Of course I've thought about stalkers, but ultimately I'm in charge of what people know about me. I don't show full shots of my face, and I don't give out too many details about myself, like what school I go to' (*Observer* 7 July 2002).

What tends to evade journalists and academics alike is that they should actually listen to young people rather than assume that the errors of their ways must stand corrected. In fact, the so-called 'camgirls' seem to have a reasonable grasp both of the commercial nature of the transaction and of the potential of the technology for removing the morally/emotionally challenging obstacle to sex work presented by the inability to split mind and body effectively. They are not selling their bodies; they are quite clear about this; they are selling pixels. The *moral* danger of their enterprise is not an issue for them. This is not an argument of the 'cyberporn revolution' type, although ironically the *Observer* published an article in 2000 which proclaimed that 'a power shift is taking place in the typically male-dominated sex industry with the arrival of a new breed of entrepreneur: the webmistress' (*Observer* 6 August 2000). But it *is* an argument against misplacing dangers with misleading notions about vulnerability. Rather than continuing to recycle simple notions of young people 'in danger', Escobar's suggestion is for an anthropological approach to cyberculture that asks:

> What are the *discourses and practices* that are generated around/by computers . . . What domains of activity do these discourses and practices create? In what larger social networks of institutions, values, conventions, etc. are these domains situated? . . . What new forms of social constructions of reality ('technoscapes'), and what new forms of negotiation of such construction(s), are introduced by the new technologies?
>
> (Escobar 2000: 57)

One view of Kerry and Kate's practices, contrary of course to 'popular' media opinion, might be that webcams have opened up relatively autonomous spaces to young women to increase their earning power from the relative 'safety' of their homes, trading images for material rewards. These practices are after all only what exist in larger networks of 'institutions, values, conventions'; in the now ubiquitous and ever-growing 'men's life-style' sections of newsagents, since, far from the politically correct days when *Playboy* and *Razzle* sat sheepishly on the top shelf of the corner shop, we are now bombarded with 'lad' culture. *GQ*, *Loaded*, *FHM*, *Front*, *Ice* and the rest parade the fleshly accoutriments of prosthetized 'fuck-me' neo-women; as virtual as they are real with digital camera technologies erasing imperfections, or implants and extensions of various kinds built into the original. The vast market among males for replicant-culture females is also evidenced in the huge popularity of icons like the 'improbably pneumatic gun-toting' gaming heroine Lara Croft on pornography websites (Brown 2003).

That girls may be naive in underestimating the actuarial risks involved in some of their cyberactivities is another matter, and one not to be taken lightly. But actually, risks can of course be lessened by improving the odds – through a more sophisticated grasp of the potential in the technologies for protection. The constant shuffling of the 'problem' of risk back onto 'the technology', then back again onto the 'dangerous dabbling' of the girls involved, or onto the need for more 'parental control' is to ignore the most telling observation. The dangers do not lie in the technology, or in the spaces and places of the cyber, or in disembodied images, or free-floating identities, but in the highly embodied world of the global trade in (real) bodies, and in the economics of male demands for sadistic and violent sexual encounters with women and other men, of which the image trade is just one node. In so far as danger is real for young females in cyberspace then a sustained critique and unambiguous criminal justice response remain as valid as ever: but most victimization of young people continues to exist within the institutions of modernity and as much in the offline as the online world.

It has been many times stated, but is worth re-emphasizing, that most danger to children arises in the context of their own homes or families, or from other people who are known to them; not from strangers, whether in physical or virtual space (http://www.nspcc.org.uk/home/information resources/). The Internet Crime Forum[1] suggests that 'the relative scale of risk of children being approached in this way via the internet is extremely difficult to establish' and that it is 'also important to note that the number of known cases to date is currently very low in proportion to the rapidly growing rate of Internet use, and that the danger of online solicitation by a stranger is thought to be relatively much lower than offline risk from someone known to the victim' (http://www.internetcrimeforum.org.uk/chatwise_streetwise.html).

Nevertheless, the Internet Crime Forum also suggests that 'evidence from the United States and the UK . . . does appear to indicate a growth of this kind of activity over recent years'. For example, the website describes how in May 2000 'a 33-year-old man was charged with 14 offences under the Sexual Offences Act and the Child Abduction Act after meeting a 13-year-old girl in a chat room. He communicated with the girl via email and mobile phone, and eventually raped her. He also sent indecent images of himself to the victim.' In the USA 'there has been a growth in reports of

---

[1] The Internet Crime Forum (ICF), like most organizations dealing with monitoring internet abuse, is a non-governmental organization. Other examples include the Internet Watch Foundation (IWF). These 'watchdogs' typically comprise membership from industry (e.g. internet service providers), law enforcement agencies, child welfare and civil liberties organizations, and regulatory bodies.

child exploitation on the internet over the past five years ... the total number of convictions between 1995 and 2000 was 740'. However disturbing such examples are, they still relate squarely to the *offline* world and its practices, and there is little evidence to suggest that children and young people are in 'more' danger from the spaces and places of the internet than in 'real' space.

The tragic irony of this was exemplified in the case of Holly Wells and Jessica Chapman in the UK in 2002. The investigation into the abduction of these two 10-year-old girls on 3 August was temporarily sidetracked when it was discovered that they had been playing on a computer on the afternoon of their disappearance. The police removed the computer, the analysis of which formed not only the focal point of wild press speculations about the culprit, but justified a flood of media reports on children and the dangers of 'net crime'. The man subsequently convicted of their murder was a caretaker at a local college, and his partner, convicted of conspiracy to pervert the course of justice after providing a false alibi, was a teaching assistant at the girls' school (http://www.nationmaster.com/encyclopaedia/Soham-murders-of-2002). In a further twist, computers were seized from the police family liaison officer in the case in connection with a child pornography investigation and the officer, Brian Stevens, was subsequently charged with three counts of indecent assault against girls, three counts of distributing indecent photographs of children and five counts of possessing indecent photographs of children. The charges were then dropped by the Crown after it emerged that there were errors in the police computer expert's analysis and the defendant's claim that he was not the sole user of the laptop concerned (http://www.guardian.co.uk/uk_news/story/0,3604,1026099,00.html).

Thus the ideological appeal of the displacement of risk onto strangers, preserving the ideal of the patriarchal family as the bedrock of social organization, obfuscates the reality of the large number of men involved in killing, assaulting and abusing children by the manipulation of close relationships and positions of trust and authority. In the case of the internet, it is moreover very unclear how offline victimization is specifically linked to online exploration. As with the *Observer* article cited above, the press is inordinately quick to seize upon any hint of such links; yet as we have seen, given the high volume of online activity by children and young people, the number of reported cases where a specific link has been made seems minimal. Furthermore, instant messaging is increasingly favoured by children over chat rooms, a form of online interaction that minimizes 'stranger danger' because it is typically constructed as a private chat room by users who know each other, and is therefore more akin to offline interaction among groups of friends.

This leads us to a further, and more prominent, area of debate regarding the notion that children and young people are in danger from the internet: that unfettered roaming exposes youth to harmful content. (Of course in this context Kerry and Kate become young people *as* danger, since they are helping to produce harmful content.) Holloway and Valentine (2003: 74) refer to this as a 'debunker' discourse:

> Debunkers [argue] that children's very competence at using ICT is placing them in potential danger. Notably some commentators ... argue that the relatively unregulated nature of cyberspace means that sexually explicit discussions ... pornography, racial and ethnic hatred, Neo-Nazi groups and paedophiles can all be found in the space dubbed by some on the right as an 'electronic Sodom'.
>
> (Holloway and Valentine 2003: 74)

A number of questions arise from this. Firstly, why is it assumed that exposure to particular forms of content is particularly harmful to children and young people; and secondly, to what extent do children and young people choose to enter an 'electronic Sodom' when they log on? Both of these questions are typically ignored in the strange leap of logic that says 'harmful' content exists on the web; therefore children online must be exposed to it; therefore children online must be adversely affected by it. None of this rhetoric refers to children and young people's own views or accounts of their online activities, but is based on a particularly crude version of the construction of childhood and youth as a highly malleable and corruptible state of fragile innocence.

The online content debate in this sense continues a long tradition of concern over 'ill effects' of the media (Barker and Petley 1997). I have discussed the notion of the 'effects' debate over the content of television and film/video at length elsewhere, and do not intend to revisit it in detail here (see Brown 2003: 107–36; also Barker and Petley 1997). The 'problem' is summarized by Fowles (1999: 20): 'It is widely believed that empirical research has absolutely demonstrated the perils of viewing televised entertainment mayhem. There is good reason for this belief: it is affirmed everywhere, creating a tight discursive skein of conventional wisdom.' Beyond this belief, there is surprisingly little (despite a vast amount of research activity) to support the notion that exposure to material of a sexual or violent nature predisposes young people to commit such acts themselves (Pearl *et al.* 1982; Newburn and Hagell 1995; Howitt 1998; http://www.cultsock.ndirect.co.uk/MUHome/cshtml/media/bbfcres. html). Murdock suggests that the notion of the 'bad' effects of media upon children and young people stems not from any scientific evidence, but rather from the pains of modernity as a more general cultural phenomenon: 'The dominant "effects" tradition has proved so resilient partly because it chimes with a deeply rooted formation of social fear, which presents the vulnerable, suggestible, and dangerous as living outside the stockade of maturity and reasonableness that the "rest of us" take for granted' (1997: 83).

This is illustrated well in the following excerpt from a recent text on *Children, Adolescents and the Media* (Strasburger and Wilson 2002). In his chapter on the internet, Donnerstein (2002: 307, 311, emphasis added) warns us:

The messages of concern on the internet do not differ from those of traditional media: those involving sex, violence, sexual violence, and tobacco and alcohol advertisements. The effects from exposure we would expect to be at least the same, if not enhanced. The interactive nature of the internet, which can lead to more arousal and more cognitive activity, would suggest that influences such as those found from media violence would be facilitated . . . More important, the *easy access to materials, which should be extremely limited for children and adolescents*, is now readily obtainable with the power of search engines . . . Terrorism is another area of concern. Some online archives provide instructions for making bombs or other weapons. The teenage school killer in Oregon, John Kinkel, described himself in his email profile as 'someone who liked watching violent cartoons on TV, sugared cereal, throwing rocks at cars', and his favourite occupation was 'surfing the web for information on how to build bombs'.

Heaven forbid that cognitive arousal should impel our children to eat sugared cereal, throw rocks and build bombs. Donnerstein's ludicrous reasoning – in a perfectly 'respectable' text – tells us a great deal about American paranoia, but little about children and young people. Moreover, its underpinning assumptions, italicized above, raise far more questions than they answer. Precisely what should be 'extremely limited' and why? Because we fear cognitive arousal? Because we fear children being transformed into cigarette-smoking terrorists? Because one unfortunate young person in Oregon who was extremely disturbed wrote rubbish on a website?

Children and young people, as we have seen, have consistently been constructed as being 'outside the stockade of maturity' throughout modernity, and thus form a locus for adult fears that bear little relation to any proper knowledge about their interaction with the media. Research on and with children and young people using new media in their everyday settings of home and school suggests a rather different picture to the fearful speculations of much public, policy and some academic discourse on netdangers. Livingstone and Bovill (1999), in a major study of young people aged 6 to 17 years, decided upon an approach that moved away from the notion of 'media effects' and towards the concept of 'media meanings and uses', the latter implying a far more child-centric and grounded methodology than 'effects'. They write:

> The main focus of our project is not on media effects but rather on the meanings, uses and impact of media in the lives of children and young people. This is partly in response to the sustained critique of the effects tradition . . . Instead . . . of regarding television viewing as a *cause* of attitudes and behaviours in children's lives, we seek to *contextualize* the uses of new media within a broad analysis of children and young people's life worlds.

(p. 5)

Similarly, Holloway and Valentine (2003) in the introduction to their study of the use of ICTs by British children aged 11 to 16, note that 'children, as symbols of the future themselves, are at the heart of debates both about how the possibilities that ICT afford should be realised, and about the "new" dangers that these technologies might also bring for the net generation' (p. 1), yet 'despite these fears in the popular imagination, little is known about how children actually employ ICT within the context of their everyday lives' (p. 2). It is essential, they argue, to depart from the essentializing model of children as 'a homogenous group defined by their biology, that in turn positions them as "other" in relation to adults' (p. 4). This can only be achieved through a detailed understanding, as with Livingstone and Bovill, of children's life worlds. A further advantage of this approach is that it avoids an overly stark distinction between children's online and offline worlds: in the rhetorics of panic it is as if children and young people suddenly become dissociated from the embodied world altogether when they enter 'into' cyberspace, whereas the reality is that relations with objects (as with computers) and people in everyday life are *symmetrical* (Latour 1993); that is to say, we live in the world with objects and with other people simultaneously, not separately. Children and young people live in a context (home, school, street etc.) *with* their peers, family and other adults, and *with* media such as mobile telephones, televisions and computers. These are interconnected and not separate interactions. As we shall see, this proves important in any discussion of netdanger.

Livingstone and Bovill concluded that: 'Nor, among those ... with access to the internet, did we encounter children upset by inappropriate materials they had found. Nor did we find children so addicted to computer games that they had become socially isolated ... notwithstanding a public tendency to scapegoat the media, our report has found that the major distinction in children and young people's leisure time is – just as it was 40 years ago – not that between media and non-media time, but rather that between time inside and time outside the home' (Livingstone and Bovill 1999, Ch. 12: 15). Parents, indeed, worried much more about their child's physical safety, their employment prospects or their schooling than they did about media use. Likewise 'children and young people express regrets regarding their freedom outside the home but only enthusiasm for the expanding media opportunities within it'. Of the internet users in this study, the main activity was looking up information (44 per cent), and surfing/browsing (33 per cent), followed quite a long way behind by 'chat groups' (18 per cent) (Livingstone and Bovill 1999: Ch. 7: 32).

Holloway and Valentine found that ICTs did not have a uniform impact on parents' views of danger. Whilst some parents regarded their children as emotionally competent to deal with 'unsuitable' content, others, especially those who were not competent in ICTs themselves, were more likely to worry. The significant point was that 'the meanings of ICT are negotiated as children, parents and technology come together in markedly different household formations or communities of practice' (Holloway and Valentine

2003: 87). It is this disparity between the homogenizing tendencies of much popular and policy discourse, and the heterogeneity and active negotiation of actual experiences, that should render us suspicious of the former. Moreover, children and young people's relationships to ICTs is far more sophisticated than the notion of the 'child-in-danger' suggests. One young respondent in this study said: 'I have, I have a lot of laws set down and I daren't break them . . . I love my mum and I have a lot of respect for her and I know they are a lot wiser than me . . . One, I know I'm gonna be in a lot of trouble if I do break, and two, it's just respect.' Another commented, 'Yeh, sometimes, Dad is . . . if I say I'm gonna go on a page, then he trusts me and lets me go on the page. Like, say I wanna go on a chat page, he says all right, and I show him what I'm going on first, and then he just goes – but most of the time he's there sitting, you know' (Holloway and Valentine 2003: 83, 88).

This is hardly the image of children wandering unsupervised into hard-core pornographic sites, or paedophile chat rooms. Holloway and Valentine point out that boys have often visited pornographic sites as a way of negotiating their masculinity within their peer group, but as one boy stated, access to pornography through satellite TV is common anyway ('I mean, your parents can't keep you under their wing all the time. You just go round your mates and they've got Sky TV and you just watch porn') (2003: 95), and this was not seen as particularly different. As regards the girls (who were more likely to chat to strangers online) and 'stranger danger', they described to the researchers strategies and precautions that they took for online safety: 'I mean you don't know who you could be talking to, you could be talking to a rapist or anything like that and you wouldn't know and if you met them you would be putting yourself at risk. It's all right to talk to him on the thingy [the internet] and on the phone' (p. 93). Holloway and Valentine conclude that 'children are often more knowledgeable and competent at managing their own lives (in particular potentially dangerous situations) than they are assumed to be . . . maturity, rationality, social competence . . . and so on are just as readily performed by a child as a grown up' (Holloway and Valentine 1999: 95).

In an extensive literature review of children's use of the internet covering over 100 articles, Livingstone (2002) identifies three broad assumptions governing rigorous empirical research in the area:

- avoidance of moral panics;
- contextualize internet use;
- children should be seen as agents, not constructed as passive or vulnerable, and not as 'incomplete adults'.

Livingstone further notes that 'media research has, throughout its history, attempted to demonstrate the cognitive, emotional, and behavioural effects on children, with only partial – and much contested – success. Thus, some of the questions now being asked of the Internet (does inadvertent exposure to pornography produce long-term harm, does playing aggressive games online make boys more aggressive ... are more or less impossible to answer' (pp. 8–9). Interestingly, Livingstone further notes that little connection is being made between content and use: in other words, when a young person, for example, visits a pornography site, there is little research into what he or she is actually making use of, or how the material is being interpreted (p. 9).

Leaving aside this latter question for the moment (as it is currently unanswerable), it seems clear that most children and young people use the internet in very ordinary ways, in very ordinary contexts. This appears to hold across a range of countries and is not just pertinent to the UK context. A survey of computer and internet use by children and adolescents in the USA in 2001 found that 'children and adolescents commonly use computers for playing games, completing school assignments, word processing, email ... and finding information' (NCES 2001: 37). Livingstone's review found a similar pattern.

The conclusion, in so far as any is possible with such a rapidly moving research area as the internet and its use, is most usefully a methodological rather than a substantive one. That is to say, we cannot assume that children and young people are never harmed by content on the internet; nor can we dismiss the notion that they can under certain circumstances be at risk of both online and offline victimization through stalking, for example. However, at the centre of any research or policy agenda must be the concept of the child or young person as a competent agent, not as 'in danger', inherently passive, or vulnerable; and the overwhelming evidence so far suggests that most children and young people's interactions with and in cyberspace are, contiguous with their offline worlds, predominantly non-criminogenic. Panic about the internet can only divert attention from what remains the greatest danger to children and young people: the institutions, practices and cultures that support abuse and physical exploitation in general. Still, the very principle of connectivity, the continuity between online and offline worlds, is also a two-way process. Wider practices and cultures of exploitation by adults extend *into* cyber victimization. This becomes particularly disturbing when the use of the internet as a tool in the exploitation of children and young people is considered, and this will be examined in the next section.

Virtual victims? Adults, cyberspace and victimization of young people

To what extent are young people subject to adult victimization via the internet? Predation, paedophiliac sexual abuse and pornography are just some forms of crime to which children and young people are subjected using the internet, as well as being open to victimizations attendant upon all users of virtual space, such as hate sites, stalking and harassment.

This is nowhere more complex than with the issue of child pornography.

Just some of the complications include the staggering volume of child pornography on the internet, the links between the trade in images, organized net crime and other forms of organized transborder crime such as human trafficking; the equally voluminous 'cottage industry' in paedophilia; the problem of morphing (computer constructed and manipulated images that are not taken from 'real' life); links to real offline child abuse; the legal conceptualization of violation through the circulation and endurance of images; and the huge *popularity* of child pornography on the net (and of pornography sites in general); and all this in relation to issues of policing, enforceability, legal definitions and varying jurisdictional contexts. Needless to say, it will be impossible to do this debate justice here. A good deal of useful information is available on the web, and some suggestions are given at the end of this chapter. Here it is intended to focus selectively on some key themes.

(Virtual) child pornography: conceptual confusions and ambiguities

Despite the very polarized reactions that the mention of child pornography tends to provoke, it is conceptually a muddy area. This is intensified in relation to the internet, as we shall see below. Firstly, it hardly needs saying that 'paedophilia' and 'child pornography' (whether or not those exact terms are used) is nothing new. 'Boy love', for example, was central to Greek homoeroticism and remains central to homoeroticism today (Tate 1990). Latter-day 'paedophiles' and child pornographers are constantly being unearthed in scholarly research, as with the case of Charles Lutwidge Dodgson (Lewis Carroll) discussed in Chapter 1 of this book, and more recently in the case of Field Marshal Montgomery, or 'Monty', Britain's famous Second World War commander. Montgomery's official biographer (Hamilton 2001) claims that the Field Marshal 'had a passion' for many boys, some of whom were not yet in their teens. Hamilton rather strangely asserted that 'his passion for young men helped him relate to his liaison officers and young staff. He felt a real concern for their welfare' (*Independent* 25 February 2001).

Fast-forwarding to the other extreme, present-day North America sees adverse reactions to almost any suggestion that children or 'minors' should be linked to sexuality. Bronski, writing in the Boston *Phoenix* newspaper (18 April 2002), reports the growing right-wing vilification of Judith Levine, author of *Harmful to Minors: The Perils of Protecting Children from Sex* (2002). Drawing on Foucault's point that repression of sexuality is characterized not by silence but rather by endless chatter, or production of discourses, about sex (Foucault 1981), Levine points out the contradictions in contemporary American attitudes toward young people, sex and censorship. These 'discourses of regulation' are dear to US culture, at the same time as the First Amendment provides a contradictory barrier to the regulation of child pornography (http://www.gigalaw.com/articles/2002-all/landau-2002-07-all.html). Levine notes that on the one hand, 'in 1996, when author Robie Harris went on radio in Oklahoma to promote her children's book *It's Perfectly Normal: Changing Bodies, Growing Up, Sex and Sexual Health*, the host requested that she not mention the S-word' (Levine 2002: see http://www.ipce.info/library_3/files/levine/lev_cens.htm). On the other hand, 'Where do you learn about sex?' a television interviewer asked a 15-year-old from a small rural town. 'We have 882 channels,' the girl replied. Levine suggests that 'our era, while producing plenty of regulatory chatter from on high, has also seen an explosion of unofficial, anarchic and much more exciting discourses down below', whilst 'as the ability to segregate audience by age, sex, class, or geography shrinks, we have arrived at a global capitalist economy that, despite all our tsk-tsking, finds sex exceedingly marketable and in which children and teens serve as both sexual commodities (Jon Benet Ramsey, Thai child prostitutes) and consumers of sexual commodities (Barbie dolls, Britney Spears)' (http://www.ipce.info/library_3/files/levine/lev_cens.htm). Complaints (over 800 telephone and email complaints) to the University of Minnesota over Levine's book – based on pre-publication releases – led to the unusual step of the university's vice-president of research announcing the establishment of an outside advisory committee to survey the peer review and acquisitions policy of the University of Minnesota Press. Such an action is unheard of, due to the tenet of academic freedom that governs all academic publishing and because an independent academic review process already takes place when a manuscript is submitted for publication (in Levine's case this comprised five reviewers from various related disciplines). Based mainly on Levine's arguments that many attempts at so-called child 'protection' through censorship do more harm than good, and her call for the acknowledgement that children and teenagers do experience sexual desire, Robert Knight of Concerned Women for America reportedly called the book 'evil', 'hideous', and 'every child molester's dream' (*Phoenix* 18 April 2002).

Liberal arguments surrounding child pornography thus tend to stress the historically and culturally relative nature of constructions both of 'childhood' (as discussed at length in this volume) and of 'obscenity'. The indubitable truth of this relativity makes it enormously difficult to defend academically *any* normative standpoint. The other indubitable truth however, is that to abandon any normative standpoint leads to an inevitable sense of collusion with practices that have been strongly argued to be exploitative and detrimental to the well-being of children and young people. In other words, the discussion and analysis of child pornography carries with it ethical entailments in a way that 'theory' does not (Brown 2003); it requires a 'normative criminology'.

Definitional difficulties: is child pornography a 'legal' or 'extra-legal' category?

In this light, although no definition of 'child pornography' can be theoretically coherent, a working definition is required. Max Taylor (2002), director of COPINE (Combating Paedophile Information Networks in Europe) at the University of Cork (http://www.copine.ie/) – a specialist

unit researching child sexual abuse on the internet – suggests that legal definitions are unhelpful, since jurisdictions define everything from childhood
to the sexual in different ways. He argues that 'an over emphasis on legal
approach [*sic*] will not therefore always assist in the development of preventative and control strategies, because the issue of producing and collect-
ing child pornography is essentially a psychological, rather than a legal
problem'.

A further problem however, is that this disciplinary 'chopping up' of
the phenomenon is not helpful either. Child pornography, as a discursive
practice, *is* a legal entity, however variously (and indeed those variations
tell us a great deal in themselves). It is *also* amenable to psychological
analysis, and it is also a sociological and a cultural phenomenon – and so on.
For definitional purposes, therefore, the most useful approach is probably
an instrumental one; that is, to make some sort of attempt to describe and/
or classify what kind of social practices are treated as child pornography by
those seeking to secure its regulation. That different communities of practice (lawyers, policy-makers, non-governmental organizations, academics)
may adopt different definitions has simply to be accepted as reflecting the
heterogeneity of their interests. In contemporary usage, driven particularly
by the growing involvement of non-governmental organizations in regulation internationally (Oswell 1998, 1999; Carr 2002; ECPAT 2002) and
by discourses on children's rights (http://www.unhchr/html/menu3/b/k/
k2crc.htm), child pornography is viewed not as a single entity, but as part
of a complex of child sexual abuse. This definition was centralized by two
World Congresses against Commercial Exploitation of Children in 1996
and 2001 (Carr 2002). Within this context it may be seen as 'the visual
record of the sexual abuse of a child, either by adults, other children or
which involves bestiality' (cited in Creighton 2003). Article 34 of the
United Nations Convention on the Rights of the Child (see Office of the
United Nations High Commissioner for Human Rights 2004 for status of
ratifications of this optional protocol) states that 'States Parties undertake
to protect the child from all forms of sexual exploitation and sexual abuse.
States Parties shall in particular take all appropriate national, bilateral
and multilateral measures to prevent . . . the exploitative use of children
in pornographic practices and materials'. Taylor (2002), based on an
analysis of many thousands of images sampled from the internet for the
COPINE database, suggests that the nature of child pornography needs to
be understood from the collector's perspective. On this basis he identifies 'a
number of different picture types that are attractive to paedophiles, not all
of which . . . readily fall into legal categories of child pornography'. Taylor
divides these into 'erotica', which may involve 'inappropriate use' of pictures of children that may not be explicitly sexual and therefore not illegal;
images involving nudity in some form, the accessing of which indicates
sexual interest in children but may not be illegal (including covert photographs taken of children at swimming pools, on beaches and so on, and
scanned into the computer); posed pictures involving nudity, suggesting

the involvement of a professional photographer, not necessarily illegal and sometimes justified on the grounds of artistic merit but highly attractive to adults with a sexual interest in children; and least ambiguous, explicitly sexual images,

> From pictures focusing on genital or anal areas, through a child or children posing in a sexually explicit way, to pictures of real or simulated sexual assaults conducted either by other children or adults. Some photographs of bestiality exist, and there are also some involving sadistic imagery, such as bondage or whipping. This category of picture is in the main clearly very sexual in character and both production and possession are illegal in all European jurisdictions.

Healy (2004), in a working paper for the first world congress on behalf of the international ECPAT (End Child Prostitution, Child Pornography and Trafficking of Children for Sexual Purposes), adopts the definition of 'a sexually explicit reproduction of a child's image' (http://www.crime-research.org/articles/536/) as distinguished from erotica, or 'any material relating to children that serves a sexual purpose for a given individual' (which may include anything from children's toys to clothing or catalogues).

In addition to this there are, of course, many legal definitions relating to different jurisdictions that are too numerous to discuss in detail here (and anyway are subject to constant change). For example in the UK, child pornography is principally regulated by the Obscene Publications Acts 1959 and 1964, Section 43 of the Telecommunications Act 1984, the Protection of Children Act 1978 as amended by the Public Order Act 1994 S.84(4), Section 160 of the Criminal Justice Act 1988, and the Criminal Justice and Public Order Act 1994. Matters in the USA are complicated by the First Amendment, so for example the US Supreme Court ruled that key provisions of the Child Pornography Prevention Act 1996 were unconstitutional in April 2002 because they violated the freedom of speech guaranteed by the First Amendment. Section 2256(8) (B) of the Act prohibited 'any visual depiction, including any video, picture or computer or computer generated image or picture' that 'is or appears to be of a minor engaging in sexually explicit conduct'. This is because US legislation cannot constitutionally prohibit pure speech; it can only legislate in relation to acts that underlie the speech. Therefore this provision, important as it relates to the computer generation of pornographic images that are entirely digitally manufactured and not 'morphs' of real photographs, is deemed unconstitutional (http://www.gigalaw.com/articles/2002-all/landau–2002-07-all.html). Article 175 of the Japanese Penal Code forbids the printed portrayal of adult genitals, but does not regulate the representation of children's genitalia in the same way (Healy 2004). The Council of Europe's Convention on Cybercrime was signed by 30 member states including the UK in December 2001, its stated aim being to pursue a 'common criminal policy aimed at the protection of society against cybercrime', including (under Article 9) offences relating to child pornography (Chase and Statham 2004). The G8 Strategy against sexual exploitation of children on the internet defines eight objectives including prevention and international cooperation, and in 2003 agreed the establishment of a new international child pornography image database (http://www.statewatch .org/news/2003/may/). This by no means exhausts the mountain of legislative and regulatory measures to deal with child pornography, and specifically internet child pornography, internationally, and the consequent numbers of definitions deployed. However, at the core of most definitions is probably now the notion that child pornography (whether production or possession) is not a victimless crime, encapsulated in this foreword by the UK Sentencing Advisory Panel Chairman on Offences Involving Internet Pornography (http://www.sentencing-guidelines.gov. uk/): 'possession of child pornography is not a victimless offence. Every indecent photograph or pseudo photograph of a child is, with limited exceptions, an image of a child being abused or exploited.' The crucial definition then rests with Taylor (2002), who writes: 'the central and important quality of child pornography that must be emphasised is that at its worst it is a picture of the commission of a sexual assault on a child. That is to say, it is a picture of the scene of a crime' (http://www.ipce.info/ library_3/files/nat_dims_kp.htm).

As we have seen in the case of the US, this definition is most problematic in relation to computer-generated images of children and young people; that is, those that are completely 'virtual' and derive from no living human being (i.e. are not 'morphed' from actual pictures, see also Brown 2003). For example, in the case of the computer-generated gaming character Lara Croft, an 'adult' website manipulated the image further to put Lara Croft into pornographic poses. The website's homepage protested against its critics, 'do you think it's scary that there are men out there *fantasising* about Lara Croft? No, because men will fantasise about anything . . . What's wrong with wanting to sleep with a computer generated character? She's got a perfect body after all' (cited in Brown 2003: 169). What happens when instead of a gaming character (who is at least cast as an 'adult' woman), the computer-generated characters are remarkably 'lifelike' representations of young children engaged in sexual acts ranging from anal intercourse to bestiality? Carr (2002: 2) has argued that 'if it looks like child pornography it should be treated as if it were child pornography' – but that approach is problematic legally. Carr argues that it is a matter of principle, not of legal technicality: 'civilized society has declared, or ought to, that any image which purports or seeks to show children being sexually abused is undesirable and unacceptable in principle' (p. 2).

Child pornography, cyberspace and cultural contestations
What the difficulties facing effective legislation on child pornography actually reflect of course are wider cultural practices and differences in relation to children, young people and sex. What the phenomena (using the plural

advisedly) of child pornography and the internet also reflect is the extent to which the social practices surrounding child pornography and computers, as well as being related to the 'special' features of cyberspace, are equally related to institutional and cultural practices of the sexual exploitation of children and young people by adults, and predominantly male adults.

Most recent reports and reviews on child pornography and the internet emphasize a marked shift in the production and consumption of child pornography between the 1970s and the 1990s that deserves careful thought. Healy (2004) notes that computer technologies have transformed the production of child pornography into a 'global cottage'. A similar point is made by Taylor (2002), Creighton (2003), Renold *et al.* (2003), Chase and Statham (2004) and numerous others. Thus in the 1970s, child pornography was largely produced commercially. Both its quantity and distribution were inevitably limited by the ability of commercial film-makers or photographers to procure young people, to distribute their commodities, and by the ability of potential consumers to locate material and be able to afford to buy it. Two technologies, the video camera/camcorder and the internet-linked PC, transformed this market-place. It is now recognized that much child pornography is traded on an amateur basis by 'collectors', often for no direct financial gain. This does not prevent there being, at the same time, a commercial market via credit card payment on the internet, but the so-called 'global cottage' (a peculiarly cosy metaphor for its abusive reality) is important because it reveals the extent of desire for child pornography and its emergence from situations of child abuse in the 'domestic' sphere of production. The 'explosion' in the child pornography market has come about not *because of the technology*, but because the technology has facilitated and revealed the *extent of child sexual abuse* actually prevalent in societies globally. A number of interesting features emerge regarding internet child pornography that indirectly increase our knowledge of previously 'hidden' sexual abuse.

The internet, according to Taylor (2002) provides not just a sense of anonymity to child abusers, but a sense of *community*. Consistent with other discussions of communities and cyberspace (Bell and Kennedy 2000), communities of practice are brought together via child pornography, forming a source of 'support, justification, information, and self help, as well as facilitating the exchange and distribution of . . . images' (Taylor 2002).

In turn, the very process of being involved in a 'community' lends sustainability and reproducibility to abusive practices. Whilst Taylor documents the many old images of children on the net that have been scanned in and recycled from earlier decades of non-computer-based pornography, the proliferation and cheapness of video capture (webcam) technologies lends an immediacy of connection to the intimate settings in which much child abuse takes place. There is thus emerging a 'seamless web' between the institutional sites of abuse offline – notably the family home, but also for example, educational and religious settings – and the production, distribution and consumption of computer-based child pornography.

Consistently with what is known about sexual abuse of children in general, police evidence suggests that the overwhelming majority of consumers of child pornography are men (Renold *et al.* 2003). Renold *et al.* conclude that 'child pornography needs to be understood, not as a separate genre by and for "paedophiles", but in a wider cultural context in which cultural ideals of beauty are youth, and [where] the media is reliant upon the sexualization of children for financial gain' (p. 3).

However disturbing it may be therefore, the internet has proved a revelatory tool: the 'freedom' of cyberspace has made visible the extent of cultural support for the sexual abuse of children and young people by men. Whilst clearly demonstrating links between child pornography and paedophile networks, it has also shown that child pornography and child sexual abuse is not necessarily a 'minority' issue. John Carr, as consultant to National Children's Homes, internet adviser to the UK Children's Charities Coalition on Internet Safety and member of the government task force on Child Safety on the internet, told the BBC Radio 4 current affairs programme *Today*, 'We've got to stop thinking about paedophiles or people who use child pornography as the dirty old man in the raincoat'. He also told the same programme that 95 per cent of 1300 people arrested under Operation Ore had no criminal record (http://news.bbc. co.uk/1/hi/uk/2652465.stm).

What is also significant is the global nature of the trade (both commercial and non-commercial) in child sexual abuse in the form of pornographic images. Cultures that on the face of it may seem to be very different – from cultures of Western Europe, the former Eastern Europe and North America, to cultures of South America, Asia and the Pacific Rim – all furnish a myriad of examples. There are (g)local (Featherstone *et al.* 1995) variations. UK images may favour domestic settings using home video/computer equipment, for example. Japan has a pre-existing history as the centre of commercial child pornography production for Asia (Healy 2004), especially for young (pre-teen) girls in school uniforms and in sexually explicit poses in teen magazines (Constantine 1994). It also has an established practice of '*enjo kosai*' or 'compensated dating' with children – including sex in return for gifts (Hyde 2004) – run formerly through telephone clubs. Japan however, is now heavily reliant on mobile phone technologies, most recently the 3G mobiles introduced by Vodafone KK in Japan in 2002. Initial evidence from Japan's National Police Agency indicates that both child prostitution through the internet and internet-enabled mobile phones, and child pornography, have increased dramatically between 2000 and 2003.

Technological convergence suggests that the global nature of the trade will develop further, and in doing so will further complicate enforcement and further intensify activity. 3G mobiles, which entered the British mass market in 2004, make the connection between child sexual abuse and child pornography even more visible. Incidents of abuse can be directly accessed from and relayed onto the Web from the phones' video features, giving real-time gratification, as well as greatly increasing the opportunities for unobtrusive and covert use (Chase and Statham 2004: 29). Indeed the word 'pornography', as suggesting a representation *separate* from actuality, begins to sound almost quaint in this context of real-time communications. The internet will also highlight the blurring of boundaries between child prostitution, child pornography, child sexual abuse and between the production and consumption of sexual abuse.

Prevalence and proliferation: how many images, how many children?

The extent of cultural support for these practices is evidenced by the sheer proliferation of images on the net. As long ago as 1995 Rimm (1995: 1914) reported on a research project at Carnegie-Mellon University that found 'paedophilic and paraphilic pornography are widely available through various computer networks and protocols ... the ... research team was able to identify consumers of these types of materials in more than 2000 cities in all fifty states in the United States, most Canadian provinces, and forty foreign countries, provinces and territories around the world'.

Far from the passage of time, legislation, and enforcement operations reducing this volume, all indications are that they have simply revealed more and more as cyberspace, or 'connectivity', has expanded. The COPINE project homepage reported in August 2004 that INTERPOL was to take over its database of child pornography images from the internet because, 'since 1997 the number of abuse images available has increased dramatically making it increasingly more difficult to maintain the database on a research budget' (http://www.copine.ie/). During a six-week period in 2002, the COPINE project came across 140,000 child abuse images, of which 35,000 were completely new. Twenty previously unseen *children* were identified – an important distinction because one incident of child abuse may generate many thousands of images: in other words, twenty *new* incidents of child abuse were identified in a six-week period. Other evidence is available from police operations. Operation Cathedral, an international operation coordinated by the National Crime Squad in London, UK, took place in 1998 to broach a paedophile ring dubbed the 'Wonderland Club' (referring to Charles Dodgson and *Alice in Wonderland*). Members of the club were reported as describing themselves as 'the cream of the paedophiles', and had to contribute at least 10,000 indecent images to join. An astounding 750,000 computer images of more than 1200 children and 1800 digitized videos of children being subjected to sexual abuse were retrieved. In interview, Detective Chief Inspector Alex Wood said 'We are talking about serious sexual abuse to young children of both sexes – and to say that it is stomach churning does not quite describe well enough what it is. We have pictures of children in hotel rooms and in private environments – there is no way of telling where they came from' (Ananova, http://www.wysiwyg://34/file:/D/Download/childporn.htm). In January 2003, the BBC reported on the Operation Ore police operation, asking whether the UK criminal justice system could handle the pressure that the volume of internet paedophile detections was putting on it (BBC News 13 January 2003) (http://news.bbc.co.uk/1/hi/uk/2652465.stm). Credit card details gave police direct leads on 250,000 people globally, and the National Criminal Intelligence Service had to sift through 7000 names given to the British police in order to prioritize the 'worst offenders'. Over 1600 arrests were reportedly made. Convictions in the UK included Nicholas Ferry, who in April 2003 admitted possessing 250,000 indecent images of youngsters (Creighton 2003: 3). Police, meanwhile, complained that the volume of work created was such that it was taking them away from child protection issues in the 'here and now'.

The volume of images on the internet suggests, as Taylor (2002) notes, that 'there is a very large demand for images of children that are either explicitly sexual, or enable sexual fantasy'. Police operations such as Operation Ore target commercial sites, being based on credit card details; but in Taylor's experience with COPINE, 'the production of hard core material in the 1990s' was 'largely a private "home" based activity ... perhaps the most disturbing quality of recent pictures is their domestic quality'.

What follows from all of this is that legislation and regulation, *however* they are formulated, can play only a relatively small part in challenging child sexual abuse in cyberspace. The real contestation must be a cultural one that challenges the *acceptability* and the *endemic nature* of the sexual exploitation of children and young people by – predominantly – men. Currently the intense focus on regulation tends to mask this hard reality, and cultural condemnation comes inappropriately from 'vigilante' name and shame websites such as 'noncewatch'. With 3G phones and internet PCs increasingly a feature of everyday life, the many men who sexually exploit young people are interpreted not as a structural and cultural feature of patriarchal societies, but as somehow 'driven by' or 'addicted to' sex and technologies, thus displacing 'the problem' to the 'out there' from its real locus 'in here'. Vigilantism meanwhile, merely perpetuates the 'evil monster' myth that there are a small number of 'those people', abhorrent, separate and different from the culture of general society.

Children, young people and discourses of cyber victimization

It is important to reiterate that children and young people are not a homogenous category, and indeed that to impose such homogeneity implies totalizing discourses that have lent themselves very often to the demonization of 'youth' as society's 'problem'. Since we have applied this critique to youthful criminality, we must also apply it to youthful victimization, as has been noted in Chapter 5. We have also insisted that children and young people are not simply passive, but are competent social actors in their own right. One problem with this in the present context is the danger of subscribing to an apologist discourse that suggests that children and young people may be complicit in their own victimization. Obvious candidates for this type of argument are the cases of the 'camgirls' cited above, or of Japanese children engaging in 'compensated dating'. The issue is further complicated because youth *is* to a large extent a socially constructed category, so that what is seen as age-appropriate behaviour may vary widely between cultures – as indeed do definitions of childhood via ages of consent to any number of activities from intercourse to drinking alcohol. This kind of argument, moreover, tends to separate out 'real' victims – the 'truly innocent'. This is implicit even in anti-child pornography discourses, which tend to define as *especially* 'disturbing' or 'horrifying' those images that depict very young children:

> The age of the children appearing in new child pornography is reducing. At the moment, there are a number of extremely disturbing new pictures emerging involving children (especially girls) who appear to be under 5 or 6 . . . These pictures are disturbing because of the age of the children involved . . . Excepting these pictures, the typical age range of all photographs tends to be in the 7–8 to 10–11 range.
> (Taylor 2002: http://www.ipce.info/library_3/files/nat_dims_kp.htm).

> Home Office Minister Hilary Benn [on Operation Ore] said in many cases the images were of very young children. The minister told *Today*: 'That is why this is such a serious issue with tough penalties.'
> (http://news.bbc.co.uk/1/hi/uk/2652465.stm)

Universal assumptions about childhood and vulnerability, childhood and lack of rationality and so on, have been subject to sustained critique in this volume. Research in childhood studies, as well as material from official and non-governmental agencies worldwide, shows huge diversity in experiences of childhood and demonstrates that such experiences are cross-cut by the North-South divide, by social class, gender, ethnicity (dis)ability and even the so-called 'digital divide' (James *et al.* 1998; Holloway and Valentine 2003; Jenks 2004). At the same time, the notion of agency underpins all childhoods. Where does this leave 'child pornography'?

Jenks (2004) suggests that whilst the 'idealist' form of the childhood studies position – that children are active agents, that children are competent – is a useful analytical tool and leads us towards a much needed child-centrism in research with (rather than on) children and young people, *in practice* it is necessary to take heterogeneity of experiences and inequalities of power into account. This is probably the best we can do in relation to child sexual abuse, exploitation and pornography. Clearly most children and young people, most of the time, *are* in a relatively powerless position, despite their agency, in relation to adult males – particularly those males who occupy a high-trust status, such as family members, teachers, priests or (sometimes) police officers. The degree of arbitrariness surrounding the ascription of 'upper' age limits is not amenable to resolution either; *is* consensuality a different matter for 7- and 16-year-olds? How young do we need to go to make an act of abuse 'totally' unacceptable (as opposed to only a bit?).

One approach, that some legislative jurisdictions adopt, is to regard the issue from the point of view of 'harms'. Both US and New Zealand law for example regard child pornography as a 'permanent record' of the exploitation and abuse of children (Healy 2004). The notion of harm goes much deeper than this of course. Here there is only space to discuss a few of its ramifications, but that should be sufficient to dispel any apologist argument that suggests child pornography is either 'acceptable' if the child 'agrees', or 'acceptable' in relation to older (i.e. teenage) young people. The caveat is that this is a normative discussion: in other words, it has no pretensions either to 'objectivity' or to strictly legal relevance, but rather relates to concerns expressed about victims by left realist and feminist victimologies.

Firstly and most clearly, under any legislature that defines it as such, child pornography – with the boundary-blurring example of virtual images excepted – records the scene of a crime, and that crime is not merely 'representational' but records sexual and physical abuse – or less euphemistically, violence. Secondly, as has been pointed out, this is not an isolated harm or incident, but has to be seen in context as part of a cycle of abuse to which the child or young person in question is subjected. In particular, the highly domestic and privatized nature of many instances suggest that the young people involved are locked into familial or other institutional abuse of a systematic nature where they are in an enduring relationship of relative powerlessness either through coercion by or trust in/love for the perpetrator. High degrees of fear and/or guilt are suggested by this scenario. In other cases, where paedophile rings or commercial sexual exploitation takes place for example, the child or young person may be enmeshed as a victim of organized crime such as prostitution and trafficking, or may find themselves being unwittingly 'groomed' for paedophiliac involvement at a later stage. Thirdly, the initial act of abuse is repeated secondarily every time the image is reproduced (often many thousands of times) and through the longevity of the image, which will still be circulating for many years in cyberspace even if the offender is apprehended.

Psychological and psychiatric discourses suggest that 'children can experience a myriad of symptoms including physical symptoms and illnesses, emotional withdrawal, anti-social behaviour, mood swings, depression, fear and anxiety' (Healy 2004: 11). Of course, these are very 'western' medicalized discourses of harmful effects, and cannot necessarily be held as universal to all. The germane issue is an ethical one as to whether or not abuse as described above is, or should be, culturally acceptable. It is crucially an issue of the exploitation of power by adult males through systematic assaults on the relatively vulnerable. Lest we be unclear about this, evidence suggests that 'in most countries, street children, poor children, juveniles from broken homes, and disabled minors are especially vulnerable to sexual exploitation', whilst at the same time, 'in many countries, including developed nations, child victims may come from homes where their own parents use them to create child pornography or where their parents offer them to others for the same purpose' (Healy 2004: 4). The only defence for a 'victimless' crime is thus left with the phenomenon of totally computer-generated images, 'pseudo-pornography' that is entirely textual (digital) and not therefore involving a 'real' child at all. Most legislatures have attempted to circumvent this as a 'loophole' in the law rather than regarding it as outside the necessity for regulation, and there are a number of cogent reasons for this. However 'virtual' the image, it commits an act against children and young people *in general*: presenting violence and abuse as acceptable and desirable. In this sense it has equivalence with 'hate' crimes. There is also the same point that can be made in relation to all such images, whether 'pseudo' or 'real', should children and young people themselves come into contact with them: that they are degrading and constitute textual or virtual victimization. Williams (2001), from a broadly linguistic perspective, makes a clear case for injuriousness in relation to virtual rape and virtual sexual assault. Following this logic, it is clear that in the case of child pornography endlessly circulating, shifting, pixels affect real children's lives and dignity. Whether real children are converted into pixels, or the pixels are generated to appear as real children, real humiliations and human pains are generated. Elsewhere Williams has also argued (2000: 103) that 'if the virtual environment is to become a "second home" for a large proportion of the population, as is the case for many already, then structures that protect their fundamental rights in the actual world must be duplicated in the virtual . . . it is hoped that enhanced methods of governance that incorporate elements of justice and fundamental human/atavar rights can be delineated'.

Discourses of regulation and governance

Over and over again it has been stressed by governments, by national and international bodies, by 'watchdogs' in numerous directives and conferences, by the internet industries and by interest groups, that legislation and conventional law enforcement alone cannot hope to control the international circulation of child sexual abuse images (child pornography) in cyberspace, for all the reasons evident in the foregoing discussion. Because of this, discourses of regulation through governance are typically invoked. Governance involves the concept of 'government at a distance' – in this context usually meaning a coalition of industry representatives, watchdogs, other non-governmental organizations such as voluntary organizations working for children, and parental controls. Policy discourses are considered critically in this context, asking whether current ways of framing and responding to the problem reflect the realities of youth, or adult idealizations and preoccupations.

Oswell (1998: 271–2) notes that 'we are often told that the Internet is ungovernable ... but this should not stop us from thinking about ... regulation ... The issue ... is not whether or not to have regulation, but *what form of regulation* (and whose interests are being served).' In other words, we should not necessarily assume that current approaches to regulation are the most realistic or effective. This applies particularly where the emphasis is upon restricting young people's access to the internet, either through filtering software or stricter parental controls. The notion of 'protecting' young people by denying or limiting access to cyberspace from the home completely misses the point that the domestic sphere is central in the production of 'harmful' content, and also assumes that the onus is upon parents and children to 'sidestep' abusive content rather than challenge it. Hence as Oswell suggests, 'given that much abuse takes place in the home, by parents, why should policy be directed toward *restricting* young people's access to new forms of knowledge and community?' (p. 283). Within such discourses the *child* rather than the adult is rendered problematic. Industry self-regulation relies on internet service providers operating their own form of 'policing' through, for example, tracking software or making censorship software available. Although to a certain extent (e.g. through involvement in hotlines and cooperation with law enforcement operations) this does target illegal material and perpetrators of abuse, again the main emphasis is on preventing 'inappropriate' content from being encountered by children.

Recent years have seen a growth in specialist law enforcement units, but also in internet hotlines. The UK-based Internet Watch Foundation was established in 1996 to provide what it describes as a 'partnership' approach to the governance of the distribution of child abuse images on the internet (http://www.iwf.org.uk/about/overview/index.html). In other words, Foundation staff receive and investigate complaints from the public about alleged illegal content including criminally 'obscene' or 'racist' material globally. The Foundation then cooperates with law enforcement agencies and 'other key stakeholders' with the aim of removing the content and tracing the perpetrators. The Foundation is funded by industry representatives (service providers and mobile network operators, hardware and software companies), the European Union and 'other organizations that have an affinity with our work'. Other hotlines now operate across Europe, Australasia, Asia and the Pacific Rim, the USA and South America. Whilst some of these are almost exclusively industry-based and funded, others receive support from the European Union, national government agencies and various international organizations. The clear problem here is that the internet and related industries indirectly make enormous profits from pornography. The Coalition Against Trafficking in Women commented of the Internet Watch Foundation's creation of a rating and filter system for internet sites to protect children from watching pornography, that 'this rating system is not aimed at ending sexual exploitation or slowing down the sex industry . . . it is only attempting to organize the content of the internet so parents can prevent children from viewing pornography, but still make pornography and sex shows readily available to buyers' (http:// www.uri.edu/artsci/wms/hughes/ppsr.htm).

Hotlines, as essentially a form of industry self-regulation, are only effective in so far as they remove content from the internet and/or are instrumental in tracking offenders, and self-interest aside, other factors militate against this. Reis (2002: 10) notes that non-governmental organizations tend to take action in isolation, whereas effective information sharing with the police is essential, as are mechanisms to make the link from information to law enforcement. However, Oswell (1999: 52–3) has argued that the trend is toward 'dispersed, individualised, and localised forms of governance which do not assume that there is a totality (i.e. society) upon which, and for which, common standards can be applied . . . the new regulatory thinking tends to be . . . in terms of . . . technological solutions to social problems'.

Concerned with the 'fragmentation and diffusion of power' (Loader and Sparks 2001: 87), the new 'governance of crime' connotes a number of things. First, changes in policing where outcomes are acknowledged as limited and the onus is placed on individual responsibility; second, the associated decollectivization of social risks, seeing citizens as not 'mere recipients of state policing but as self-calculating, risk-monitoring actors' (p. 89), including encouraging people to 'deploy their judgement and means as consumers' in personal crime prevention; and third, advocating avoidance and preventative behaviours by individuals, all of which may be subsumed under the notion of 'responsibilization strategies' (following Garland 2001). The shift to governance as it has so far applied to the regulation of internet crime against children and young people, or regulating the dangers of young people being incited to crime by the internet, has demonstrated the lessening of either the will or the ability of the state to 'protect' young citizens; and a concomitant responsibilization of policing through the family or industry. This, despite the exhaustive evidence that both these sites of regulation are precisely the sites of production of internet criminality against youth. Thus the 'new' spaces of the cyber produce a range of responses to the victimization of children and young people and the risks and dangers of their becoming criminals or victims, which retain the rhetoric of paternalism and protection characteristic of modern state regulation, but are at the same time re-framed through the rhetorics of governance.

Moreover, and centrally, the child is treated as the *object* of representation by regulatory bodies and not the *agent* (Oswell 1999: 59). As both significant users of the internet, and as the victims of crime, the involvement of children and young people in the processes of internet governance is essential. Even more than this, the inherent notion that *children* need more supervision is bizarre, when clearly *adults* require more supervision and children require more autonomy!

'For kids by kids online?' Risk and autonomy

Contrary to much popular and policy discourse, the general conclusion, whether in terms of children and young people victimized whilst *using* the internet, or children and young people as victims of abuse and exploitation *through* the internet, must be that cybertravel is only dangerous because of children's and young people's relative powerlessness in the face of adult practices on- and offline. Netdangers, therefore, are better combated by increasing, not decreasing, young people's involvement and autonomy both in using the internet and in representing their views on and through it. 'Communities of practice' support paedophiles, pornographers and sexual predators in providing justification, self-help, information sharing and belonging, thereby reinforcing their power; yet we do not apply the same logic to children and young people themselves.

Instead, when girls especially, tunnel out of bedroom culture and the confinements of family life through cyberspace, we regard them as either 'risky' or 'at risk'. We represent them as isolationist or addictive, whereas use of the internet is in fact frequently communitarian and enskilling – and therefore empowering. We try to separate out 'good' use of the internet by children and young people (educational, 'informative') from 'risky' use (in other words accessing skills, content and other people of whom we do not 'approve'). Industry abdicates responsibility through discourses of 'governance'.

The virtual 'community' however offers unprecedented opportunities for a lesser-policed childhood and youth. 'Grrlpower', for some time now a popular cultural category referring to the cooption of 'feminine' cultural categories in empowering ways, has reached the internet. As a case study in cultural geography, Leonard (1998) explains that the grrl phenomenon shows how zines (defined by Leonard as 'self-published, independent texts devoted to various topics including hobbies, music, film and politics': 103), firstly printed and later electronic, formed the basis of a geographically transcendent and dispersed network of girls and young women embracing 'feminist' gender politics. This is very much tunnelling out of bedroom culture, for whilst zines as textual productions locate the girls in privatized domestic space, that space is rearticulated through the textual 'spaces of articulation' (Leonard 1998: 106–7). Leonard cites the 'Friendly Grrls Guide to the Internet': 'Girls are not girls, but grrls, super kewl young women who have the tenacity and drive to surf the net, network with other young women online and expand the presence of young women in new and emerging technologies' (p. 111). To avoid an overly idealistic presentation of such phenomena, it is important to note that Leonard acknowledges the largely white, middle-class base of grrls. Moreover, since Leonard was writing this particular phenomenon has been subject to extensive internet commercialization, using grrl 'power' as a marketing tool. Nevertheless, many 'grrl' chat sites and zines continue to exist; and principally the grrl movement is interesting in its demonstration of the possibilities that the internet offers girls and women to form networks that challenge and provide some escape from 'dangers', hence articulating space through 'spaces of articulation'.

Another positive, if limited, development has been the growth of child and youth-centred sites encouraging young people to become involved themselves in internet governance. For example, the US volunteer-based WiredSafety WiredKids site (http://www/wiredkids.org/news/wiredkids/index.html) claims that 'when wired kids was first launched in 1998, we knew that kids and teens needed to be the leaders of our content development'. Similarly the UK-based For Kids By Kids Online (FKBKO), a European-funded project based at the University of Central Lancashire, 'works with children, parents, teachers, industry and the government to help make the internet a better and safer place for children and young people' (http://www.fkbko.co.uk/). Despite working 'with' children and young people, however, such sites are inherently paternalistic, guided and 'led' by adults concerned with 'protecting' 'their' children. The emphasis is on 'educating' rather than skilling children, and the focus is always on parents and teachers; even the 'kids' sections of these sites centre on providing 'kids' with material to download to give to their parents so that their parents can guide them! Such convolutions seem aimed at doing anything *except* empowering young people themselves. Children are 'guided' by the sites as to what is suitable for them through (adult devised) rating systems and filtering of appropriate chat sites and so on. This is not an attempt to dispute that children and young people may find some of the information on the sites useful (such as how to report illegal content, or how to find help in cases of stalking or harassment); but the assumption behind them is made explicit on the ONCE project website (of which FKBKO is a partner): 'Mission Statement: Empowerment of parents, teachers and carers with the knowledge they need to educate children to navigate safely on the internet . . . furthermore, we aim to raise awareness of the positive aspects of the internet by inviting parents and teachers to compile a database of web sites that they would recommend for children' (http://www.once.uclan.ac.uk/home.htm). The tone of these sites cannot help but be patronizing; they attempt to use terminology that adults think children and young people will relate to ('kewl' for example) and succeed in sounding as if they are drafted by twenty-something postgraduates or youth leaders.

Other 'youth centred' initiatives include examples such as Tingog sa Kabataan, a 30-minute Filipino radio broadcast focusing on internet safety and combating internet child sexual abuse, coordinated by ECPAT Philippines Inc., and run by young amateur broadcasters who mostly seem to be aged between mid-teens to early twenties. ECPAT itself has an international children and youth advisory committee, but only at an international board meeting in March 2002 was it agreed that a young person would be elected onto the board of directors.

In general it seems that, as with the offline world, discourses of protection abound in relation to children and young people, but effective participation is largely lacking. 'Listening to youth' takes the usual form of 'youth councils', 'kids divisions' and so on, magnanimously inviting children and young people to 'have a say' in matters that are fundamental to their own lives. Perhaps most optimism can be derived from young people's self-skilling in using the internet, however much adults might try to restrict it. As one of Holloway and Valentine's young respondents commented, 'Children . . . do know a lot more about the internet and different things like that than adults do at the moment. Even though it's the adults that design most of the things that go on the internet' (interview in Holloway and Valentine 2003: 78). Of course this will change as these children shortly become adults, and it is unclear what impact that might have upon the issues discussed in this chapter; similarly at the moment many children and young people are still excluded from both the risks and opportunities of cyberspace through the 'digital divide'; and children and young people as a heterogeneous group are differentially exposed to the effects of internet crime. Moreover, in an adult world cross-cut by the imperatives of commercial exploitation, political expediency and patriarchal masculinities, it is difficult to see how an effective and lasting reduction in crimes of sexual exploitation and abuse can be achieved. What is clear in general is that netdangers are not simply dangers of the net. Legislative and regulatory discourses need to recognize centrally that this is the case rather than shifting responsibility back and forth in the rhetoric of governance and partnership, back and forth from blaming the technology to scapegoating minorities, to responsibilizing families and the internet industry – whilst simultaneously noting that the source of much abuse is male, adult and domestic on the one hand, and commercially motivated on the other.

Further reading

Holloway and Valentine (2003) provide an excellent introduction to the issues surrounding children's use of the internet, based around an empirical research study. David Oswell has written widely on children and internet regulation. See for example Oswell (1998), but a simple internet search will reveal numerous other examples. Donnerstein (2002) provides a perspective opposite to the one presented in this chapter. At the time of writing there is no one definitive text in this field. The nature of the subject itself however lends itself to internet research. Good starting points are the Internet Watch Foundation website (http://www.iwf.org.uk), ECPAT (End Child Prostitution and Trafficking, http://www.ecpat.net/eng/index.asp),

NSPCC (National Society for the Prevention of Cruelty to Children, http:// www.nspcc.org.uk/home/), the Internet Crime Forum (http://www. internetcrimeforum.org.uk/), the COPINE project home page (http:// www.copine.ie/) and Wired Patrol (http:// www.wiredpatrol.org/). Alternatively you can use any of the internet references in this chapter, or perform a keyword search using search terms suggested by the chapter. Many campaigning and non-governmental organization website pages have links to bibliographies of both research and campaigning literature, as well as media sources.

chapter eight

Beyond boundaries: understanding global youth and crime

Most of this book, along with the vast majority of English-language texts on youth and crime, is strongly oriented toward a western perspective and focuses chiefly on the Anglo-American context. In this chapter we ask the deceptively simple question of what happens if we try to take into account the rest of the world. Once we begin to think about this in more depth a number of problems emerge. Firstly, since childhood and youth, as we have repeatedly argued, are not universal categories, then it is clear that despite western attempts to homogenize and totalize them into a universal ideal, childhood and youth in reality are constitutive of diversity. We therefore need to think about what such categories might mean from a viewpoint *other* than the 'we' of western culture. Since childhood and youth in reality mean different things globally, can there be one way of thinking about them in relation to something the western criminologist may call 'crime'?

And since it is obvious that 'crime' means many different things in different contexts, we seem to have two fragmenting categories here.

Secondly, it is important to ask what is meant by 'global'. The phenomenon of 'globalization' has become a frequent focus of academic, policy and political discourses, but the concept is used to refer to a myriad of different, complex processes. What are the most important 'globalizing' trends for understanding youth and crime?

Third, what new and different ways of thinking about and defining a criminology of and for young people are suggested once we attempt a more global perspective? Is 'traditional' criminological theorizing about youth and crime thrown into disarray, and if so in what sense? What might be some of the future key questions for understanding youth and crime, and listening to youth, if we abandon a narrowly domestic perception for a broader horizon? The questions asked in this chapter are *not* an attempt to move toward a comparative criminology of youth; they are rather an attempt to move toward a diversity and plurality of perspective that denies a unitary logic to academic disciplines such as 'criminology': that is to say, 'criminology' itself may fragment as a category if we try to apply it to a global context; it may come to mean many different things. This rejection of unitariness however, also brings with it problems, most notably that of cultural relativism and the question of standards of social justice and human rights for children and young people. For if we do not have *some* common way of describing the harms that are done to young people, or the harms done by them, then how can the vulnerable be protected?

A view from childhood studies: the 'many childhoods' debate

An important 'many childhoods' question has been posed within childhood studies (James *et al.* 1998; Jenks 2004). It has long been recognized in this field that childhood and youth are framed differently in different social contexts. As noted previously childhood and youth are cross-cut by many other modes of stratification (Jenks 2004: 5) such as class, gender, ethnicity, the North-South divide, physical and mental health and so on. Equally important, it has also been noted that as children and young people are part of those social contexts, they are also *agents themselves* in constructing and reconstructing society. This does not necessarily imply symmetry of power between children, young people and adults, since age itself, as we have seen in Chapter 1, is also an independent variable of power stratification. Nevertheless, the young do have agency and are not merely passive recipients of culture. So for example, a criminologist from the West studying street children in Central America may make the mistake of firstly assuming that childhood in Central America is or should be the same as western childhood and secondly, that the child is *merely* a passive object in this process. Exponents of the 'new childhood studies' therefore not only reject the notion that childhood is a unitary phenomenon; they assert that 'children are and must be seen as active in the construction and determination of their own social lives' (James and Prout 1990: 9). We saw in Chapter 7 how often this point has been missed in approaches to children and cyberspace. It is frequently completely ignored in discourses surrounding global childhood and youth in general, even by international organizations responsible for producing directives and guidelines on issues such as human rights. The present chapter therefore has the task of acknowledging this whilst retaining the position that as an analytical tool the concepts of childhood and youth as loosely cohesive formations remain useful. We are on the one hand studying commonality (which helps us to frame concepts of 'human rights' and 'social justice' for example) and on the other acknowledging diversity of social structures and cultures.

Questions of counting: no straight answers

It is always tempting to begin tackling questions of basic definitions in the hope of clarifying debates. If we can define our terms, the argument goes, then we can measure, and that is the road to objectivity. The difficulty is that this usually reveals deeper and more complex questions that actually muddy the waters further. 'Childhood(s?)' and 'youth(s?)' are no exception to this, especially where a macro context, the 'global', is concerned. Yet, the 'global' seems to demand that two things be possible: firstly a universal measurement of the phenomena of childhood and youth, and social issues in relation to these groups, such as welfare, poverty and delinquency; and secondly, that a comparative approach then be taken to assess the relative positions of various regions or countries in relation to these. Yet in truth this is highly problematic.

Many global and local 'facts' are available through which to frame or shape a picture of childhood and youth in relation to economics and social policy. However, they do not (and could not) produce a uniform picture. This is because, whether using statistical or cultural indicators, the definition of childhood and youth is produced differently in different regions of the world, across different countries and across (and within) different international bodies. For example, whilst the United Nations General Assembly defines 'youth' as an age group of 15–24 years, and childhood as 14 years old and under, Article 1 of the *United Nations Convention on the Rights of the Child* defines 'children' as those aged 18 and under because the *Convention* is directed at protecting the rights of as large an age group as possible (there is no UN Convention on the rights of youth). Then again, the UN's own 'frequently asked questions' website (http://www.un.org/esa/socdev/unyin/qanda.htm) notes that within the category of 'youth' 'it is important to distinguish between teenagers (13–19) and young adults (20–24) since the sociological, psychological and health problems they face may differ'. Individual nation states may define childhood and youth differently, and operate numerous different definitions in relation to different areas of governance and legislation: the age of majority in general for example, is often different from the level of criminal responsibility, or from legal age limits relating to any number of social behaviours from smoking to the age of sexual consent (which in turn may differ according to sexual orientation). It is also fair to say that the subjectivities of age groups are differentiated in many ways, as refracted through cultural identities: psychologically and socially for instance, a 12-year-old boy in one region of one country may be in an entirely different space of identity than a 12-year-old boy in another region of the same country, or continent, or part of the world. How then can either universal or comparative measures be possible?

All formal delineations appear arbitrary from this position and for this reason, 'age' as a chronological entity alone cannot be taken as a conceptually useful tool. This is not only a methodological but also a broadly theoretical problem. Statistical indicators, the basis of social accounting (James *et al.* 1998), hide diverse methods of applying definitions, or counting practices. Thus, it cannot be assumed that data gathered from one country or region are actually comparable with others. Where standard indicators have been developed by organizations such as the UN UNICEF division, some kind of useful comparisons may be made about, for example, life chances, poverty, involvement in warfare and so on. However, many other categories are highly dependent upon normative interpretations, such as what counts as exploitation or criminality, and many statistics in this respect obscure the cultural dynamics behind the social structure. The UN for example identified in its World Programme of Action for Youth to the Year 2000, ten 'youth issues' that 'should be of the highest priority to governments': education, employment, hunger and poverty, health, environment, drug abuse, juvenile delinquency, leisure time activities, girls and young women, and full and effective participation of youth in the life of society and in decision-making (http://www.un.org/). But how can these things possibly have the same meaning in highly diverse cultures? It is unrealistic to suppose that 'leisure activities' or 'juvenile delinquency' could mean the same thing in say, Paraguay and Paris. Any statistics relating to such general categories make sense only if they are considered alongside studies of specific localities, viewed from the perspective of local cultures and economic and social structures.

Moreover there is – we have touched on this point before and shall return to it later in the chapter – an implicit assumption within international organizations that whilst there may be different 'models' or experiences of childhood and youth, the 'First World' or 'western' model is *better*. As James *et al.* note, 'childhoods in the developing world are ... cast as unfortunate, even outrageous, violations of some universal, natural childhood. In such a game plan Western childhood acts as a normative basis, the springboard, for remedial action elsewhere.' (James *et al.*

1998: 141). Thus, western-oriented definitions and mores about childhood, youth, and social policy are used as a basis for proclamations about 'what should be done' in other parts of the world. As we shall see, this becomes crucial when trying to unravel ideas about victimization, rights and crime from a global perspective. Before we tackle these issues in more depth however, it is important also to ask what we mean by 'global' and 'globalization'.

Global, 'globalization' and the (g)local: tackling diversity and convergence

Defining 'globalization' is far from a simple task. It represents a huge and still growing corpus of knowledge that it is impossible to embrace in this section. However, we need to distil at least some main features of the debate.

The idea of the 'global' refers to a number of processes. Firstly, there is the shrinking of the world due to factors such as the electronic communications revolution and rapid mass transit – in other words, telecoms and jet planes. This means that not only bodies, but also ideas, are no longer distanced and separated in the way they once were. This is known rather grandly as the 'collapse of time-space distanciation' (Giddens 1991). Secondly, and consequent upon this, is the notion that this entails a homogenization of culture. Both of these processes are seen to take place within a framework of the expansion of global capital: flows of money, the reach of big business corporations, expand and extend. Involved in all of this is an erosion of national borders so that *transborder flows* of money and people occur more rapidly and with more ease.

However, this is to oversimplify by far, because globalization also produces another phenomenon: that of resistance to homogeneity – as is seen in the growth of nationalist movements and ethnic- or religious-based resistance and demands for independence, in attempts to reassert identities and borders threatened by global processes.

The academic debate thus runs roughly as follows. Featherstone *et al.* (1995) divide globalization theorists into two types: homogenizers and heterogenists. They write: 'the *homogenizers* tend, ideal-typically, to subscribe to some notion of world system. They look primarily at the presence of the universal in the particular' (p. 4). For Featherstone *et al.* this includes theorists such as Anthony Giddens.

Giddens (1990) identifies a fourfold typology of globalization that comprises the nation-state system, the world capitalist economy, the world military order and the international division of labour. He sees nation states as the principal actors in the world order, and corporations as the dominant agents within the world economy. Military industrialization and alliances and conflicts are, he argues, increasingly global in nature. The international division of labour, as a dimension of stratification based on unequal access to the means of production is a principal axis of global inequalities (1990: 70–5) – or put crudely, there are those who produce the global cake and those who eat it. Giddens also argues that a further and 'quite fundamental' aspect of globalization is the global impact of the media (1990: 77). He especially notes the centrality of electronic communications:

> Instantaneous electronic communication isn't just a way in which news or information is conveyed more quickly. Its existence alters the very texture of our lives, rich and poor alike. When the image of Nelson Mandela is maybe more familiar to us than the face of our next door neighbour, something has changed . . . Globalisation isn't just about what is 'out there', remote and far away from the individual. It is an 'in here' phenomenon too, influencing intimate and personal aspects of our lives.
>
> (Giddens 1999: 3)

Nederveen Pieterse (1995) by contrast argues a strongly *heterogenist* position. The focus on homogenization, he suggests, implies that globalization equates with westernization. Instead, he says, we should see globalization as 'a process of hybridization which gives rise to a global melange' (1995: 45). Most importantly for present purposes, Pieterse is concerned here with both the weakening of nation states in the context of economic globalism *and* with the resurgence of nationalism.

Giddens himself later emphasized in his Reith Lecture on globalization that 'globalisation is the reason for the revival of local cultural identities in different parts of the world . . . Local nationalisms spring up in response to globalising tendencies' (Giddens 1999: 3). A crucial aspect of this is the separation of cultural forms from local particularities, or the global in the local: 'think globally, act locally' (Nederveen Pieterse 1995: 49 – and one might equally say 'think locally, act globally', as with the Afghanistan-US conflict and the second Gulf War).

As we noted previously then, globalization may be defined in terms of *flows*, crucially of economics and culture – through the compressed spatialities of electronic landscapes and weakened borders – and at the same time as a dynamic of *blockages* through attempts to reinforce particularity. Featherstone points out that this does not refer to the global *versus* the local, but the local in the global and the global in the local. Whereas one argument sees a 'McWorld' of homogenizing globalization as against a 'Jihad world' of particularizing Lebonanization (Featherstone *et al.* 1995: 33) Featherstone *et al.* assert that 'globalization – in the broadest sense, the compression of the world – has involved and increasingly involves the creation and incorporation of locality' (p. 40). In the light of this it has been suggested that *glocalization* is a more accurate term than globalization. Nederveen Pieterse (1995: 49) argues for example that glocalization 'is at work in the case of minorities who appeal to transnational human rights standards beyond state authorities, or indigenous peoples who find support for local demands from transnational networks'.

In this chapter we shall adopt a broadly (g)local orientation. A homogenizing position would assume that it *is* now possible to speak of *one* childhood and youth, and that consequently understanding youth and crime amounts to the same thing the world over. But this is simply not the case. If anything, the blockages, the resistances to homogenization have increased the diversity of experiences of children and young people. At the same time, factors such as weakened national borders and the increases in flows of capital and bodies have facilitated such atrocities as the mass trafficking of children and young people for commercial gain. A grounded study of childhood, youth and crime in the global context – necessary if we are to avoid joining the 'totalizers' – requires an ethnographic perspective as well as a more overarching, systemic view. We need to ask both what it means to be a child or young person in the local sense, and what problems and potential arise from the global dimensions of childhood and youth.

The local in the global: exploitation or independence? Economics or crime?

Behind many western concerns with childhood and 'crime', or delinquency, in developing countries such as Central America is the assumption that non-western childhoods are deviant (and therefore criminogenic) because of the particular way in which children are placed economically. Instead of the 'schooled' child and the 'contained' (i.e. within the home) child, a problem is seen of children who are 'exploited' for labour and 'on' the streets.

UNICEF proclaims in its campaign against child labour exploitation that 'over and above the multiple threats of poverty, disease, violence and war, [children] also face direct exploitation by adults who abuse their innocence and vulnerability ... Adults can make children work long hours in homes, factories, in fields or on the streets, rather than sending them to school – denying them their fundamental rights to education and protection, and to a regular and healthy process of development' (http://www.endchildexploitation.org.uk/faces_of_exploitation.asp). Whilst acknowledging that many western children work 'after school hours' and usefully contribute to family life and income, preparing 'themselves for the responsibilities of adult life', the UNICEF campaign differentiates the latter from 'child labour', a particular form of child work that 'implies that children are doing things that are harmful to their healthy development ... labouring long hours, sacrificing time and energy that they might have spent at school or at home, enjoying the free and formative experiences of childhood'. Hence as James *et al.* point out, 'organizations concerned to protect children from abuse and exploitation mobilize the child labour/ child work difference in order to classify some of what children do as harmful' (1998: 108).

Unfortunately, despite the 'common sense' appeal of this distinction – and its utility for framing practical points of action against the most extreme forms of child economic activity – it places an idealized and generalized western template unrealistically over specific economic and cultural settings. The distinction between child labour and child work is not an analytical one, but is 'primarily a moral one' (James, Jenks and Prout 1998: 110).

It is suggested that around 2.5 million children aged 5–14 (or 2 per cent of this age group) are economically active worldwide. This varies from 2 per cent in industrial countries, to 4 per cent in 'transitional' countries, to, for example, 16 per cent in Latin America and the Caribbean, to sub-Saharan Africa, where 29 per cent of children are economically active. Inadequate education is seen by UNICEF as a central element in perpetuating child labour because 'the skills acquired in school may lead directly to the sort of gainful employment that will help children rise above the poverty into which they were born'.

This fails to take into account the unpaid work carried out by children in *most* economies within the 'private' sphere of the home. Neither is it possible simply to assume that poverty and inadequate education are the unique motivators to child work: for example, regional studies carried out in the UK between 1972 and 1994 found between 30 and 50 per cent of children were in paid employment (cited in James *et al.* 1998: 113) – and much of this work was undertaken illegally. Thus it seems that child 'labour' is at least in part a way of problematizing the economic activity of children in developing countries, whereas child 'work' in western countries by contrast is less visible and is seen as unproblematic because it does not stand (for the most part) in *place* of the educational institutions of the state.

By imposing western assumptions about the undesirability of child 'labour' therefore, organizations such as UNICEF both ignore the realities of child 'labour' in the West and make non-western childhoods inherently deviant, unschooled and subject to delinquency and criminality. Such assumptions also make children appear as passive subjects of exploitation and deny any possibility that children themselves might make any active choices about their lives. The non-western child is by definition a delinquent child, but is also a passive, exploited child. 'Delinquency', in other words, has become a global export of the West, but so has the notion of the 'unfortunate' child – both are direct legacies of colonialism.

This is not to derogate the efforts of intergovernmental organizations such as UNICEF, or those of many non-governmental organizations with similar aims. Nevertheless, it does suggest that a closer analysis is needed of (g)locality in attempting to understand the social world of the 'exploited' or the 'delinquent' child in non-western countries.

The case of street children: a metaphor for 'non-western' childhood out of control

The case of street children is perhaps the most well-known example of the way in which the economic activity and extra-familial existence of non-western childhoods has been condemned in the West. Indeed 'street children' have almost become a metaphor for everything that is wrong about non-western childhood. Whilst in countries such as the UK the problematization (and criminalization, as seen in Chapter 4) of 'our own' young people 'hanging around' the streets has long been a staple of 'respectable fears', it has nevertheless been a fairly domestic, mild affair in comparison to some of the responses to children's use of the streets in other parts of the world.

A dramatic image of street children in the urban centres of developing countries has been portrayed in the popular media of the West. This is the image of 'feral children', who, like feral cats, are domestic animals gone wild on the fringes of urban society. For example, *The Guardian* in the UK reported on 29 May 2003 from Honduras: 'Selvyn says he is 14 but he looks about 8. His feet are bare, his clothes torn and his eyes heavy with the effects of sniffing a powerful glue. His home is nearby, beneath the stars and beside a municipal rubbish dump. His neighbours are other street children – equally feral . . . and the hovering vultures which compete with them for scraps of food on the dump.' This particular report is concerned with an 'epidemic' of murders that, it claims, is sweeping Central America. The principal victims are the street children and the perpetrators are said to be vigilante groups, the police, and 'gang related' (a term left unexplicated). With characteristic inaccuracy, the article in fact conflates the issue of street children with gun violence against young people in general in Central America, and in effect we are left with little more information than that 'there are thousands of street children in Tegucigalpa and thousands more in Guatemala city and in San Salvador whose chances of making it out of their teens alive are sometimes seen as slim as their malnourished frames'. In a slightly more contextualized *Guardian* piece aimed at UK schoolchildren the following month ('Resources Key Stage 3 Age 11–14' *Guardian Education* 10 June 2003), the reader is told that since in Latin American countries 'the authorities have often resorted to violence and intimidation against their opponents . . . It is not surprising that in such places the life of street children is devalued and crimes against them overlooked.' The media also come in for some of the blame: 'thanks to sensational articles calling for the savage treatment of street children and stories about young gang members that fuel people's fear and intolerance'. These statements lack any irony: clearly we are meant to see the obvious – that such terrible places and such irresponsible media, and such intolerant attitudes toward youth, are far removed from anything that exists in western developed, *civilized* nations and exhibit no continuity at all. Such children – such *feral* children – are to be pitied and anguished over, lacking the privileged and safe childhoods of the West.

Unsurprisingly, research studies of 'street children' provide a somewhat different scenario. Firstly the notion that 'street children' are exclusively part of Central American (or Latin American) cultures and economies is inaccurate. Although UNICEF reports that 50 per cent of street children are found in Latin America, this leaves an estimated 50 million in other parts of the world. Moreover, this figure conceals a number of important differentiations. The World Bank for example, notes the distinction between 'market children' and 'street children' in Central America, the former being defined as those who work in the streets but generally live with their families, and the latter being those who live, work and sleep in the streets and often lack regular contact with their families (Takashi and Cederlof 2000: 1). Similarly Hewitt and Smyth (1999: 212–13) suggest at least two categories of children who are normally referred to as 'street children': working children who are highly visible because of what they do, or 'children on the street', and a smaller group of children who have no contact with families and relatives and have no shelter, or children 'of' the street. Glauser (1997) further points out that there are many children who do not fit simply into either category. For example, some children move between home and street and back again; some live mainly on the street because of their work in the night-time economy, from shoe shining to prostitution; some spend part of the time living in institutional homes or shelters. Many 'street children' are aware, and make instrumental use of, varying kinds of support from non-governmental organizations such as Save the Children, whether this is residential or some other form of semi-structured institutional support (Southon and Dhakal 2003).

Such distinctions are important, not just for accounting purposes, but because they enable us to examine the complex realities behind the stereotypes of 'street children' as a lumpen, 'feral' mass that violates western preconceptions of everything childhood stands for. They enable us to ground the concept and reveal the metaphor for what it is: another projection of western fear of the Other. They also enable us to assess more realistically what an analysis of street children's relationship to crime and victimization might consist of.

As Hewitt and Smyth point out (1999: 212), most reactions to street children are tinged by 'two, often co-existing emotions: pity and fear'. The pity of western societies is for a 'lost childhood', deprived of a proper family life, education, play and adequate socialization, echoing the UNICEF campaign to 'end child exploitation'. There is an assumption embedded in this pity that such children need helping toward a 'normal' childhood, and that 'being on the street is the worst of all options available to children' (Hewitt and Smyth 1999: 216). At the same time, in a now depressingly familiar pattern, street children are also viewed with fear and loathing, as marginals and vagabonds. Vagabondage of course has a long history and a long stigma attached to it in many parts of the world, but the negative perceptions of street children have dire consequences. Inciardi and Surratt (1997: 1) record that just some of the colloquial names for street children in Brazil include *marginais* (non-essentials or criminals), *pivetes* (little farts) and *abandonados* (children who have nowhere else to go). In the West 'feral' (the domesticated gone wild and teeming in the streets like vermin) is the popular term. Because criminality (typically petty thefts and robberies) forms one part of the economic life of street children, delinquency and the state of street childhood have become interchangeable in many popular and indigenous legal and policy discourses. In a number of areas this has been used to justify vigilante and police killings of children and young people. As long ago as 1989, Hewitt and Smyth contend, 'the number of children killed by "death squads" in Brazil reached an average of approximately one a day' (1999: 217). They report a case in Rio de Janeiro where a boy was strangled 'and a note left on his body which read: "I killed you because you don't go to school and have no future" ' (p. 218). The stamping out, or more horrifyingly, 'cleansing' of street children continues in the twenty-first century despite the efforts of intergovernmental and non-governmental organizations.

Beyond pity and fear?

It is clear that western emotions of pity, and the applications of western ideals of childhood, have little relevance to life as street children themselves experience it. Firstly, the criminality of street children needs to be placed in economic context. It is children 'of' the street who are most typically involved with crimes from robbery and theft to prostitution and drug trafficking. Inciardi and Surratt (1997: 3) suggest that while 'younger children often begin their careers on the street by begging', they 'rely increasingly on crime to support themselves as they age and become less successful at panhandling'. Criminal occupations intermingle with shining shoes, hauling garbage and selling small items such as newspapers and flowers. For example, a 14-year-old respondent in Southon and Dhakal's study explains, 'at the moment I collect plastics and sometimes beg, sometimes steal . . . I earn money but I do not save any . . . Sometimes I take drugs like glue' (2003: 13). Crime is only one part of a complex economy within which children of the street live. Street life has also to be related to the broader structure and economy of the locality. Children enter street life through various dynamics. Changes in the economic infrastructure of particular countries may mean that rural families are fragmented through the impulse to urbanization, and that as this occurs children choose to leave destitute rural environments for the city streets. Inciardi and Surratt (1997), for example, note that almost half of all Brazilian families live below the poverty line. Children also choose to leave the family home because of violence and abuse from adults (Takahashi and Cederlof 2000).

Takahashi and Cederlof identify a reinforcing loop between poverty and market and street children, whereby poverty leads to migration/urbanization, that in turn exacerbates family disintegration, in turn exacerbating poverty, and around again; the 'by-product' of this is market children and street children, who in turn produce a feedback loop into this cycle. Nevertheless, this is to draw too stark a distinction between 'family' and 'non-family' life. The boundaries of the family, Howitt and Smyth suggest, are often fluid in any case in many developing countries, and children may belong to a broad range of kin and non-kin 'socializing agents'. They are also accustomed to a cultural view of life on the streets as central to sociality. Within the picture of limitation and deprivation however, children are agents, they can and do make decisions: 'In short, children may decide that they will be better off if they go it alone or make an allegiance to a gang on the streets than if they stay with their family or relations' (Hewitt and Smyth 1999: 215).

In their lives on the streets, children have a degree of autonomy and independence. Southon and Dhakal point out that much of the work of 'development' agencies is aimed at working against dependency, but 'when it comes to children our tendency is first to encourage dependence on our own terms before we can support their own independence ... Street children have access to income and are in control of their day-to-day decision making. They will not accept strict rules, restrictions on their freedom, low standards of service provision, and organizations which do not respect them. These children have a choice and can survive without organizations' (2003: 24).

This is why organizations seeking to impose notions of western institutions will fail. A key finding of the Southon and Dhakal study was that 'organizations are very much seen as a part of street life and not a way out. Different organizations are used for different services – food, shelter, medical treatment, emergency support, clothes, shelter and recreational facilities. It is these open access services, supporting their independent living, which were positively assessed by children' (2003: 22, a similar conclusion was reached by Hewitt and Smyth 1999).

None of this can negate a number of startling facts. Firstly, as we have seen, street children, especially children 'of' the street, are frequent victims of an arbitrary, violent and sometimes murderous vigilante *and police* 'popular justice' that largely goes unpunished. Secondly, certain forms of crime, notably theft and prostitution, are endemic among children of the street, putting them at risk of both vigilantism *and* severe juvenile justice responses such as imprisonment, as well as, of course, HIV/AIDS and other sexually transmitted diseases. Thirdly, children have often been partially precipitated into street life because of abusive and violent family circumstances. Fourthly, drug and solvent use is extremely high among street children, although it is difficult to estimate numerically. Takahashi and Cederlof (2003: 1) write that 'it is estimated that up to 90 per cent of the street children sniff glue'; while it is not at all clear that such a figure is reliable, Inciardi and Surratt (1997: 5) for example, confirm that in the case of Brazil 'anecdotal accounts of drug abuse among street youths . . . are commonplace'.

These issues can *only* be understood, and acted upon effectively, through firstly a research approach that is (g)local, and secondly that recognizes the importance of children's own agency and voices. In this section the material presented has as far as possible been limited to studies based on research *with* and *by* street children themselves; but such studies are still far too few in number and tend to be small in scale. Glauser's point of 1997 is still pertinent: it is unacceptable on the part of those who 'feel entitled to intervene in the lives of children with problems [to] do so on the basis of . . . unclear and arbitrary knowledge about the reality of these children's lives . . . there is very little knowledge about the way children who are themselves directly affected by serious problems of life and survival think about their situation' (pp. 150–1).

'Corrupting' and 'co-opting' the bodies of the young: challenging the boundaries of criminology

Despite its complexities, the study of street children at least provides some familiar 'criminological' material with which to work. We have questions of the relationship of poverty and economics to involvement in juvenile crime; questions of vigilante and formal justice; questions of drug abuse; and so on. We may need to shift the paradigmatic prism of criminology somewhat to accommodate factors such as non-western approaches to the family and the street, to children as agents, to summary 'justice' and traditions of execution, but the terrain is conceptually surmountable. In this section however, the traditional boundaries of youth criminology are more fundamentally challenged.

Two strands within this will be emphasized in particular. Firstly, what happens (analytically speaking) when transborder crimes against children and young people occur? Globalization, in implying economic and cultural flows, also implies flows of people. Starting from this perspective, we shall examine some of the possible implications of such flows for the victimization – both legalized and criminalized – of the young.

The trade in young bodies: global trafficking and children

Human trafficking – the contemporary phrase for slave trading – clearly has a long history, intimately tied up with flows of capital and economic demand for cheap or free physical labour (including sexual labour). Global capitalism is not new, as we have seen, and bodies, including young bodies, have long been commodities; the trade has been worldwide for centuries. Nor has it ever disappeared completely, finding some outlets in the smuggling of illegal immigrants, a related business, and smaller-scale operations across regional rather than international borders, as well as being an enduring part of the sex trade in one form or another.

Thus it is hardly surprising that, with the more recent global restructuring of economies and borders (e.g. the dismantling of the 'old' Soviet and Eastern European blocs) and the resultant opportunities for transborder flows, there should be a resurgence of the trade in bodies. On the one hand control over borders has weakened, on the other both pre-existing local conditions of poverty, or the dismantling of economies causing unemployment and political instability, has resulted in large numbers of people unemployed and desperate. Gionti (2004: 70) argues that 'human trafficking has become a global business bringing huge profits to organized criminal syndicates ... characterised by high profits, small expenditures, and minimal risk of punishment'. The UN in their 'fact sheet on human trafficking' claim that 'over the past decade, trafficking in humans has reached epidemic proportions ... the search for work abroad has been fuelled by economic disparity, high unemployment, and the disruption of traditional livelihoods. Traffickers face few risks and can earn huge profits' (http://www.unodc.org/unodc/en/trafficking_victim_consents.html). Thus the UN Office on Drugs and Crime realistically assesses trafficking in humans in economic terms: 'trafficking in human beings is a crime in which victims are moved from poor environments to more affluent ones, with the profits flowing in the opposite direction ... it is believed to be growing fastest in Central and Eastern Europe and the former Soviet Union [although Nepal, Bangladesh, Thailand and the Philippines are also cited] ... Europol estimates that the business is now worth several billion dollars a year' (http://www.unodc/en/trafficking_victim_consents.html).

Trafficking victims are merely a commodity in global organized crime, or 'criminal commerce', in tandem with drug trafficking, the illegal weapons/firearms trade and money laundering; indeed as Shelley (2002) notes, these activities are often interwoven in the activities of organized crime networks. And, of course, trafficking is not simply a global, but rather a (g)local, phenomenon. For example, Shelley (2003a) suggests that the problems of transition in the Soviet Union resulted in the large-scale trafficking of women and children from Russia, Moldova and the Ukraine. Part of this has its roots in the nature of the former Soviet system, which was characterized by centralized economic planning. Shelley argues that 'the economic transition removed women's social safety net, however restrictive and deficient it was, without providing them with any means to acquire and maintain property. The privatization of state property resulted in the mass transfer of wealth, primarily to men. Women were left without capital or the non-wage supports that allowed them to survive' (Shelley 2003a: 234). Poverty was 'feminized' and particularly in Far Eastern regions, Shelley notes, 'women were left with limited opportunities to function in the legitimate economy, a situation which served the traffickers who thrived on the vulnerability of women' (p. 234). Thus local conditions act in complex interplays with the globalizing impetus to produce a situation where trading in bodies continues to expand. Moreover, the organization of trafficking varies: 'organized' or 'transborder' crime covers a number of forms of criminal organization and varying degrees of relationship between criminal and state organizations. The trade may be conducted by small networks, by large cartels or by some other networked set of operators lying between these extremes. As Levi (2002: 906) points out, forms of organized crime need to be understood as a 'business process'; and indeed Shelley (2003b: 119) proposes a 'business model' approach to the study of trafficking in young women: 'behind the egregious human rights violations of trafficking lie intricate enterprises, each with business characteristics that influence the severity of human rights violations. The business structures of the crime groups have historical roots in the respective society but are also shaped by the contemporary conditions in the societies from which individuals are recruited and ultimately the countries to which they are transported.'

The profits of trafficking may also feed back into legitimate economies through money laundering, meaning that their economic impact may actually fuel development and, however unpalatable, provide incomes for families without any other means of subsistence.

A more complex understanding of its organization and dynamics helps us to see why legal control of trafficking is limited in both its coverage and enforceability. Trafficking is intricately tied to the 'legitimate' economic process and to state involvement or that of corrupt agents of states. It crosses several legal jurisdictions and many countries have no specific laws against it. Indeed, until 2002 and the entering into law of the Nationality, Immigration and Asylum Act (making the trafficking of people for prostitution a crime), the UK had no legislation specifically criminalizing human trafficking. This lack of legal definition and regulation itself has been one of the reasons behind the growth of the human trafficking industry. However, in 2004 the trafficking of people for sexual exploitation became illegal in the UK under the Sexual Offences Act (2003), whilst the Asylum and Immigration (Treatment of Claimants etc.) Act (2004) introduces a new offence of human trafficking for non-sexual exploitation (http://www. endchildexploitation.org.uk/issue_child_trafficking.asp, http://www.ind. homeoffice.gov.uk/). International conventional law on trafficking in persons by contrast has a longer history and moreover under recent changes now presents an unambiguous criminalization of human trafficking, particularly in relation to women and to children. The *International Convention for the Traffic in Persons and of the Exploitation of the Prostitution of Others* of 1949 was principally concerned with trade in women for prostitution but it was not until 1989 that the *United Nations Convention on the Rights of the Child* explicitly prohibited trafficking of children and child prostitution (defining children as those aged 18 years old and under) among states parties. In December 2000, the UN *Protocol to Prevent, Suppress and Punish Trafficking in Persons*, especially women and children, was introduced to supplement the *United Nations Convention*

Against Transnational Organized Crime (see Article 3, paragraph (a), http://www/unodc.org/unodc/en/trafficking_human_beings.html). The precise wording of this instrument is interesting:

> 'Trafficking in persons' shall mean the recruitment, transportation, transfer, harbouring or receipt of persons, by means of threat or use of force or other forms of coercion, of abduction, of fraud, of deception, of the abuse of power or of a position of vulnerability or of the giving or receiving of payments or benefits to achieve the consent of a person having control over another person, for the purposes of exploitation. Exploitation shall include, at a minimum, the exploitation of the prostitution of others or other forms of sexual exploitation, forced labour or services, slavery or practices similar to slavery, servitude or the removal of organs . . .

The language used is framed to minimize the notion of agency in relation to trafficking, and is aimed at defining the 'trafficked' person as a victim of crime. Moreover, within the terms of UN legislation, children – persons under 18 years old – cannot by definition consent to trafficking. Power is defined as a relative matter in relation to this ('vulnerability', 'abuse of power', 'control over') so that coercion does not have to be regarded as absolute or physical.

Hence the legal discourse of the West has shifted considerably toward the criminalization of a section of the global economy that is highly profitable *and* perhaps for the first time in history has recognized children as victims of global organized crime. At the same time, a more complex approach to the study of organized crime in general, and trafficking in particular, under conditions of globalization and glocalization, has begun to emerge in contrast to older mainstream western criminology that typically treated 'organized crime' as a glam, 'lads' area of analysis, concerned with the mafia, narcotics, terror and the operation of the illegal and often violent politics of this supposedly subterranean world.

Recently there has been a rapidly growing scholarship in transnational or transborder criminology (Nevala and Aromaa 2004), including criminology from a non-western perspective, that has included human trafficking in its analysis of global and transborder organized crime (Shelley 2002). Nevertheless, the concentration has been largely on the impact of globalization processes on the organization of crime, on economic and political processes and on the changing place of the state in an era of 'transovereign' crime. Despite the importance of both Levi's and Shelley's points that organized crime needs to be seen from the perspective of the analysis of business process, the idea of a victim's – especially a child's – voice in relation to organized crime is very much absent in criminology. The impact on children of trafficking has still only become visible through the news media and popular representations such as television dramas and documentaries, which still largely present young people as passive victims in this particular context (or else link them to the 'threat' of disorder from asylum seekers). In addition to this is a relatively large output from non-governmental organizations, which varies in content, approach and quality, but whose emphasis tends to be on the extent of the problem and on the kinds of harm experienced by victims.

Much of this output also relates primarily to trafficking for sexual exploitation, which whilst by far the most predominant form in Europe, by no means accounts for all trade in children's bodies. Also, whilst such research is extremely valuable, there has been little concern with the notion of children and young people as agents, in terms of their engagement with trafficking. Since they are deemed incapable of consent, they are also implicitly deemed incapable of agency. Moreover, since the harm inflicted through trafficking is frequently very psychologically as well as physically traumatic, it has tended to be assumed that victims are so damaged that their sense of agency has been 'taken away'. A coherent victimology of trafficking in children and young people – both boys and girls and young women – is long overdue. A research agenda is needed that is driven by those most closely affected by human trafficking – young people – *and* which recognizes trafficking as an economic sector of organized crime.

War games, real deaths: children and global conflicts

What happens if we open up the perspective of criminology to include perhaps the most global of all phenomena: international armed conflicts? More precisely, what happens if we centralize children and young people within this frame?

> The most widely used weapons of mass destruction are not nuclear or biological – they are the estimated 500 million small arms and light weapons that are fuelling bloodshed and mayhem around the world . . . the growing privatisation of security and warfare . . . contributes to the trade in small arms. The militarisation of daily life adds to general levels of instability, blurring the boundaries between warfare, crime, and local disputes . . . Small arms and light weapons kill and maim thousands of children each year . . . and millions more children suffer indirectly from the emotional consequences of armed violence.
>
> (Machel 2001: 120–1)

Almost certainly, a criminology of warfare needs to be developed in order to take account of the massive involvement in – and death and injury from – armed conflicts on the part of children. Once again, the global and the local execute their inimitable dance. The battle for global supremacy and national and religious identities presents a backdrop so complex and so demanding of interdisciplinary skills that it is almost impossible to know where to start. From an international relations point of view, analysts of militarism for example have little to say about humanitarian concerns with casualties. Unfortunately, discourses of human rights cannot but come into conflict with indigenous beliefs and states' and superpowers' hypocrisies in defence of their own actions.

Armed conflict is divided into the hard and the soft. The hard deal with precisely that: hardware, hard men (*sic*), gameplans and strategic analysis. The soft are left with the images of the 'tragic', as if victims of conflict, especially children, were some kind of awful, sad but inevitable and inexorable consequence of the actions of 'bad' aggressors such as Saddam Hussein. The obvious need for some connection between the two is almost never acknowledged in public debate or in hegemonic forms of conflict analysis.

The example of Ali Ismael Abbas, better known to the West as 'Little Ali', is a case in point. 'Little Ali', as he was dubbed by the western media, became an icon when as a young boy he was maimed by shrapnel in the Gulf War of 2003. He did not ask for this conflict, which was deemed illegal under international law and was waged allegedly from the UK point of view over Saddam Hussein's famous 'weapons of mass disappearance' (Brown 2003). Ali Ismael Abbas, who suffered pain and trauma, whose family was killed, and whose dreams and memories will probably always be filled with those images, was 'discovered' by the western media and made into a star. 'Little Ali', the archetypal child victim, and not Ali Ismael Abbas, became the reference point for global media representation. The West was presented with a broken child body, soft brown eyes staring into the cameras, white bandages around the stumps of arms; not a person but a grotesque parody of innocence abused. The image was appropriated to salve the western conscience and reinforce Saddam's evil-ness as western medical expertise was mobilized to 'save' this child through magnanimous prosthetic rehabilitation. Under the pretence of showing the 'real' effects of war on children, or 'a living example of "collateral damage" ' (*Guardian* 19 April 2003), the allure of the 'Little Ali' images was, as Sam Jones neatly put it in the *Guardian*, their ability to fascinate and appal. Unwittingly providing a steady stream of soundbites for popular consumption ('I can't go to school any more because I don't have arms'; 'If I had hands I would shake your hand'), the image was irresistible, adorable, passed as a token from one faction to another for processing: 'Little Ali' made civilian casualties attractive on any number of levels. Photographed bravely eating a shish kebab (his 'favourite food') in hospital, he was made to stand proxy for the countless others who were not selected to prove how much the West cares despite the ugly 'necessity' of war, but merely left to die unglamorously.

UNICEF estimates that 2 million children died in armed conflict in the decade up to 1996 and a further 4–5 million disabled (http://www.unicef. org; Kuper 1997). It is not, of course, just direct casualties from weapons that need to be taken into account, but indirect deaths from deprivations and disease, family disintegration, infrastructure collapse and so on. An estimated half million Iraqi children had already died during the sanctions regime by 2001 and 'the infant mortality rate rose from 47 per 1,000 live births, during the pre-sanctions period, to 108,000 in the period after the sanctions were imposed' (Machel 2001: 132). A report published by medical charity Medact (*Guardian* Online 11 November 2003) claims an 'alarming deterioration' in the health of the Iraqi people, based on a 'comprehensive survey assessing the health and environmental impact of the war'. The author of the report stated that 'limited access to clean water and sanitation, as well as poverty, malnutrition, and disruption of public services – including health services – continue to have a negative impact ... the environment is littered with mines, and they are killing humans. A lot of unexploded bomblets are continuing to injure civilians, particularly children.'

The question of children's participation in armed conflict as soldiers is equally, if not more, vexed. Almost every pitfall possible faces those who both seek analytical clarity and yet at the same time have a moral commitment to social justice. We cannot simply assume that 'child soldiers' are nothing more than pitiful, passive and exploited. Most definitions of 'child soldier' used by the international non-governmental organizations follow the UN in classifying anyone under the age of 18 years as a child. Vast cultural differences regarding the nature and boundaries of childhood affect the concept of young people's agency in joining conflicts, and many ideological passions and commitments as well as more pragmatic concerns may bear upon a child or young person who volunteers, or 'volunteers', for armed service. Moreover, it has to be remembered that the West has a very long history of child conscription and press-ganging, viewed under the 18-and-under definition, and most countries today regard 16 or 17 as a viable voluntary enlistment age for state armed forces. Graca Machel, frequently cited as one of the principal authoritative voices in the field, contends that 'A child soldier is any child – boy or girl – under the age of 18, who is compulsorily, forcibly, or voluntarily recruited or used in hostilities by armed forces, paramilitaries, civil defence units or other armed groups' (Machel 2001: 7). Whilst the wide scope of this definition is useful in that it enables many different local and regional situations to be included in debate and pressure for action, it is less helpful in that it paves the way for a universalization of very different realities. The experience of a 17-year-old joining the army in the UK or the USA cannot be simply compared with the experience of a 10-year-old child soldier in a highly unstable conflict zone. The number of child soldiers is estimated at around 300,000 worldwide (Machel 2001), and we have research data on only a tiny proportion of these. What data (quantative or qualitative) there is, is disturbing. A 2004 report from the major international campaigning organization against child soldiers, the Coalition to Stop the Use of Child Soldiers (CSUCS), found that fighters under the age of 18 have been used in 22 conflicts in the last three years (http://www.child-soldiers.org/; individual country reports can be downloaded at www.child-soldiers.org/regions/).

A plethora of children's own voices in interviews gathered by this and other organizations (see Further Reading at the end of this chapter for a brief guide to resources) show a variety of experiences of child soldiering, and a variety of processes by which children come to be soldiers. Some of these are nothing less than horrific. Forcible abduction of children as young as 9 years old occurs in some countries (www.child-soldiers.org/childsoldiers/some-facts.html). 'Voluntary' enlistment has to be placed in inverted commas because of the large number of cases where children see no viable alternative, either economically or because of fear of reprisals if they do not join; or because of the need to leave abusive or life-threatening situations in their own families. CSUCS reports that many girls enlist to escape domestic servitude, violence and sexual abuse (www.child-soldiers.org/childsoldiers/some-facts.html). This is cruelly ironic because of the evidence from some girl soldiers of their experiences. For example:

> There was no-one in charge of the dormitories and on a nightly basis we were raped. The men and youths would come into our dormitory in the dark, and they would just rape us – you would just have a man on top of you, and you could not even see who it was. If we cried afterwards, we were beaten with hosepipes . . . The youngest girl in our group was aged 11 and she was raped repeatedly in the base.
>
> (19-year old Zimbabwean describing her experience in the National Youth Service Training Programe; data from http://www.child-soldiers.org/childsoldiers/voices-of-young-soldiers.html)

Other reports cite girls from the age of 10 years used as sexual slaves for military leaders, in addition to performing 'duties' of domestic serfdom and participating in armed conflict themselves; the widespread rape and torture of boy soldiers to enforce their subjection; children being forced to watch brutal killings, including of their own family members and other children, to 'prepare' them for war; adults forcing children to participate in war crimes such as executions; and children being used as informants, spies and messengers (see e.g. Machel 2001; http://www.essex.ac.uk/human_rights_centre/research/projects/cacu.shtm; see also Further reading).

Despite all of this, more research is needed to understand the role of children themselves in these processes, and to grasp their diversity. Some children and young people will have strongly formulated beliefs and reasons for wishing to participate in armed conflict, whether or not adults (especially western adults) approve. Others make the kind of active, if constrained, choices made by street children, in search of autonomy or freedom from hardship and abuse at home or from local political oppressions. Responses need to be as diverse as the dynamics that impel children into participating in armed conflict and this is no more apparent than when they cease to be needed as combatants. Beyond the vicissitudes of involvement in conflict comes demobilization and disarmament, leaving in its wake children and young people with often intolerable psychological and physical legacies of warfare, as well as economic, cultural and geographical dislocation. The assymetry of power between adults and children makes it inevitable that what we blithely term 'post-traumatic stress syndrome' is a living hell for ex-child combatants. At the same time, resources to support some kind of autonomy and reconstruction for the very different needs exhibited by these young people are lacking. Although demobilization, disarmament, and reintegration (DDR) programmes aimed at child soldiers exist in many countries, CSUCS reports that these lack long-term investment and rarely include girls (www.child-soldiers.org/childsoldiers/some-facts.html).

Current responses to the question of children as combatants include the *Optional Protocol to the Convention on the Rights of Child on the Involvement of Children in Armed Conflict*, which entered into force in February 2002 (http://www.unhchr.ch/html) and outlaws the involvement of those aged under 18 in hostilities, whilst CSUCS called in November 2004 for the prosecution of recruiters of child soldiers by the international criminal court (http://news.bbc.co.uk/2/hi/africa/4019087.stm). A wide range of campaigning groups, human rights organizations, and legal and academic organizations are currently working in alliance to broaden the research and educational base on child soldiers, as well as exerting policy and legal pressure (www.essex.ac.uk/human_rights_centre/research/projects/cacu.shtm). One encouraging facet of this movement is a definite emphasis on research gathering children's own accounts, and on taking the debate into youth forums and schools. However, problematic aspects remain: an assumption that children and young people under the age of 18 who participate in armed conflict lack agency, and a lack of combatants' voices in the formulation of campaigning demands and legislation. Too often, children's 'voices' are used only to reflect the horror of their experiences in support of campaigners' aims, and can easily slide into hand-wringing voyeurism rather than a realistic appraisal of choices made and choices available. A useful research guide is provided by CSUCS (see Further Reading), which includes advice on interviewing children in a 'non-judgemental' way, but the assumption remains that child soldiering is always and of necessity worse than adult participation in conflicts, and is of necessity less informed. The most fundamental assumption, after all, is that there could not be a worse abrogation of the condition of a universal childhood than the deliberate involvement of children in killing other human beings – a quandary that would have been recognized by very few people as recently as 200 years ago.

However, child soldiers and child civilian victims of war are not icons in all of this reality, and while the mass media makes them toys of the simulacra of politics that is war, they are heading for an early grave. As the journalist Mary Riddell put it (*Observer* 20 April 2003), 'just as Ali is the comfortably bogus proof of how much we care for Iraqi children, the devastation of the past becomes a minor matter of chipped or mislaid pottery. When illusion is more seductive than facts war can make barbarians of us all.' Does this make armed conflict a subject for the criminology of childhood and youth? Currently the discourses surrounding children and war are humanitarian/rights based, and to that extent come under the purview of international legal studies, but rarely enter criminological discussion. Although 'terrorism' has long received attention as an 'anti-state' crime (Levi 2002), war has not. The problem here is that in bracketing war *off*, criminology reinforces the discipline's continuing obsession with children and young people as problem populations, and ignores its role of critique in relation to the actions of states, in much the same way it ignored for a long time the areas of other state crime and of environmental crimes.

It is probably true that the attack destroying the World Trade Center on 11 September 2001 has changed the scenario somewhat. The rapid construction of the 'war against terror' in the wake of the atrocity placed the USA implacably at the centre of a normative structure which outlawed a great deal of the non-western peoples of the world. This global exercise in vilification and criminalization, appearing as it has to justify every and any breach of international human rights treaties and international law, as in the war against Iraq, could not but provoke interest among at least some criminologists. The task now is to extend analyses of states, wars, and crime to embrace children and young people.

Children's rights and the wrongs of adults: a voice for young people?

The principal response to the harm inflicted on children through conflict and through human trafficking, to the vigilante violence and stigmatized, delinquent status of 'street children', and to the negative consequences for children of many other aspects of adult actions has been operated through a human rights discourse. In this section we shall consider the possibilities and limitations of 'children's rights' as a means of 'listening to youth'. On the face of it, the language of a universal recognition of the 'rights' of children and young people provides a means through which a voice for children to demand minimum levels of care, respect and autonomy can be mobilized. Indeed, the postulation of 'the rights of *the child*' asserts firstly the possibility of universal rights and secondly the ideal of a universal child.

There is a fundamental problem with the notion of 'human rights' in general, as many commentators have noted. Gaete (1999: 195) for example states that 'inherent in the concept of human rights is the old Judeo-Christian idea of a transcendent God "beyond the world" and of a law beyond the law of the State'. In practice, discourses of human rights have typically been used rhetorically to justify the practices of western states:

> Human rights became, during the cold war, a State ideology that was used selectively against what the West saw as its external enemies. The West presented itself as a post-imperialist, ethical force, encapsulated, in the 'Free World' formula, as a homogenous and coherent ethical entity . . . that is the rhetoric. But the . . . practice of human rights [in the US] revolves mainly around the Supreme Court, which is the

> political agency with the authority to determine the meaning of
> human rights concepts and principles . . . it is the Supreme Court that
> decides what cruelty is and what is cruel. Is the death penalty cruel?
>
> (Gaete 1999: 196)

Similarly, Gaete argues, the European Court of Human Rights is strongly influenced by particular cultural conceptions, whilst for example some feminists critique 'human rights' as a masculinist discourse, since it prioritizes a metaphysical subject of humanity 'anterior and separate from less "relevant" aspects such as gender, ethos, culture or wealth' (1999: 196). It is doubtful whether this tension between the notion of metaphysical 'rights' and the problem of ethnocentrism – or culture bound hierarchization – can ever be resolved. Even the notion of rights itself, from some feminist perspectives, is masculinist since it presumes the moral supremacy of individualism rather than the feminist ethic of mutual care and collectivism. Should 'I' have rights over and above the needs of the collectivity? In other words, there is a good deal of doubt as to whether 'rights' can ever be universal, or are always relative to features of history and culture and the distribution of power in practice.

We further have to remember that children's 'rights' are based on a relatively novel idea of childhood rooted in western modernity, and as such can themselves be seen as one feature of globalization (Ennew and Morrow 2002). Stephens (1995) points out the importance of 1979 as the 'Year of the Child', when the concept of the 'world's children' emerged in the discourses of UNICEF and the World Health Organization. This was also the real beginning of the global mass mediation of children's lives under famine, war and poverty that has continued to be used to delineate non-western childhoods as impoverished and inadequate in relation to the West. Reaching all the way back to colonialism, this impetus ensures that 'we' in the West continue to think of progress as being one of movement toward the universalization of the western ideal of childhood, and it is that ideal that has largely been encapsulated in 'children's rights'. This runs the risk of designating non-western childhoods as 'deviant childhoods' (Stephens 1995: 19) involving 'differences' which 'are frequently glossed as "loss" and contamination'.

The biggest landmark in the assertion of children's rights is of course the *United Nations Convention on the Rights of the Child*. Adopted by the UN General Assembly resolution 44/25 on 20 November 1989, it entered into force on 2 September 1990. The *Convention* consists of some 54 articles and as of June 2004 had been signed by all 191 UN member states. Two additional protocols, the optional protocol on the involvement of children in armed conflict, and the optional protocol on the sale of children, child prostitution and child pornography, had been ratified by most but not all members (http://www.unhchr.ch/html). It might be anticipated that any appeal to 'fundamental' human rights would come under criticism given the foregoing discussion of the problems inherent in appeals to the metaphysical subject. One needs only to read the preamble of the *Convention* carefully to see how this would arise:

> Recalling that, in the Universal Declaration of Human Rights, the United Nations has proclaimed that childhood is entitled to special care and assistance . . . Convinced that the family, as the fundamental group of society and the natural environment for growth and well being of its members and particularly children, should be afforded the necessary protection and assistance so that it can fully assume its responsibilities within the community . . . Recognizing that the child, for the full and harmonious development of his or her personality, should grow up in a family environment, in an atmosphere of happiness, love and understanding . . . Considering that the child should be fully prepared to live an individual life in society, and brought up in the spirit of the ideals proclaimed in the Charter of the United Nations, and in particular in the spirit of peace, dignity, tolerance freedom, equality and solidarity . . . *Taking due account of the traditions and cultural values of each people for the protection and harmonious development of the child . . .*
>
> (http//www.unhcr.ch/html/ emphasis added)

The text of the *Convention* is on the one hand loaded with cultural assumptions regarding an idealized state of childhood and the 'family', and yet on the other it emphasizes the need to take into account cultural diversity, with one hand giving recognition to divergent viewpoints and interests regarding what childhood is and what 'rights' such a state carries, and with the other hand taking these away by appealing to universalism. The great difficulty with this western universalization is in the kind of idealism that it imports to the notion of rights for children. The notion that there is some kind of ideal family, for example, where children are best located to be protected and nurtured, is simply belied by the extent of physical and sexual abuse of children within families; by the facts of serious victimization of children – *including* in the West; by the fragmentation of families driven by western capitalist exploitation of developing countries' economies, and the ensuing poverty and violence; by the endemic *instability* engendered by the pressures under which families come in liberal individualist 'developed' societies, and the consequent high divorce rates, mental health problems, splitting of families and associated behavioural consequences for children. Indeed, one is hard put to locate instances of the ideal family, whether in 'developed' or developing societies and it is difficult to see how 'protection' for children stems naturally from this institution where perhaps children have *fewer* rights in practice than anywhere else. Some feminist theorists have gone further by suggesting that in fact the principal exploitation of, and source of oppression and damage to, children – especially girls – arises inevitably from the nature of the family as the principal institution of patriarchy (Johns 1995) and/or patriarchal capitalism (Barrett and McIntosh 1991).

The *Convention* also assumes a universal definition of individualism. The 'individual', or the properties of the self, by contrast have been strongly argued by many theorists across a variety of disciplines to be both fluid and culturally relative (Johns 1995: 107). The idea that there could be one ideal process of socialization 'into' the individual ignores work in social theory, social psychology and cultural anthropology that suggests otherwise. Giddens' work on self and society in late modernity for example (1991) delineates an intricate relationship between the 'trajectory of the self' and macro features of social structures and cultures. Under late modernity there is a prevalent uncertainty and ethos of choice that can in turn lead to a reaching back to an imagined past of 'tradition' but which belies the notion of a 'single answer' to questions such as child-rearing practices. Then there is the question of agency and negotiation in the construction of self, long pointed out by micro sociologists such as Erving Goffman. The very notion of an 'individual' suggests at once coherence and difference, the former denoting a coherent sense of the world and one's place in it and the latter that every agent could see themselves in multiple ways in relation to society and the ability to act in it, could tell many 'stories' about who they are (Giddens 1991: 54–5). Within this, the notion of the child as an individual sits uncomfortably in the *Convention*.

Related to this is the question of to what extent, if children are individuals with rights, they are also accorded *agency*, as we have noted in relation to street children. Article 12 states that: 'States Parties shall assure to the child who is capable of forming his or her own views the right to express those views freely in all matters affecting the child'; and Article 13 states that 'the child shall have the right to freedom of expression . . . regardless of frontiers, either orally, in writing or in print . . . or through any other media of the child's choice'. But in effect, these 'rights' are contradicted by Article 14, which states that 'States Parties shall respect the rights and duties of parents and, when applicable, legal guardians, to provide direction to the child in the exercise of his or her right in a manner consistent with the evolving capacities of the child'.

Of course, since different cultural contexts will produce adults with different notions of the 'evolving capacities' of the child (and this will typically be gendered), there can be no 'universal' right signified here. Similarly the 'freedoms' granted by such articles are always limited by loose definitions of legalities that may supersede the legalities of right. For example, 'freedom to manifest one's religion or beliefs may be subject only to such limitations as are prescribed by law and are necessary to protect public safety, order, health, or morals, or the fundamental rights and freedoms of others'. This kind of 'rights talk' could of course go on for ever, pitting one right against another, one set of obligations cancelling out another set of rights, and so on.

This is a crucial problem particularly in so far as children are concerned, precisely because by definition they are seen as imperfectly formed, something less than adults, in capability and judgement, and therefore their fundamental 'right' to *agency* is already compromised by their ascribed status of relative powerlessness in relation to adults. This has direct implications for effective implementation of any rights accorded under the *Convention*. In relation to implementation, Article 4 states that 'States Parties shall undertake all appropriate legislative, administrative and other measures for the implementation of the rights recognized in the present Convention', whilst 'General Comment No. 5' from the 34th session of the Committee on the Rights of the Child (United Nations 2003) states under point (1) that 'when a State ratifies the *Convention on the Rights of the Child* (CRC), it takes on obligations under international law to implement it', and 'its task of implementation – of making reality of the human rights of children – needs to engage all sections of society and, of course, children themselves'.

This is simply unrealistic in relation to many states parties – including, as we have seen, the UK. The cultural resistance to children's autonomy is enormous in many societies and downright hostility toward young people amounts at times to paranoia. There is, cumulatively, a far larger body of legislation allowing for the containment and punishment of children and young people than there is provision for the participatory ethos of the *Convention*. Moreover, as Johns (1995: 105) notes, 'children did not participate in the deliberations or the drafting of the Convention. This indicates how the international community still implicitly regards children.' Franklin (1992) however, suggests that the *Convention* remains important if we do not view it from a narrowly legalistic perspective. It represents a *symbolic* authority that is empowering, and is a significant moral document regarding the treatment of children and young people. Despite the obvious shortcomings of the *Convention*, it has become the focus of international pressure from many directions for the empowerment of children and young people in many different contexts, giving a baseline that can be used as leverage by a wide range of campaigning groups, non-governmental organizations, and intergovernmental agencies in working with and for children and young people.

There has been increasing movement toward child and youth participation in campaigning groups globally, not least because transformation in ICTs has enabled better, faster, and more globally dispersed communications and sharing of experiences, ideas and resources to take place – proving again that cyberspace is not simply a site of danger but is also a site of resistance.

But can international 'rights' and legislative instruments protect children and young people from the criminogenic and often just plain *lethal* processes of globalization? There is a wide array of instruments relating to international law that can be applied in these contexts, and it would not be possible to summarize them here. Two specific optional protocols of the *Convention* have already been mentioned – on child prostitution and child pornography and on the involvement of children in armed conflict. In addition there a number of UN and other instruments that set out to protect child victims and witnesses of crime (Saris 2002) and children impacted upon by armed conflict (Harvey 2003). Much general international provision (i.e. not specifically aimed at children or young people) is also relevant. The International Bureau for Children's Rights has compiled guidelines on justice for child victims and witnesses of crime (IBCR 2003) as part of its ongoing programme on justice for child victims and witnesses of crime, to 'bring together ... the major international and regional norms, standards and principles' within this field. Their comprehensive guide to international and human rights law relating to children and armed conflict demonstrates the breadth of the impact that global militarism has upon children and young people. It is however the very mass and breadth of such documents that is testament to the fundamental problem. The document on children and armed conflict for example covers topics from child soldiers, refugees, trafficking, landmines and cluster bombs, to the role of children in peace processes. Saris' compilation of selected provisions on the rights of child victims and witnesses of crime provides 264 pages and a comprehensive bibliography over 11 broad areas from the right to be treated with 'dignity and compassion' to witness protection, reparation, professional cooperation and so on (Saris 2002). There is a massive task at hand, one that needs to recognize children and young people more fully as social actors and to incorporate this within the rubrics of 'rights' and within legislatures. It is almost certainly true to say that children and young people are beginning to figure more centrally in global politics and in debates over global issues, and that if viewed from an international perspective the disempowerment of youth has at least become a problematic. When the (g)local perspective is adopted however, the problems of child/youth victimization, of crimes committed against children and young people, of the impacts of the illegal activities of states on children and young people, and of the abrogation of the rights of children and young people who find themselves in contravention of the law, remain enormous. Nation states continue to exist and continue to assert their localized practices of harm and exploitation whilst the increased permeability of borders facilitates crimes against children and young people as much as it opens up questions of 'rights' *for* them. At the same time, the far reaching impact of flagrant disregard for international law leads to escalating global/(g)local armed conflicts that daily puts millions of children and young people in danger of their lives and livelihoods.

The International Criminal Court, based on a treaty ratified by 66 countries in 2002, is principally aimed at the prosecution of crimes against humanity, war crimes and genocide, but is also intended to help defend the rights of women and children. It is intended to combat the unwillingness of nation states to bring their own prosecutions, and thereby to be an instrument in support of human rights (Morrison 2004). As yet, it is too soon to comment upon the functioning of the court, and indeed, the court itself should be a focus of criminological study, part of a necessary shift in the emphasis of criminology generally and youth criminology in particular, toward a greater concern with global childhood and youth.

The demise of youth criminology?

The Anglo-American ethnocentrism of youth criminology has, it seems, reached the limits of its usefulness. This is so on a number of counts. It has relied on a definition of 'youth' either explicitly or implicitly that has restricted most of its research to teenage boys. It has relied on a definition of youth crime, implicitly or explicitly, that has concerned itself with the delinquescent activities of these disaffected young men and placed such activities at the heart of criminological analysis. Meanwhile, the world has left it behind. Whilst (mainly male, western) criminologists are studying (mainly male, western) behaviours in public places – and thereby effectively following the agenda set by domestic preoccupations (e.g. in the UK, of the British media, the British government and the British tradition of respectable fears) – the transformative processes of globalization have set in train irreversible trends, both positive and negative, in definitions of crime and victimization, in the central agendas facing those who are concerned with youth, and in the landscapes of law, crime and society.

Criminology has begun to tackle the theoretical challenges thrown up by globalization in its broadest sense – issues of 'risk', 'governance', 'agency' and 'identity' for example (Loader and Sparks 2002) but these still tentative explorations represent little more than a glimmer of recognition that the boundaries of criminology should and must become far more fluid than hitherto. What has typically been regarded as the main corpus of youth criminology in particular can in future be no more than a tiny subdivision. A global (or (g)local) youth criminology will have a far broader scope. Morrison, indeed, sees a recognition of this as no more than acknowledging the colonial legacy that criminology in any case bears, as we have tried to point out in the case of the construction of childhood and youth as 'other'. Writing on globalization, human rights and international criminal courts in a 'student handbook' of criminal justice and criminology, Morrison (2004: 153) says:

> This is an unusual chapter for a criminology text because criminology historically has been separate from international relations and has only studied actions and processes internal to the nation-state. It is no longer possible to defend this separation in a world of global communication networks and where all activities are interconnected . . . Criminology normally recognised its basic subject matter – crime – as that which was prohibited and punished by the state, but many atrocities and almost all genocidal actions have been conducted by state-sponsored persons and have almost never been punished. While much

current discourse holds up ... human rights as a reference point to judge state action by, the reality is much more ambiguous.

Traditional criminology operated separately from the question of international relations and human rights discourses: it can no longer do so. Moreover, human rights discourses, for the reasons discussed in this chapter, cannot of themselves provide an effective analysis of 'crimes' in relation to children and young people; they are rather the *subject* of a global/(g)local youth criminology. International law must likewise be the focus of criminological and socio-legal critique, as must the setting up of the International Criminal Court (Morrison 2004). The criminological 'fraternity' (*sic*) moreover, traditionally largely ruled by an elite, male- and white western-dominated academia and the state-sponsored organizations of administrative criminology, must expand to include the increasingly complex and high quality research and analysis carried out by or on behalf of non-governmental organization and intergovernmental organizations, and crucially, to include research by and with children and young people. Whether more 'traditional' criminologists want to accept it or not, all this *effectively redefines criminological issues in global terms*. What is being presented here is a more challenging agenda to that traditionally tackled by western youth criminology, especially when we return to our central question and ask what it now means: that of 'listening to youth'.

Further reading

The 'many childhoods' debate is presented succinctly in an editorial by Jenks (2004) and at more length in James *et al.* (1998). The journal *Childhood* is an excellent source of articles and in this context see especially Volume 11(1). Globalization is discussed in its most accessible form in Anthony Giddens' 1999 BBC Reith Lectures, available on the internet at the BBC online network. The UNICEF (http://www.unicef.org/) and Save the Children (http://www.savethechildren.net) websites link to numerous resources on street children and trafficking in children. ECPAT links to resources on trafficking.

UNICEF again is a central link to sources on children and armed conflicts. The main campaigning organization specifically aimed at the issue of child soldiers is CSUCS which is made up of several major non-governemental and intergovernmental organizations. The steering committee includes among others Amnesty International, Human Rights Watch and the International Save the Children Alliance. The CSUCS website contains links to research and many related organizations and is an excellent starting point. The CSUCS 2004 report on child soldiers can also be downloaded, as can a guide to research methodology for working in the area of children and armed conflict (http://www.child-soldiers.org/). The

University of Essex in the UK has a Children and Armed Conflict Unit within its Human Rights Centre, a joint project with the Children's Legal Centre, and works with governments, UN bodies and other organizations to carry out research and information activities and to reform legislation. Again, useful information on research and organizations can be found on its website at http://www/essex.ac.uk/armedcon. This website also links to a very useful list of media and shorter analytical and campaigning pieces. Machel's (2001) book on *The Impact of War on Children* is accessibly written and useful factually.

Stephens (1995) provides a context for a discussion of globalization and children's rights. The *United Nations Convention on the Rights of the Child* may be consulted at http://www.unchr.ch/html/, while Johns (1995) provides a critique of the Convention. Information on the International Criminal Court can be found at http://www.icc-cpi.int.

As criminology has not generally regarded the topics discussed in this chapter as part of its subject matter, little reading matter will be found in criminology textbooks generally. As discussed in the chapter, it will be necessary to regard the boundaries of 'understanding crime' in a more fluid way, and the internet – as with cybercrime issues – can be an excellent resource. Morrison (2004) is an exception to the above comments, and is an interesting analytical piece on the challenges posed to criminology by global issues and international human rights. This piece also provides a brief useful bibliography, although it is not related specifically to children and young people.

chapter nine

Conclusion: listening to youth?

**Revisiting the domains of youth and crime: discarding the
   comfort blanket**
Disparate histories, enduring themes: the powers of articulation

In this chapter we summarize the arguments presented in the preceding
eight chapters, not simply as an aid to memory for the dazed and confused,
but with a wider purpose in view. We have attempted, through a presentation of some of the central ways in which 'youth and crime' has been
constructed in the popular, policy and academic worlds to indicate the
problems which arise once the shackles of 'what we all know' are discarded.
At the same time, this can be a discomfiting experience. How do these
different insights into different worlds fit together to provide us with an
'answer' about youth and crime? What is it we are supposed to 'know' or
'believe' at the end of it all? The field of 'youth and crime' has been presented as one which shifts according to the perspective taken upon it; that
perspective, in turn, shifts with history, culture, economic and political
circumstances, institutional interests and priorities. Some of these twists
and turns in perspective appear to operate at the broadest level of collective
consciousness, others at the micro level of individual interest, and at many
levels in between. The chapters appear as a series of 'domains': territories
of knowledge which belong to no single individual or social grouping, but
which nevertheless, at different times and in different ways, seem to produce distinctive tendencies. The task of this chapter is to briefly revisit each
domain, and then to consider whether we can identify, if not unifying
threads, at least some enduring themes. Last but not least, we address some
of the deliberate absences in our own textual treatment of youth and crime,
and consider some potential future directions for 'understanding'.

Revisiting the domains of youth and crime: discarding the comfort blanket

It is, then, comforting to think that the 'youth crime problem' is an obvious one. Surely most crimes are committed by young people, therefore the answer is to explain why, and to do something about it. The astute reader will have noticed that we do not, in fact, address either of these apparently central issues in the text. Instead, we have chosen to focus upon the way in which the 'youth crime problem' became seen in this light, and to highlight other possible ways of seeing which seem to have got lost in the obsession with the youthful offender and his (*sic*) punishment. The relatively disparate domains which we confront in the separate chapters can, in fact, be re-presented as a fairly coherent narrative of the historical articulation of one version of a 'problem' and the corresponding lack of articulation of other possible 'problems'. This section revisits our earlier chapters in this light.

Age as a social category and childhood and youth as 'other'

This may be considered the prehistory of youth and crime. Without particular conceptions of childhood and youth, we would have no question to address. While the cultural and historical variability of the definitions of crime have become a staple issue within criminology and sociology, less attention has been paid to the definitions of childhood and youth. This prehistory is important, not for the sake of mere pedantry, but because historically specific conditions produced our taken-for-granted assumptions that childhood and youth are 'given' states of human development. It forms the basis for a framing of the youth crime question throughout the twentieth century, which has largely taken for granted the dependency of childhood and the troublesomeness of youth. It also forms the basis for assumptions about the respectability of middle age and the vulnerability of old age. Quite tangible results occurred as a result of this prehistory: most notably an ever ready eagerness to project the troubles of any given era onto the state of youth as some kind of barometer of the general health of society, and a concomitant reluctance to admit the destructive or criminogenic tendencies of the middle aged and elderly. Childhood and youth – productions of adult desires and longings – were made to represent the dichotomy of the hopes and fears of a nation: a quite impossible role for the marginalized to fulfil. Beyond the margins lies another fundamental concern of the text. It is of crucial importance that the notion of a universal 'childhood' and 'youth' is a *western* notion with its roots firmly in colonialism, and latterly, imperial colonialism. Just as the idealized notion of childhood has come to represent the norm, so non-western childhoods have been constructed as unfortunate and inferior, and non-western youth as doubly deviant, doubly troublesome, doubly dangerous.

Enter criminology: science and objectivity?

It is then hardly surprising that criminology – as an eclectic disciplinary field with one foot in academia and one in the regulatory concerns of the state – should have, from its inception, focused overwhelmingly on youth and crime. Throughout the formative decades of the 1920s to the 1970s Anglo-American criminology in its various guises reflected and reinforced 'official' (and popular) concerns with youth-as-problem. 'Youth and the health of the nation' remained very much related to criminological and sociological concerns well into the period of post-Second World War reconstruction. This stemmed partly from the institutional contexts within which these disciplines developed in a transatlantic interchange, and partly from the internal dynamics of their academic concerns. Despite the limited challenges of radical and critical criminologies in the 1960s and 1970s, the centrality of the 'youth problem' to criminological knowledge was never to be transcended. In academic discourse as elsewhere, 'crime' continued to imply youth, and 'youth' to imply crime. Young people were to remain the problematized and the criminalized and – with the exception of radical cultural studies – youth criminology (in effect) the handmaiden of official and popular concern. The voices of young people themselves were rarely heard, and then only through the more or less elaborate reconstructions of their lives presented by (adult male) academics. 'Scientific' and 'objective' social inquiries for the large part accepted the foundations laid down in prehistory unproblematically.

I read the news today: youth crime and the popular media

Our third domain is that of 'popular' representation. Increasingly, academic criminology operates in relation to media and popular cultural constructions of youth and crime. The proliferation of popular media in the electronic, globalized era comes to form a most important context for understandings of youth and crime. Through the complex processes of the production and consumption of cultural images, a hegemonic constellation of everyday knowledges has emerged. From specific 'moral panics' surrounding young people not dissimilar to those seen in our prehistory domain, through the 1970s to the 1990s, ever more reciprocal relationships between the media, the political and the populace fostered an explosion of panic concerning the young. Qualitatively and quantitatively more pervasive, the new wave of media representation first generalized, and then totalized, the assumed relationship between young people, crime and the state of society. Tied into escalating anxieties over the collapse of the welfare state and late modern capitalism, the youth 'crisis' reached fever pitch. Adult worries over everything from unemployment to consumer boom, urban degeneration to video nasties, were to find expression in a lament for the lost generation. Again there was nothing intrinsically new that was not there in embryo in the prehistory, but by the 1990s it had dispersed into every corner of everyday life; the distinction between 'factual' and 'fictive' categories had collapsed as surely as the distinction between direct and mediated experience. It had become ever more difficult to frame 'youth' outside 'crime'. More recently this process of media demonization has expanded to cover almost everything young people do, reflecting and reinforcing policy-makers' drive, at the behest of politicians 'governing through crime', to criminalize the everyday lives of young people. In a seemingly unbreakable feedback loop, public (adult) fears demand more and more containment and control of young people, politicians driven by popular authoritarianism and penal populism respond, the press make capital out of this situation, and in turn feed and help construct the popular demand, responded to by politicians . . . and so on. It is no longer possible to separate cause and effect: the media *are* everyday life, and the consequences are typically negative in so far as justice for young people is concerned.

The comforting pragmatics of policy?

The policy domain should surely provide refuge for those who do not wish to engage with the discomfiting relativities of cultural analysis. For surely policy is about pragmatics, finding the most effective solutions to practical social problems? Yet in the tortuous twists and turns of criminal justice policy, children and young people have been subject to 'care' and 'control', 'treatment' and 'punishment'. Lying behind all of the policy provisions of the twentieth century were the strategies of politicians, criminal justice agents and agencies to harness young people in the regulation of society through moral (and thereby cultural) languages. Whether stemming from good intentions (such as philanthropic concern), naked self-interest (winning adult votes), the pragmatics of governance (controlling public spending) or the desire for the maintenance and strengthening of hierarchies of existing power (authoritarianism), 'youth' has been dragged along by adult institutions in their quest to secure a complex web of political interests. The young have been constructed through policy not as citizens, but as objects of increasingly repressive modes of governance. As adult anxiety and punitive desire escalate, the (metaphorical) body of the delinquent is carved up to serve to political and popular appetites, and effectiveness and rationality are increasingly subsumed under ideological imperative.

Out of sight: young people as victims

If young people have been selectively constructed as 'problem' and 'other', if their concerns have been marginalized, their lifestyles problematized and their voices subdued, what has been lost in our understanding of youth and crime? One largely neglected set of issues relates to the unpopular notion of children and young people as victims of crime. Because the idea of the 'victim' connotes blamelessness, it is very difficult to conceptualize young people in this way. Except in conjunction with the ideology of childhood 'innocence' – itself increasingly shaken by the demonization of ever younger age groups – the predominant categorizations of youth do not sit easily within a 'victim' discourse. 'True victims' – except for child victims of random killers or sex attackers – are culturally reserved spaces for the infantilized elderly. Where children and young people are constructed as 'true' or 'acceptable' victims they tend to be constructed in such a way as to divert attention away from the real extent of the problem of victimization of young people, and such constructions operate rather to satisfy adult idealizations of childhood and youth. The idea of young people as victims of social or legal injustice, as victims of widespread incidences of assault within institutional contexts (whether the family, the school, or residential state institutions), or as victims of everyday crimes in public space – these are areas of relative silence. Only recently has criminology itself begun to challenge these omissions in any concerted fashion, and in popular and policy discourse such issues are often treated with cynicism, disdain or vehement denial. Indeed, it is possible to argue that this is a symptom of society in denial, a society so attached to a psychic need to project fears and failures onto the young that it is afraid to acknowledge the scale of adult crimes against them.

Gender and beyond: challenging youth and crime

The idea of youth victimization raises important questions about subjugated or denied knowledges. However refracted through other formations such as class and race, it is the dyad of (male) youth and (criminal) youth which above all characterizes any vision of what it means to understand youth and crime. Thus although subconscious ideas of race and class also impinge, youth is fearfully personified within the popular psyche as *male* and *criminal*. Criminology has only recently begun to deconstruct this conflation, helped by the gender-based analysis of the last two decades. Perhaps then it is not so much 'youthfulness' as 'masculinities' which are at issue; perhaps not so much 'offending' as 'victimization'? This is not to suggest simply replacing one exclusionary set of obsessions with another. It is to suggest that the framing of the 'youth crime problem' as 'the crime problem' – however comprehensible as a historical and cultural phenomenon – has created a kind of subsidence in the foundations of understanding crime which will not be easily amenable to quick repair.

Virtual worlds: autonomy and threat

Virtuality, or cyberspace, throws out another set of challenges for understanding youth and crime. Adult fears that young people may be 'at risk' from the internet not only echo decades of such preoccupations since the advent of television, but also conceal a deeper anxiety that adults hold about young people and cyberspace. For cyberspace and internet use by young people is hard to 'police', and more than the physical spaces and places of the street, it puts young people in control of their own geographies. This autonomy is threatening, and still mysterious even in the twenty-first century to many over-35s, who do not know what young people are 'up to' out there in cyberspace. Tunnelling out of bedroom culture, girls too can find virtual travel empowering in ways that adults find worrisome. Challenging boundaries of childhood, youth, gender and 'appropriate' behaviour, the 'deviant' possibilities of the cyber can prove good news for youth. The reverse side of this coin is the victimization of children and young people through internet pornography. The vast proliferation of pornography on the internet reveals just how endemic the abuse of children and young people is in society, both on- and offline. Internet pornography is seen to be closely intertwined with the widespread cultures, institutions and practices that support child sexual abuse, and its popularity dispels once and for all the myth that child pornography is the province of a few isolated individuals. Once again adults are focusing on the dangers of children and young people using space (and the problems they may cause when 'out' in space) and paying insufficient attention to the real problem: the use of the internet by adults to further their already widespread criminal and abusive activities against youth.

Beyond the western horizon: the global and the fragmentation of 'youth criminology'

Because 'youth criminology' has been a western phenomenon, based on universalized, western constructions of childhood and youth, and focused on the problematics of urban, western, (adult) society, it fragments when the question of 'understanding global youth and crime' is raised. Not only are all of traditional criminology's definitional assumptions challenged, but so are its normative assumptions. Traditional youth criminology has little to say to a global context. The answer is not a 'comparative' youth criminology, for this would be a futile task beyond the western horizon. From labour exploitation to street children to trafficking in humans, the application of western ideals of childhood and youth, or western aetiologies of behaviour, has little relevance to the lives of young people in non-western cultures and economies. Nor can it speak to a criminology of war, and the problem of young people as victims of states in armed conflict. Nor, traditionally, has youth criminology concerned itself with questions of human rights. Moreover, in a global context, 'childhood' assumes a much greater importance, whereas traditional criminology has concerned itself largely with teenagers.

Unless youth criminology opens its boundaries to accept the centrality of these issues, and accepts interdisciplinarity with, for example, international relations and areas such as peace studies, and makes more research and policy links with humanitarian organizations and non-governmental organizations, then it remains what it has always been: a small parochial enclave of male-dominated white adults studying for the most part western male teenagers (or male teenagers in the West) with one eye on the administrative policy concerns of the state and state nodes of governance and one eye on the comfort of the university office.

Disparate histories, enduring themes: the powers of articulation

If there is one overarching theme of this text, it is that the 'youth crime problem' as it has conventionally been approached is neither more nor less than a product. It is not a product of absent fathers or single mothers, nor a product of unemployment or lack of discipline, but a product of the production and consumption of knowledges.

To avert the outrage of realists, and to avoid as far as possible the sin of contributing to the aetiological crisis, it is important here to insert a timely caveat. Careful empirical analysis has (and will continue to) show distinct correlations between specific social circumstances, specific personality traits, specific situational dynamics and the commission of specific criminal acts. Since the commission of these acts is not only real, but real in its effects, we have no desire to take refuge in cultural relativism in the sense of attempting to wave away crime (whether committed by young people or not) as being merely linguistic or definitional. Nor are we assuming a comparable moral relativism in relation to the sanctioning and control of acts which are deleterious to social well-being. What this text has endeavoured to demonstrate is that the framing of the 'youth crime problem' in particular ways has produced specific ways of seeing and responding to youth and crime which are also real in their effects.

If we are to be 'realist' about the crimes *of* young people, why are we not equally realist about crimes and social injustices *against* young people? In the end, the answer lies within the powers of articulation. Since the young are a marginal category (or a constellation of marginal categories, if preferred, refracted through other social positionings and hierarchies of power), they are non-persons. Since they are non-persons, they are outside of claims to citizenship. Since they are not enfranchised, they stand outside of formal polity. Their 'powers' are inarticulated and thereby accorded qualities of danger without reference to the voices of young people themselves.

Policy-makers, academics, the popular media and politicians still speak as if there were an obvious 'community' – which young people as non-citizens stand outside – whose interests can be identified and operationalized and set against the 'enemy' (the marginal groups) in the form of practical strategies (e.g. of punishment or crime prevention). A study of the notion of 'community' or 'society', however, quickly reveals that the concept typically operates to obfuscate ideological and material divisions in social life and obscure the interests on which they are based (Bankowski and Mungham 1981). Power operates in relation to the life course to produce 'youth' as the problematic section of the population to which 'community' or 'society' must address itself in order to protect itself from crime and disorder. Yet 'safety' for some is secured at the cost of silencing others. Policy-makers and academics alike 'represent' not 'community' but their own aspirations and the organizational conventions of the institutions within which they daily work. Excluded from the voice of 'community' or 'society', children and young people occupy a discursive domain foregrounded by popular images of trouble-making, rioting, incivility and rebellion. Much academic endeavour has focused on the same preoccupations as popular discourse with youth as a 'threat' to social order. Psychological and biological languages have in parallel fashion represented young people within a developmental cycle of troublesomeness, turbulence and hormonal anarchy. The gendered character of these discourses has exacerbated these tendencies. Young people are largely excluded from the languages of human rights, legal rights and formal political enfranchisement; they are increasingly marginal to the waged labour force. Even their centrality to the consumer lifestyle market of popular culture has been defined negatively rather than creatively. The cultural and political investment in the production, silencing and scapegoating of the marginal usually ensures their continued marginality, while subordinated young people come to recognize and enjoy their own 'dangerousness', which itself becomes a creative force for the reproduction of marginality.

Two sets of spaces and places – the spaces and places of the cyber, and those of the global landscape – have transformed the question of articulation further. In the case of cyberspace, young people are able to negotiate their own geographies without reference to adults. Here they are even able to redefine and control whether they *are* 'young' in the sense in which the adult world likes to construct them. Marginality can become ever more creative. In the case of young people globally, diversity of experiences makes a nonsense of the unitary, totalizing categories of youth criminology, and many ways are seen in which youth negotiates its course through a world that bears no resemblance to the typecast scenarios of criminology texts. But young people worldwide are *agents*. Whether victimized, silenced or scapegoated, denied a voice or not, they generate resistances, practise survivalism and find ways of becoming people despite all our attempts to mould them into the unitary logic of a frequently spurious knowledge formation.

The reframing of 'understanding youth and crime' requires either a dissolution of 'youth' as a special object of knowledge and policy, or an inclusion of young people in the social enterprise through the legitimation of their voices and a recognition of their agency and potential for active participation. As yet there is very little recognition of this problem in any of the ways in which adults speak of youth and crime. The processes of critical excavation, however, may at least provide us with a starting point for debate. Of all the current enterprises engaged in by criminologists, youth criminology perhaps remains the field most trapped by its past and most confounded by uncritical presupposition. It is hard to leave behind the comfort blanket.

Glossary

Aetiology In criminology, the notion of the causality of crime. In a critique of 'Left idealist' criminology, proponents of Left realism have claimed that criminology has encountered an 'aetiological crisis' whereby the discipline has lost sight of a concern with crime causation (Young 1994).

Agency In the context of this volume, it is important to understand the concept of agency as applied to children and young people. Whether as 'victims' or 'villains' children and young people have tended to be treated as the *objects* of policy, rather than as active members of society who take part in producing and reproducing the cultures and meanings of that society. As a result, they are rarely seen as productive individuals capable of autonomous decision-making or as full 'persons'. Instead they are relegated to the marginal status of the 'other'. By acknowledging youthful agency we may be led to challenge many existing policies and practices surrounding children and young people, whether in relation to the criminal justice system, or in relation to broader issues of human rights and social participation. This is the basis of 'listening to youth'.

Archaeology As used in social science or cultural analysis, the excavation of layers of knowledge by a process of 'peeling' back layers of discourse and belief rather like the skins of an onion to reveal the historical and cultural organization of a society.

Biologism A form of reductionism which seeks to explain human characteristics and behaviours in terms of underlying biological factors such as genetic composition. It is often used to challenge critical analyses which emphasize the role of cultural values in shaping personality and behaviour.

Cultural construction The process by which discourses are produced and sustained within any particular culture by the dominance of certain beliefs and practices.

Cultural transmission theory The notion that norms and values are passed on through peer groups, familial groups, or territory-based groups, so that one's form of association with others is the locus of the reproduction of culture.

Cyberspace crime Sometimes less accurately called 'cybercrime'. This can comprehend crimes committed *in* cyberspace, such as stalking, paedophiliac predation, hate crimes and the like, and crimes committed *through* cyberspace, such as fraud, the circulation of illegal child pornography and so on. In practice of course the distinction is very blurred. For example, there is a clear link between the online and offline context, such as cases where webcams are used in domestic settings to transmit 'realtime' images of child sexual abuse onto the web for consumption by online paedophiles or other 'communities'. In this case the internet becomes the circulatory system for images of scenes of crime offline. And yet these endlessly circulating images then take on an autonomous character in cyberspace almost independently of the offline world. In this context the consumption of images must also be considered – that is, the crimes committed by those who access and download depictions of child sexual abuse.

Darwinian Named after Charles Darwin, a theory based on the concept of natural selection, whereby species evolve to best enable them to survive in changing environments, and the strongest and most adaptable species will survive and develop into higher forms as others die out.

Deconstruction A method or process by which the taken-for-granted nature of representation is questioned, particularly by examining the interests which particular types of representation serve, or their role in upholding certain cultural practices and beliefs. Deconstruction reveals the ideologies which inhere within representations.

Delinquency Coleman and Moynihan (1996) define delinquency as 'law violations (usually of juveniles)', but the term is sometimes used more loosely to refer to any kind of youthful misconduct. In the USA, 'status offences' are 'those acts which are offences only if committed by a person within a certain age category' (p. 146). More broadly, one might add that delinquency implies the notion of a 'fallen' or 'subterranean' character.

Deviancy amplification A description of a process whereby societal reaction to deviance indirectly exacerbates the level of deviance, in particular the ways in which the reactions of official agencies of control (the police, the courts, politicians) and the popular media produce a heightened sensitivity toward certain forms of deviance, render people committing those deviant acts more likely to apprehension, and make people more likely to see themselves as deviant and further reinforce their deviant identity.

Discourse A much debated term within social sciences and humanities. It typically involves a notion of a series of related beliefs and values articulated through language. It is often used on the basis that discourse is by its nature public.

Domain A term used in this volume to denote a bounded space of culture and practice: for example, the family domain, the policy domain, the media domain.

Ecology A method of inquiry which stresses the need to map a system (whether biological or social), specifying the precise operation of its component parts and the relationships between them. Using an organic metaphor, it is assumed that ecological systems are essentially self-regulating, different forms of adaptation occurring as component parts interact with each other. It is a social science application particularly in the work of Chicago School sociology, where the ecology of the city is the object of inquiry.

Empirical science A form of scientific practice which stresses the importance of experimentation and practical application of scientific principles. It is particularly central in the development of Victorian industrialism in Britain.

Ethnography A method of study which emphasizes qualitative observation and the immersion of the researcher in the 'field' – i.e. the society or subsection of society being studied. The ethnographer deliberately sets out to 'climb into the shoes of other people and walk around in them'. The assumption is that it is not possible to understand society fully without collapsing the distinction between researcher and researched. Both the researcher's own personal biography, and the biographies of the researched, must be taken into account.

Fragmentation Because traditional criminology has been dominated by white, male, western knowledge and assumptions, a question must be asked as to whether youth criminology is *fragmenting* as global and g(local) dimensions of the social world are increasingly having to be acknowledged. Neither 'youth' nor 'crime' can be seen as having a universal meaning, being defined and understood very differently in different cultures. Hence universalism is under threat, and with it the bedrock of the 'old' youth criminology. The question of fragmentation therefore forms a central point of debate for the future of youth criminology: can there any longer be an argument for *a* youth criminology at all? If not, what would replace it? A myriad of 'local' criminologies, or more interdisciplinary boundaries and dialogue between criminology and, say, human rights discourses, international relations, globalization studies, and so on? Is there still a role for some notion of the 'universal', as in say, universal children's rights to protection from exploitation and victimization? All of these aspects of the fragmentation debate lie at the hub of contemporary youth criminology.

(G)localism Refers to the complex relationship between the global and the local in the contemporary world. While globalization tends to imply the 'shrinking' of the world through electronic and other communications systems, and a homogenization of cultures as national boundaries and cultures are increasingly eroded, localism implies the specific cultural ways in which global products and global events are interpreted and used. The ubiquity of McDonald's for example, implies the global, while the use of Coca-Cola bottles in Mexican shamanist rituals implies the (g)local. In order to understand global youth and crime, it is essential to grasp the idea of the g(local) because, while youth and childhood, and crime, may seem to be universal, global categories, they are at the same time subject to many specific interpretations and resistances at local level.

Hegemonic ideology 'Hegemony' in this instance is a term used by Antonio Gramsci (1978). It entails the notion that systems of economic and political power differentiation are maintained because the belief systems which reinforce the interests of the powerful appear to the individual as powerful and taken-for-granted 'truths', even though they may operate to secure the continued disadvantage or oppression of that individual.

Interactionism A methodological and theoretical position based on the notion that meanings are only created as people act and react towards each other. A deviant act, for example, only becomes deviant when it is reacted to as such by others. An act itself has no inherent meaning; such meaning has to be actively constructed as actors negotiate with each other in specific social settings. Similarly a criminal statistic is a product of a series of interactions, rather than an objective measurement of reality.

Justice approach (in juvenile justice) Based on a critique of welfarism which, the proponents of the justice model argued, resulted in the collapse of due process and unjustifiable levels of intervention in the lives of children and their families. Re-emphasized (in the 1980s) the importance of legal process and rights, and proportionality in sentencing rather than unbridled discretion.

Left realism Sometimes referred to as 'radical realism', Left realism is based on a critique of constructionist criminology's emphasis on the role of the state, the law and the mass media in constructing notions of criminality which disadvantage the poor, young people and ethnic minorities. In emphasizing the notion of crime as a social and ideological construct, argue the realists, criminologists have failed in their duty to 'take crime seriously'. Crime is real in its effects, from the Left realist perspective; fear of crime is rational not irrational; and very often it is the poor and the young who are the perpetrators of those offences which disproportionately affect the poor, whose quality of life is already low. It must be seen in the context of its proponents' research activities, which developed local crime surveys in association with local authorities as a means of mapping patterns of victimization and policing practices. It also emphasizes the role of police accountability in democratic societies (Young 1997). It stems in part from the inspiration of feminist criminologists concerned with putting violence and sexual assault against women on the criminological agenda (Heidensohn 1996).

Masculinities Usually now used in the plural to denote the diversity of masculine subjectivity. A growth area in criminology, 'masculinities' theory emphasizes the achievement and management of self-identity and the social constraints upon the formation of identity. In particular, masculinities theory attempts to explain the relationship between the subjective inner self and the public outer self, and the importance of this for understanding different forms of criminality, such as 'joyriding' or white-collar crime (Newburn and Stanko 1994). 'Hegemonic masculinity' is seen as a particular form of 'doing' manhood which can be damaging to the individual and criminogenic in its consequences.

Medicalization Related to biologism in so far as it refers to the use of scientific knowledge to explain behaviour. The practical implication is, for example, that if delinquency may be seen as a disease, then it may be treated and 'cured', (e.g. through drug therapy). It also implies that if a person is 'sick', then any curative methods can be justified, and the person can therefore be denied the rights accorded to 'healthy' people.

Metaphorical The sense in which language is symbolically laden to express far more than a simple description of the 'real'. Language is always imagery and is redolent of culture: for example, we feel 'up' or 'down', things cannot be reduced to 'black and white'. Any word, however apparently descriptive, relies on a whole system of shared meanings and assumptions and is often emotionally laden: for example, the description of young offenders as 'animals' dragging society 'down'. Metaphorical analysis can therefore be used to help deconstruct social discourse.

Netdangers This term refers to both the dangers *of* the net – for example, the dangers posed by adults to young people using the internet – and to the discourses of danger surrounding the net. In some ways the latter are more worrying than the former. For example, the languages of control and fear through which adults attempt to regulate children and young people's use of the internet may *appear* as a simple concern with the safety and well-being of the young; but often a closer examination of such 'panic' talk reveals a deeper concern of adults with blocking the autonomy of the young. The spaces and places of the internet can provide liberating and empowering opportunities for young people outside of adult control, a less easily policed space than say, the local street corner. At the same time, the need to control adult behaviour on the internet is implied by netdangers, where very real threats may be posed to the young in a small number of cases – stalking and predation, for example. The biggest netdanger is of course the exponential growth of internet based child sexual abuse.

New criminology The early 1970s in the UK saw the emergence of 'new criminology' or 'critical criminology', which, although drawing upon new deviancy, went further by insisting upon the need to place the study of deviance within a Marxist economic and political framework. The law was to be treated as a tool of the ruling class, and definitions of crime questioned in so far as they served these interests and so perpetuated capitalist oppression. Deviant acts themselves could be seen as rational forms of rebellion against oppression, and criminology should have a socialist agenda which insisted on the importance of eradicating economic exploitation. It is most closely associated with Ian Taylor, Paul Walton and Jock Young (the last – in an interesting turn of events – was later to become the prime advocate of Left realism).

New deviancy theory A critique of orthodox sociology of delinquency originating in the USA in the 1950s and 1960s. Based theoretically around interactionism, 'new deviancy' focused on definitional issues (who defines whom as deviant? how? how is it possible that for some the deviant label sticks, and for others it does not? what kind of social interactions and settings frame the definition of some as deviant and others as not?). Similarly, the world of the social actor was to be taken seriously, and actors' own accounts of deviant motivations given credence. Strongly associated with the work of Matza and Sykes and Howard Becker, new deviancy was subsequently to provide inspiration for radical criminology in Britain (see Chapter 2).

Paradigm A general framework of knowledge, or an orientation toward the study of natural or social phenomena which shares common features despite the differences within it, and whose general features are systematically related to each other in some way: for example, the 'scientific paradigm'. 'Paradigm shifts' are said to occur when a major or fundamental change in the basis of knowledge and understanding occurs, usually implying philosophical shifts underpinning the way of seeing embraced by the paradigm.

Pathology A pathological approach to crime suggests that there is an inherent organic malfunction within the offender which causes the offending behaviour. As with medicalization, it takes not only responsibility away from the actor, but also civil rights.

Patriarchy Again, a much debated term, literally meaning 'the rule of the father'. It refers to the systematic ordering of gender relationships into hierarchies whereby the masculine controls the feminine through the appropriation of material and cultural resources including money, political power, language and knowledge. It is not, however, simply a system in which men control or oppress women; it is a system in which masculinity is the dominant cultural form, and through which men also control other men.

Policy Populism A process whereby policy is driven by political expediency. In particular, a 'punitive' policy populism is common in relation to young people where successive governments seek to appeal to popular demand for tighter controls over young people and 'law and order', typically fanned by the media.

Policy populism leads policy making away from rational goals of effectiveness in the pursuit of electoral and media endorsement. It is frequently antithetical to social justice as a result, and exacerbates processes of social exclusion.

Positivism A methodological position within the social sciences which assumes that criminals are demonstrably different from non-criminals, and that causative factors within the individual or their life circumstances may be identified and quantified. Positivism may be either biological, psychological or sociological. The methods of empirical science are stressed: quantification, experimentation, statistical correlation and prediction.

Postwar reconstruction In this volume this term refers to the period after the Second World War and the attempts to rebuild the economic and social infrastructure of the UK, in particular the development of a welfare state under Beveridge and programmes for the expansion of the public education system.

Realism see Left realism

Representation A term with a specific meaning in the sociology of knowledge, cultural studies and similar fields. It assumes that knowledge is never unmediated by cultural values and beliefs. Although 'reality' is 'out there', it can never be truly or objectively described. Thus for example the representation of childhood relates to something real (a chronologically young person) but the notion of what constitutes childhood varies from culture to culture and over historical time. Indeed, some cultures would not recognize the term at all. Representations may be produced through the media, through public policies, in popular culture – indeed, through all aspects of social life – and may be produced through language or image.

Stereotype A schematic portrayal, usually of a 'type' of person, which produces a generalized image (e.g. a 'thug') which plays down individual difference between people and scales up a small number of (usually undesirable) attributes. It is often used pejoratively and in a dehumanizing way to demonize certain groups in society.

Subcultural theory A perspective concerned with the culture and behaviour of subsets of groups within societies. There are several different strands of subcultural theory but all have in common the notion that there are distinct and identifiable smaller groupings within wider society who share particular values and focal concerns specific to them, as well as values and beliefs of wider society. It is used to explain youth crime and delinquency in terms of the resistances and oppositions towards the parent culture generated, for example, among economically disadvantaged males in authority settings such as the school. Radical subcultural theory, as with the Centre for Contemporary Cultural Studies (CCCS) at the University of Birmingham in the 1970s, emphasizes the symbolic importance of subcultures in creating a sense of belonging and community, and the deep meaning of subcultural forms (such as music, dress, sport fandom): what you see is not what you get, hence skinhead culture may be 'read' as the magical recovery of community.

Universalizing discourse A process by which individual differences are subsumed under a powerful generic definition which is assumed to apply across a population irrespective of any dissimilarities. It has the effect of making a particular notion seem natural or 'common sense', hence the universalization of childhood.

Utilitarianism An approach to social policy which would, in theory at least, secure 'the greatest good for the greatest number'.

Welfarism (in juvenile justice) A concept that children who commit criminal offences are not merely criminals, but have unmet social needs. The issue for the state should not therefore be one of 'punishment' but of 'treatment'. Using metaphors of sickness in this way, it is assumed that social work or psychiatric intervention in the 'sick' family can address the offending behaviour. As with 'pathology' and 'medicalization' the effect can be to deny the offender citizenship rights, so that effectively more painful and intrusive measures (such as removal into care) could be justified on the grounds that even a minor offence could be seen as a symptom of unmet 'need'.

Zero tolerance A concept first imported to the UK from the USA. In the early 1990s it had a specific application in relation to campaigns against violence against women: the 'Z' campaign which began in Edinburgh and was subsequently adopted by UK local authorities. The aim of this campaign was to use graphic representation (advertising hoardings, the 'Z' logo on local authority minibuses, public service vehicles etc.) to draw attention to the physical and sexual abuse of women and children and to call for 'zero tolerance' of domestic violence. This original and specific application has since been lost as 'zero tolerance', firstly, became taken up in various ways by police forces to characterize more intensive policing of minor infractions, and, secondly, passed into general parlance and political rhetoric as a social attitude. It has now become a cultural and rhetorical device of popular authoritarianism.

References

Abrams, M. (1959) *The Teenage Consumer*. London: London Press Exchange.

Alcock, P. and Harris, P. (1982) *Welfare Law and Order*. London: Macmillan.

Allen, F.A. (1964) *The Borderland of Criminal Justice: Essays in Law and Criminology*. Chicago: Chicago University Press.

Anderson, S., Kinsey, R., Loader, I. and Smith, G. (1994) *Cautionary Tales: Young People and Policing in Edinburgh*. Aldershot: Avebury.

Aries, P. ([1960] 1973) *Centuries of Childhood*. Harmondsworth: Penguin.

Audit Commission (1996) *Misspent Youth: Young People and Crime*. Abingdon: Audit Commission Publications.

Audit Commission (2004) *Youth Justice 2004: A Review of the Reformed Youth Justice System*. London: Audit Commission.

Baden-Powell, R. (1930) *Rovering to Success: A Book of Life Sport for Young Men*. London: Herbert Jenkins.

Bailey, V. (1987) *Delinquency and Citizenship: Reclaiming the Young Offender 1914–1948*. Oxford: Clarendon Press.

Balagopalan, S. (2002) Constructing indigenous childhoods: colonialism, vocational education and the working child, *Childhood*, 9(1): 19–34.

Baldwin, J. and Bottoms, A. (1976) *The Urban Criminal*. London: Tavistock.

Bankowski, Z. and Mungham, G. (1981) Lawpeople and laypeople, *International Journal of the Sociology of Law*, 9: 85–100.

Bannerji, H. (2002) *Inventing Subjects: Studies in Hegemony, Patriarchy and Colonialism*. London: Anthem.

Barker, M. (1997) The Newson Report: a case study in common sense, in M. Barker and J. Petley (eds) *Ill Effects: The Media/Violence Debate*. London: Routledge.

Barker, M. and Petley, J. (eds) (1997) *Ill Effects: The Media/Violence Debate*. London: Routledge.

Barrett, M. and McIntosh, M. (1991) *The Anti-Social Family*, 2nd edn. London: Verso.

Bean, P. (1976) *Rehabilitation and Deviance*. London: Routledge & Kegan Paul.

Beck, U. (1992) *Risk Society*. London: Sage.

Bell, D. (2000) Introduction I: a user's guide, in D. Bell and B. Kennedy (eds) *The Cybercultures Reader*. London: Routledge.

Bell, D. and Kennedy, B. (eds) (2000) *The Cybercultures Reader*. London: Routledge.

Benedikt, M. (2000) Cyberspace: first steps, in D. Bell and B. Kennedy (eds) *The Cybercultures Reader*. London: Routledge.

Beynon, J. and Solomos, J. (eds) (1987) *The Roots of Urban Unrest*. Oxford: Pergamon.

Bottomley, A.K. and Pease, K. (1986) *Crime and Punishment: Interpreting the Data*. Milton Keynes: Open University Press.

Bottoms, A.E. (1974) On the decriminalisation of the English Juvenile Courts, in R. Hood (ed.) *Crime, Criminology and Public Policy*. London: Heinemann.

Bottoms, A.E. (1995) The philosophy and politics of punishment and sentencing, in C.M.V. Clarkson and R. Morgan (eds) *The Politics of Sentencing Reform*. Oxford: Oxford University Press.

Bottoms, A.E. and Pratt, J. (1989) Intermediate treatment (IT) for girls in England and Wales, in M. Cain (ed.) *Growing up Good: Policing the Behaviour of Girls in Europe*. London: Sage.

Bottoms, A.E. and Stevenson, S. (1992) What went wrong? Criminal justice policy in England and Wales, 1945–1970, in D. Downes (ed.) *Unravelling Criminal Justice*. Basingstoke: Macmillan.

Bowlby, J. (1951) *Maternal Care and Mental Health*. London: HMSO.

Box, S. (1981) *Deviance, Reality and Society*, 2nd edn. London: Holt Reinhardt.

Box, S. (1983) *Power, Crime and Mystification*. London: Tavistock.

Braithwaite, J. (1989) *Crime, Shame and Reintegration*. Cambridge: Cambridge University Press.

Brake, M. and Hale, C. (1992) *Public Order and Private Lives*. London: Routledge.

British Journal of Criminology (1988) Special edition, 28(2).

Brody, S.R. (1976) *The Effectiveness of Sentencing*, Home Office Research Study No. 35. London: HMSO.

Brown, S. (1992) Doing time: crime and everyday life on Blue Hall. Unpublished report to Banks of the Wear Housing Association. Middlesbrough: Research Action.

Brown, S. (1994a) Whose challenge? Youth, crime and everyday life in Middlesbrough. Published report to Middlesbrough City Challenge Partnership. Middlesbrough: City Challenge Partnership.

Brown, S. (1994b) Time of change? Adult views of youth and crime in Middlesbrough. Published report to Middlesbrough City Challenge Partnership. Middlesbrough: Middlesbrough City Challenge.

Brown, S. (1995) Crime and safety in whose 'community'? *Youth and Policy*, 48: 27–48.

Brown, S. (2003) *Crime and Law in Media Culture*. Buckingham: Open University Press.

Brown, S. (2004) *The Sciences and Cultures of Detection: Policy Promises, Popular Representations and Crime Processing Realities*. Unpublished research report.

Burt, C. (1925) *The Young Delinquent*. London: University of London Press.

Cain, M. (ed.) (1989) *Growing up Good: Policing the Behaviour of Girls in Europe*. London: Sage.

Campbell, A. (1984) *The Girls in the Gang*. Oxford: Blackwell.

Campbell, B. (1988) *Unofficial Secrets: Child Sexual Abuse: The Cleveland Case*. London: Virago Press.

Campbell, B. (1993) *Goliath: Britain's Dangerous Places*. London: Methuen.

Carlen, P. (1988) *Women, Crime and Poverty*. Milton Keynes: Open University Press.

Carlen, P. (1996) *Jigsaw – A Political Criminology of Youth Homelessness*. Buckingham: Open University Press.

Carlen, P., Hicks, J., O'Dwyer, J., Cristina, D. and Tchaikovsky, C. (1985) *Criminal Women*. Cambridge: Polity Press.

Carr, J. (2002a) Child pornography. Theme paper, 2nd World Congress Against Sexual Exploitation of Children, Yokohama, Japan, 17–20 December.

Carr, J. (2002b) Pseudo Pornography and Freedom of Speech, *ECPAT Newsletter* (39: 2).

Carter, M. (1966) *Into Work*. Harmondsworth: Penguin.

Castells, M. (2001) *The Internet Galaxy: Reflections on the Internet, Business and Society*. Oxford: Oxford University Press.

Cavadino, M. and Dignan, J. (1997) *The Penal System*, 2nd edn. London: Sage.

Cavadino, P. (2003) The harshest punishment: young offenders and suicide, *Criminal Justice Matters*, 54: winter.

Centre for Crime and Justice Studies (2003) Youth and crime edition of *Criminal Justice Matters*, 54: winter.

Chase, E. and Statham, J. (2004) *The Commercial Sexual Exploitation of Children and Young People: An Overview of Key Literature and Data*. London: Thomas Coram Research Unit.

Chesney-Lind, M. (1989) Girl's crime and woman's place: toward a feminist model of female delinquency, *Crime and Delinquency*, 35(1): 5–29.

Chibnall, S. (1977) *Law and Order News*. London: Tavistock.

Christie, N. (1985) Punishment, in A. Kuper and J. Kuper (eds) *The Social Science Encyclopaedia*. London: Routledge & Kegan Paul.

Clarke, J. (1976) The skinheads and the magical recovery of community, in S. Hall and T. Jefferson (eds) *Resistance through Rituals*. London: Macmillan.

Clarke, J. (1980) Social democratic delinquents and Fabian families, in National Deviancy Conference (NDC) (eds) *Permissiveness and Control*. London: Macmillan.

Clarke, J. (1985) Whose justice? The politics of juvenile control, *International Journal of the Sociology of Law*, 13: 407–21.

Cloward, R. and Ohlin, L. (1960) *Delinquency and Opportunity*. London: Collier Macmillan.

Cockburn, T. (1995) *The Devil in the City: Working Class Children in Manchester 1860–1914*. Paper presented to the British Sociological Association, University of Leicester, April.

Cohen, A.K. (1955) *Delinquent Boys*. London: Free Press.

Cohen, P. (1997) *Rethinking the Youth Question: Education, Labour and Cultural Studies*. London: Macmillan.

Cohen, S. (1973) *Folk Devils and Moral Panics: The Creation of the Mods and Rockers*. St Alban's: Paladin.

Cohen, S. (1985) *Visions of Social Control*. Cambridge: Polity Press.

Cohen, S. (1988) *Against Criminology*. New Brunswick, NJ: Transaction Books.

Colebourne, C. (2001) Making 'mad' populations in settler colonies: the work of law and medicine in the creation of the colonial asylum, in D. Kirkby and C. Colebourne (eds) *Law, History, Colonialism: The Reach of Empire*. Manchester: Manchester University Press.

Coleman, C. and Moynihan, J. (1996) *Understanding Crime Data*. Buckingham: Open University Press.

Connell, R.W. (1987) *Gender and Power: Society, the Person and Sexual Politics*. Cambridge: Polity Press.

Constantine, P. (1994) *Japan's Sex Trade: A Journey Through Japan's Erotic Subcultures*. Tokyo: Charles E. Tuttle.

Cook, D. and Hudson, B. (1993) *Racism and Criminology*. London: Sage.

Cook, F. (2003) Children in prison: advocating for the human rights of young offenders, *Criminal Justice Matters*, 54: winter.

Corby, B. (1997) The mistreatment of young people, in J. Roche and S. Tucker (eds) *Youth in Society*. London: Sage.

Corrigan, P. (1976) Doing nothing, in S. Hall and T. Jefferson (eds) *Resistance through Rituals*. London: Hutchinson.

Creighton, S.J. and Noyes, P. (1989) *Child Abuse Trends in England and Wales 1983–1987*. London: National Society for the Prevention of Cruelty to Children.

Creighton, S. (2003) Child pornography: images of the abuse of children, *NSPCC Inform* November. www.nspcc.org.uk/inform

Creighton, S. and Tissier, G. (2003) Child killings in England and Wales, *NSPCC Information Briefings*, January. http://www.nspcc.org.uk/Inform.

Critcher, C. (2003) *Moral Panics and the Media*. Buckingham: Open University Press.

Crowther, C. (2000) *Policing Urban Poverty*. Basingstoke: Macmillan.

Davies, B. (1986) *Threatening Youth: Towards a National Youth Policy*. Milton Keynes: Open University Press.

Davis, J. (1990) *Youth and the Condition of Britain: Images of Adolescent Conflict*. London: Athlone Press.

de Alwis, M. (1991) Seductive scripts and subversive practices: 'motherhood', nationalism, and the state in Sri Lanka. Proposal for Doctoral research, Department of Anthropology, University of Chicago.

de Haan, W. (1990) *The Politics of Redress: Crime, Punishment and Penal Abolition*. London: Unwin Hyman.

DfES (2003) *Every Child Matters: The Next Steps*. London: Stationary Office.

Ditchfield, J. (1976) *Police Cautioning in England and Wales*, Home Office Research Study No. 37. London: HMSO.

Donnerstein, E. (2002) The internet, in V.C. Strasburger and B.J. Wilson (eds) *Children, Adolescents and the Media*. London: Sage.

Donzelot, J. (1981) *The Policing of Families*. London: Hutchinson.

Douglas, M. (1994a) *Purity and Danger: An Analysis of the Concepts of Pollution and Taboo*. London: Routledge.

Douglas, M. (1994b) *Risk and Blame: Essays in Cultural Theory*. London: Routledge.

Downes, D. (1966) *The Delinquent Solution*. London: Routledge & Kegan Paul.

Downes, D. (1988) The sociology of crime and social control in Britain, 1960–1987, *British Journal of Criminology*, 28(2): 45–55.

Downes, D. and Rock, P. (1988) *Understanding Deviance: A Guide to the Sociology of Crime and Rule Breaking*, 2nd edn. Oxford: Clarendon Press.

Duff, R.A. and Garland, D. (eds) (1994) *A Reader on Punishment*. Oxford: Oxford University Press.

ECPAT (2002) *Newsletter 39*, April.

Ennew, J. (1986) *The Sexual Exploitation of Children*. Cambridge: Polity Press.

Ennew, J. and Morrow, V. (2002) Releasing the energy: celebrating the inspiration of Sharon Stephens, *Childhood*, 9(1): 5–17.

Escobar, A. (2000) Welcome to cyberia: notes on the anthropology of cyberculture, in D. Bell and B. Kennedy (eds) *The Cybercultures Reader*. London: Routledge.

Farrington, D.P. (1994) Human development and criminal careers, in M. Maguire, R. Morgan and R. Reiner (eds) *The Oxford Handbook of Criminology*. Oxford: Clarendon Press.

Farrington, D.P. (2002) Developmental Criminology and risk-focused prevention, in M. Maguire, R. Morgan and R. Reiner (eds) *The Oxford Handbook of Criminology*, 3rd edn. Oxford: Oxford University Press.

Farrington, D.P. and West, D.J. (1990) The Cambridge Study in Delinquent Development: a long-term follow-up of 411 London males, in H.J. Kerner and G. Kaiser (eds) *Criminality, Personality, Behaviour, Life-History*. Berlin: Springer-Verlag.

Featherstone, M., Lash, S. and Robertson, R. (eds) (1995) *Global Modernities*. London: Sage/TCS.

Ferrell, J. (1996) Slash and frame, in G. Barak (ed.) *Representing O.J.: Murder, Criminal Justice and Mass Culture*. Guilderland, NY: Harrow and Heston.

Fitzpatrick, P. (2001) Terminal legality: imperialism and the (de) composition of law, in D. Kirkby and C. Colebourne (eds) *Law, History, Colonialism: the reach of Empire*. Manchester: Manchester University Press.

Förnas, J. and Bolin, G. (eds) (1995) *Youth Cultures in Late Modernity*. London: Sage.

Foucault, M. (1981) *The History of Sexuality*. Harmondsworth: Penguin.

Foucault, M. (1977) *Discipline and Punish: The Birth of the Prison*. London: Allen Lane.

Foucault, M. (1990) *The History of Sexuality: Volume I*. Harmondsworth: Penguin.

Foucault, M. (1991) Governmentality, in G. Burchell *et al.* (eds) *The Foucault Effect: Studies in Governmentality*. Hemel Hempstead: Harvester Wheatsheaf.

Fowles, J. (1999) *The Case for Television Violence*. London: Sage.

Franklin, B. (1992) Children and decision making: developing empowering institutions, in M.D. Fortuyn and M. de Langen (eds) *Towards the Realization of Human Rights of Children*. Amsterdam: Children's Ombudswork Foundation and Defence for Children International.

Furnham, A. and Gunter, B. (1989) *The Anatomy of Adolescence: Young People's Social Attitudes in Britain*. London: Routledge.

Fyvel, T. (1963) *The Insecure Offenders*. Harmondsworth: Penguin.

Gaete, R. (1999) The west, its other, and human rights, in T. Skelton and T. Allan (eds) *Culture and Global Change*. London: Routledge.

Garland, D. (1994) Of crimes and criminals: the development of criminology in Britain, in M. Maguire, R. Morgan and R. Reiner (eds) *The Oxford Handbook of Criminology*. Oxford: Clarendon Press.

Garland, D. (ed.) (2001) *The Cutlure of Control: Crime and Social Order in Contemporary Society*. Oxford: Clarendon.

Garratt, D. (1997) Youth cultures and subcultures, in J. Roche and S. Tucker (eds) *Youth in Society*. London: Sage.

Gaskell, E. ([1848] 1981) *Mary Barton: A Tale of Manchester Life*. Harmondsworth: Penguin.

Gelsthorpe, L. and Morris, A. (1994) Juvenile justice 1945–1992, in M. Maguire, R. Morgan and R. Reiner (eds) *The Oxford Handbook of Criminology*. Oxford: Clarendon Press.

Gibbons, S. (1996) Reclaiming the streets, *Police Review*, 13 September: 18–22.

Gibson, B. (1995) Young people, bad news, enduring principles, *Youth and Policy*, 48: 64–70.

Gibson, B. *et al.* (1994) *The Youth Court – One Year Onwards*. Winchester: Waterside Press.

Gibson, W. (1984) *Neuromancer*. London: Victor Gollancz.

Giddens, A. (1990) *The Consequences of Modernity*. Stanford, CA: Stanford University Press.

Giddens, A. (1991) *Modernity and Self Identity: Self and Society in the Late Modern Age*. Cambridge: Polity.

Giddens, A. (1999) Lecture 1 – Globalisation, *The BBC Reith Lectures 1999: Runaway World*. BBC Online Network.

Gill, O. (1977) *Luke Street: Housing Policy, Conflict and the Creation of the Delinquent Area*. London: Macmillan.

Gionti, G. (2004) Human trafficking: concept, classification, and questions of legislation regulation, in S. Nevala and K. Aromaa (eds) *Organized Crime, Trafficking, Drugs*. Selected papers presented at the Annual Conference of the European Society of Criminology, Helsinki 2003, Publication Series 42. Helsinki: European Institute for Crime Prevention and Control/United Nations.

Glauser, B. (1997) Street children: deconstructing a construct, in A. James and A. Prout (eds) *Constructing and Reconstructing Childhood*. Brighton: Falmer Press.

Goldson, B. (ed.) (2000) *The New Youth Justice*. Dorset: Russell House.

Goldson, B. (2004) Youth crime and youth justice, in J. Muncie and D. Wilson (eds) *Student Handbook of Criminal Justice and Criminology*. London: Cavendish.

Goodey, J. (1994) Fear of crime: what can children tell us? *International Review of Victimology*, 3: 125–210.

Goodey, J. (1995) *Boys Don't Cry: Masculinities, Fear of Crime, and Fearlessness*. Paper presented to the American Society of Criminology Conference, Boston, MA, November.

Goodey, J. (2005) *Victims and Victimology: Research, Policy and Practice*. Harlow: Pearson Longman.

Gramsci, A. (1978) *Selections from the Prison Notebooks*. London: Lawrence & Wishart.

Greek, C. (1996) O.J. and the internet: the first cybertrial, in G. Barak (ed.) *Representing O.J.: Murder, Criminal Justice and Mass Culture*. Guilderland, NY: Harrow & Heston.

Greenleaf ([1998] 2003) An endnote on regulating cyberspace: architecture vs law? in D. Wall (ed.) *Cyberspace Crime*. Aldershot: Ashgate.

Griffin, C. (1993) *Representations of Youth: The Study of Youth in Britain and America*. Cambridge: Polity.

Guardian/ICM (1996) Dream teens, *Guardian*, 14 May.

Gunter, B. (1998) *The Effects of Video Games on Children*. Sheffield: Sheffield Academic Press.

Hagan, J. (1989) *Structural Criminology*. New Brunswick, NJ: Rutgers University Press.

Hagan, J., Simpson, J.H. and Gillis, A.R. (1979) The sexual stratification of social control: a gender-based perspective on crime and delinquency, *British Journal of Sociology*, 30: 25–38.

Hagell, A. and Newburn, T. (1994) *Persistent Young Offenders*. London: Policy Studies Institute.

Hall, G.S. (1904) *Adolescence: Its Psychology and Its Relation to Physiology, Anthropology, Sociology, Sex, Crime, Religion and Education*, 2 vols. New York: D. Appleton.

Hall, S. and Jefferson, T. (eds) (1976) *Resistance through Rituals: Youth Subcultures in Post-War Britain*. London: Hutchinson.

Hall, S., Critcher, C., Jefferson, T., Clarke, J. and Roberts, B. (1978) *Policing the Crisis: Mugging, the State, and Law and Order*. London: Macmillan.

Hamilton, N. (2001) *The Full Monty*. London: Allen Lane.

Harris, J. (1993) *Private Lives, Public Spirit: Britain 1870–1914*. Harmondsworth: Penguin.

Harris, R.J. (1985) Towards just welfare, *British Journal of Criminology*, 25(1): 31–45.

Harris, R. and Webb, D. (1987) *Welfare, Power and Juvenile Justice*. London: Tavistock.

Hartless, J., Ditton, J., Nair, G. and Philips, S. (1995) More sinned against than sinning: a study of young teenagers' experiences of crime, *British Journal of Criminology*, 35(1): 114–33.

Harvey, R. (2003) *Children and Armed Conflict: A guide to international humanitarian and human rights law*. Montreal: International Bureau for Children's Rights.

Harwin, J. (1982) The battle for the delinquent, in *The Yearbook of Social Policy in Britain 1980–1981*. London: Routledge & Kegan Paul.

Healy, M. (2004) Child pornography: an international perspective, *Computer Crime Research Centre*, working paper for the World Congress against Commercial Sexual Exploitation of Children, August. http://www.crime-research. org/articles/536/

Heidensohn, F.M. (1968) The deviance of women: a critique and an enquiry, *British Journal of Sociology*, 19(2): 160–75.

Heidensohn, F. (1994) Gender and crime, in M. Maguire, R. Morgan and R. Reiner (eds) *The Oxford Handbook of Criminology*. Oxford: Clarendon Press.

Heidensohn, F. (1996) *Women and Crime*, 2nd edn. London: Macmillan.

Heim, M. (1998) *Virtual Realism*. Oxford: Oxford University Press.

Hendrick, H. (1990) Constructions and reconstructions of British childhood: an interpretive survey 1800 to the present, in A. James and A. Prout (eds) *Constructing and Reconstructing Childhood*. London: Falmer.

Hewitt, T. and Smyth, I. (1999) Street lives and family lives in Brazil, in T. Skelton and T. Allen (eds) *Culture and Global Change*. London: Routledge.

Himmelweit, H. *et al*. (1958) *Television and the Child: An Empirical Study into the Effects of Television on the Young*. Oxford: Oxford University Press.

Hirschi, T. (1969) *Causes of Delinquency*. Berkeley, CA: University of California Press.

HMSO (2000) *Report of the Tribunal of Enquiry into the Abuse of Children in Care in The Former County Council Areas of Gwynedd and Clwyd since 1974: 'Lost in Care'*. London: The Stationery Office.

Hockey, J. and James, A. (1993) *Growing up and Growing Old: Ageing and Dependency in the Life Course*. London: Sage.

Holland, P. (1997) Living for libido; or, 'Child's Play IV'; the imagery of childhood and call for censorship, in M. Barker and J. Petley (eds) *Ill Effects: The Media/ Violence Debate*. London: Routledge.

Holloway, S.L. and Valentine, G. (2003) *Cyberkids: Children in the Information Age*. London: RoutledgeFarmer.

Home Office (1927) *Report of the Departmental Committee on the Treatment of Young Offenders*, Cmd 2831 (The Molony Report). London: HMSO.

Home Office (1946) *The Care of Children Committee*, Cmd 6922 (The Curtis Report). London: HMSO.

Home Office (1960) *Report on the Committee on Children and Young Persons*, Cmnd 1191 (The Ingleby Report). London: HMSO.

Home Office (1965) *The Child, The Family and the Young Offender*, Cmnd 2742. London: HMSO.

Home Office (1968) *Children in Trouble*, Cmnd 3601. London: HMSO.

Home Office (1976) *The Children and Young Persons Act (CYPA), 1969: Observations on the Eleventh Report of the Expenditure Committee*, Cmnd 6494. London: HMSO.

Home Office (1980) *Young Offenders*, Cmnd 8045. London: HMSO.

Home Office (1984) *Tougher Regimes in Detention Centres: Report of an Evaluation by the Young Offender Psychology Unit*. London: HMSO.

Home Office (1990) *Crime, Justice and Protecting the Public*, Cm 965. London: HMSO.

Home Office (1995a) *National Standards for the Supervision of Offenders in the Community*. London: Home Office.

Home Office (1995b) *Young People, Victimization and the Police: British Crime Survey Findings on Experiences and Attitudes of 12–15 Year Olds*, Home Office Research Study No. 140. London: HMSO.

Home Office (1996) *Protecting the Public*, Cm 3190. London: HMSO.

Home Office (1997) *No More Excuses: A New Approach to Tackling Youth Crime in England and Wales*. London: The Stationery Office.

Home Office (2003) *Respect and Responsibility: Taking a Stand Against Anti-Social Behaviour*. London: The Stationery Office.

Home Office (2004) *The British Crime Survey 2001–2*. London: The Stationery Office.

Hood, R. (1974) Criminology and penal change: a case study of the nature and impact of some recent advice to governments, in R. Hood (ed.) *Crime, Criminology and Public Policy*. London: Heinemann.

Hornby, N. (1992) *Fever Pitch*. London: Gollancz.

House of Commons Expenditure Committee (1975) *Eleventh Report from the Expenditure Committee: The Children and Young Persons Act (CYPA), 1969*. London: HMSO.

Howitt, D. (1998) *Crime, the Media and the Law*. Chichester: John Wiley & Sons.

Hudson, A. (1989) Troublesome girls, in M. Cain (ed.) *Growing up Good: Policing the Behaviour of Girls in Europe*. London: Sage.

Hudson, B.A. (1996) *Understanding Justice: An Introduction to Ideas, Perspectives, and Controversies in Modern Penal Theory*. Buckingham: Open University Press.

Hunt, D.M. (1999) *O.J. Simpson Facts and Fictions: News Rituals in the Construction of Reality*. Cambridge: Cambridge University Press.

Hyde, S. (2004) Planning ahead for the mobile generation, *ECPAT Newsletter* 48, July: 1–2.

IBCR (2003) *Guidelines on Justice for Child Victims and Witnesses of Crime.* Montreal: International Bureau for Children's Rights.

Inciardi, J.A. and Surratt, H.L. (1997) Children in the streets of Brazil: drug use, crime, violence and HIV risks. (http://www.udel.edu/butzin/articles/child. html).

Inglis, F. (1993) *Cultural Studies.* Oxford: Blackwell.

James, A. and Prout, A. (eds) (1990) *Constructing and Reconstructing Childhood.* London: Falmer.

James, A., Jenks, C. and Prout, A. (eds) (1998) *Theorizing Childhood.* Cambridge: Polity.

Jefferson, T. (1976) Cultural responses of the teds: the defence of space and status, in S. Hall and T. Jefferson (eds) *Resistance through Rituals.* London: Hutchinson.

Jefferson, T. (1994) Theorising masculine subjectivity, in T. Newburn and E.A. Stanko (eds) *Just Boys Doing Business: Men, Masculinities and Crime.* London: Routledge.

Jenks, C. (1996) *Childhood.* London: Routledge.

Jenks, C. (2004) Editorial: many childhoods?, *Childhood*, 11(1): 5–8.

Johns, M. (1995) Children's rights in a free-market culture, in S. Stephens (ed.) *Children and the Politics of Culture.* Princeton, NJ: Princeton University Press.

Johnston, L. (1997) New Labour and the usual suspects, *Chartist*, March–April: 14–15.

Jones, T., Maclean, B. and Young, J. (eds) (1986) *The Islington Crime Survey.* Aldershot: Gower.

Kelly, L. and Radford, J. (1987) The problem of men: feminist perspectives on sexual violence, in P. Scraton (ed.) *Law, Order and the Authoritarian State.* Milton Keynes: Open University Press.

Kidd-Hewitt, D. and Osborne, R. (eds) (1995) *Crime and the Media: The Postmodern Spectacle.* London: Pluto Press.

King, M. (1991) The political construction of crime prevention: a contrast between the French and British experience, in K. Stenson and D. Cowell (eds) *The Politics of Crime Control.* London: Sage.

Kinsey, R. (1985) *First Report of the Merseyside Crime Survey.* Liverpool: Merseyside County Council.

Kuper, J. (1997) *International Law Concerning Child Civilians in Armed Conflict.* Oxford: Clarendon.

Latour, B. (1986) The powers of association, in J. Law (ed.) *Power, Action and Belief: Towards a New Sociology of Knowledge?* London: Routledge & Kegan Paul.

Latour, B. (1993) *We Have Never Been Modern.* Cambridge, MA: Harvard University Press.

Lees, S. (1989) Learning to love: sexual reputation, morality and the social control of girls, in M. Cain (ed.) *Growing up Good: Policing the Behaviour of Girls in Europe.* London: Sage.

Leonard, E.B. (1982) *Women, Crime, and Society: A Critique of Theoretical Criminology.* New York: Longman.

Leonard, M. (1998) Paper planes: travelling the new grrrl geographies, in T.

Skelton and G. Valentine (eds) *Cool Places: Geographies of Youth Cultures*. London: Routledge.

Levi, M. (1994) Masculinities and white-collar crime, in T. Newburn and E.A. Stanko (eds) *Just Boys Doing Business: Men, Masculinities and Crime*. London: Routledge.

Levi, M. (2002) The organization of serious crimes, in M. Maguire, R. Morgan and R. Reiner (eds) *The Oxford Handbook of Criminology*, 3rd edn. Oxford: Oxford University Press.

Levine, J. (2002) *Harmful to Minor: The Perils of Protecting Children from Sex*. Minneapolis, MN: The University of Minnesota Press.

Lipton, D., Martinson, R. and Wilks, J. (1975) *The Effectiveness of Correctional Treatment: A Survey of Evaluation Studies*. New York: Praeger.

Livingstone, S. (2002) *Children's Use of the Internet: A Review of the Research Literature*. Report commissioned by the National Children's Bureau: March. London: Media@LSE. http://www.lse.ac.uk/depts/media/people/slivingstone/index.html.

Livingstone, S. and Bovill, M. (1999) Young people new media. Report of the research project *Children, Young People and the Changing Media Environment*. London: London School of Economics and Political Science.

Loader, I. and Sparks, R. (2001) Criminology, social theory and the challenge of our times, in D. Garland and R. Sparks (eds) *Criminology and Social Theory*. Oxford: Clarendon.

Loader, I. and Sparks, R. (2002) Contemporary landscapes of crime and control: governance, risk and globalization, in M. Maguire, R. Morgan and R. Reiner (eds) *The Oxford Handbook of Criminology*, 3rd edn. Oxford: Oxford University Press.

Lombroso, C. and Ferrero, W. (1895) *The Female Offender*. London: T. Fisher Unwin.

Lury, C. (1996) *Consumer Culture*. Cambridge: Polity Press.

Machel, G. (2001) *The Impact of War on Children*. London: Hurst & Co.

Maguire, M., Morgan, R. and Reiner, R. (eds) (1997) *The Oxford Handbook of Criminology*. Oxford: Clarendon Press.

Matthews, R. and Young, J. (eds) (1992) *Issues in Realist Criminology*. London: Sage.

Matza, D. (1964) *Delinquency and Drift*. New York: Wiley.

Matza, D. (1969) *Becoming Deviant*. Englewood Cliffs, NJ: Prentice Hall.

Matza, D. and Sykes, G. (1961) Juvenile delinquency and subterranean values, *American Sociological Review*, 26: 712–19.

Mawby, R.I. (1979) The victimization of juveniles: a comparative study of publicly owned housing in Sheffield, *Journal of Crime and Delinquency*, 16: 98–114.

McInerney, J. (1993) *Bright Lights, Big City*. London: Penguin.

McLaughlin, E. and Muncie, J. (1993) Juvenile delinquency, in R. Dallos and E. McLaughlin (eds) *Social Problems and the Family*. London: Sage.

McRobbie, A. (1991) *Feminism and Youth Culture: From Jackie to Just Seventeen*. London: Macmillan.

McRobbie, A. and Nava, M. (eds) (1984) *Gender and Generation*. London: Macmillan.

Mead, M. (1929) *Coming of Age in Samoa*. London: Jonathan Cape.

Merton, R.K. (1993) Social structure and anomie, in C. Lemert (ed.) *Social Theory: The Multicultural Readings*. Boulder, CO: Westview Press.

Messerschmidt, J.W. (1993) *Masculinities and Crime: Critique and Reconceptualization of Theory*. Lanham, MY: Rowman and Littlefield.

Messerschmidt, J.W. (1994) Schooling, masculinities and youth crime by white boys, in T. Newburn and E.A. Stanko (eds) *Just Boys Doing Business? Men, Masculinities and Crime*. London: Routledge.

Miller, W.B. (1958) Lower class culture as a generating milieu of gang delinquency, *Journal of Social Issues*, 14(3): 5–19.

Millham, S., Bullock, R. and Hosie, K. (1978) *Locking up Children*. Farnborough: Saxon House.

Ministry of Education (1959) *15–18* (The Crowther Report). London: HMSO.

Morgan, J. and Zedner, L. (1992) *Child Victims: Crime, Impact and Criminal Justice*. Oxford: Clarendon Press.

Morgan, P. (1981) The Children's Act: sacrificing justice to social worker's needs? in C. Brewer *et al.* (eds) *Criminal Welfare on Trial*. London: Social Affairs Unit.

Morgan, R. (2003) Offender trucking funds: to reverse the punitive sentencing trend, *Criminal Justice Matters*, 54: winter.

Morley, D. and Robins, K. (1995) *Spaces of Identity: Global Media, Electronic Landscapes and Cultural Boundaries*. London: Routledge.

Morris, A. (1987) *Women, Crime and Criminal Justice*. Oxford: Basil Blackwell.

Morris, A. and Giller, H. (1987) *Understanding Juvenile Justice*. London: Croom Helm.

Morris, A. and McIsaac, M. (1978) *Juvenile Justice?* London: Heinemann.

Morris, A., Giller, H., Szwed, E. and Geach, H. (1980) *Justice for Children*. London: Macmillan.

Morrison, W. (2004) Globalisation, human rights and international criminal courts, in J. Muncie and D. Wilson (eds) *Student Handbook of Criminal Justice and Criminology*. London: Cavendish.

Morse, M. (1965) *The Unattached*. Harmondsworth: Penguin.

Muncie, J. (1984) *The Trouble with Kids Today*. London: Hutchinson.

Muncie, J. (1987) Much ado about nothing? The sociology of moral panics, *Social Studies Review*, 3(2): 42–7.

Muncie, J. (1999) *Youth and Crime: A Critical Introduction*. London: Sage.

Muncie, J. (2001) A new deal for youth? Early interventionism and correctionalism, in G. Hughes, E. McLaughlin and J. Muncie (eds) *Crime Prevention and Community Safety: New Directions*. London: Sage.

Muncie, J. (2004) *Youth and Crime*, 2nd edn. London: Sage.

Muncie, J. and McLaughlin, E. (eds) (1996) *The Problem of Crime*. London: Sage.

Murdock, G. (1997) Reservoirs of dogma: an archaeology of popular anxieties, in M. Barker and J. Petley (eds) *Ill Effects*. London: Routledge.

Murray, C. (1990) *The Emerging British Underclass*. London: Institute of Economic Affairs.

NCES (National Center for Educational Statistics) (2001) *Computer and Internet Use by Children and Adolescents in 2001*. NCES Electric Catalog. http://nces.ed.gov/pubsearch/pubsinfo.asp.pubid=2004014.

Nederveen Pieterse, J. (1995) Globalization as Hybridization, in M. Featherstone and R. Robertson (eds) *Global Modernities*. London: Sage.

Neill, S. (1966) *Colonialism and Christian Missions*. London: McGraw-Hill.

Nevala, S. and Aromaa, K. (eds) (2004) *Organised Crime, Trafficking, Drugs*. Selected papers presented at the Annual Conference of the European Society of Criminology. Helsinki, 2003, Publication Series 42. Helsinki: European Institute for Crime Prevention and Control/United Nations.

Newburn, E. and Hagell, T. (1995) *Persistent Young Offenders*. London: Policy Studies Institute.

Newburn, T. (1995) *Crime and Criminal Justice Policy*. London: Longman.

Newburn, T. (2002) Young people, crime and youth justice, in J. Muncie and D. Wilson (eds) *Student Handbook of Criminal Justice and Criminology*. London: Cavendish.

Newburn, T. and Stanko, E. (eds) (1994) *Just Boys Doing Business? Men, Masculinities and Crime*. London: Routledge.

Nichols, B. (1994) *Blurred Boundaries: Questions of Meaning in Contemporary Culture*. Bloomington, IN: Indiana University Press.

Office of the High Commissioner for Human Rights (2004) *Status of Ratifications of the Principal International Human Rights Treaties*, 9 June 2004. http://www.unchr.ch.pdf/report.pdf

Oswell, D. (1998) The place of 'childhood' in Internet content regulation, *International Journal of Cultural Studies*, 1(2): 271–291.

Oswell, D. (1999) And what might our children become? Future visions, governance and the child television audience in postwar Britain, *Screen* 40(1): 66–87.

Parker, H. (1974) *View from the Boys*. Newton Abbot: David & Charles.

Parsloe, P. (1978) *Juvenile Justice in Britain and the United States*. London: Routledge & Kegan Paul.

Patrick, J. (1973) *A Glasgow Gang Observed*. London: Eyre Methuen.

Pearl, D., Bouthilet, L. and Lazar, J. (eds) (1982) *Television and Behaviour*. Washington, DC: Institute of Mental Health.

Pearson, G. (1983) *Hooligan: A History of Respectable Fears*. London: Macmillan.

Pearson, G. (1985) Lawlessness, modernity and social change: a historical appraisal, *Theory, Culture and Society*, 2(3): 15–36.

Pearson, G. (1994) *Youth, Crime and Society*, in M. Maguire, R. Morgan and R. Reiner (eds) *The Oxford Handbook of Criminology*. Oxford: Clarendon Press.

Pease, K. (2002) Crime reduction, in M. Maguire, R. Morgan and R. Reiner (eds) *The Oxford Handbook of Criminology*, 3rd edn. Oxford: Oxford University Press.

Penal Affairs Consortium (1995) *Boot Camps for Young Offenders*. London: Penal Affairs Consortium.

Phillips, D. (1977) *Crime and Authority in Victorian England*. London: Croom Helm.

Pilcher, J. (1995) *Age and Generation in Modern Britain*. Oxford: Oxford University Press.

Pinchbeck, I. and Hewitt, M. (1973) *Children in English Society, vol. 2*. London: Routledge & Kegan Paul.

Pitts, J. (1988) *The Politics of Juvenile Crime*. London: Sage.

Pitts, J. (1993) Thereotyping: Anti-Racism, Criminology and Black Young People, in D. Cook and B. Hudson (eds), *Racism and Criminology*. London: Sage.

Pitts, J. (1995) Scare in the community: Britain in a moral panic, *Community Care*, 4–10 May.

Pitts, J. (2001) *The New Politics of Youth Crime: Discipline or Solidarity*. London: Routledge.

Pollak, O. (1950) *The Criminality of Women*. Philadelphia, PA: University of Pennsylvania Press.

Porter, R. (1991) History of psychiatry in britain, *History of Psychiatry*, 2: 279.

Pratt, J. (1983) Intermediate treatment (IT) and the normalisation crisis, *Howard Journal*, 22: 19–37.

Pratt, J. (1990) Crime, time, youth and punishment, *Contemporary Crises*, 14(3): 220–42.

Radzinowicz, L. and Hood, R. (1986) *A History of English Criminal Law*, Vol. V: The Emergence of Penal Policy. London: Stephens & Sons.

Redhead, S. (1990) *The End-of-the-century-party: Youth and Pop Towards 2000*. Manchester: Manchester University Press.

Redhead, S. (ed.) (1993) *Rave Off: Politics and Deviance in Contemporary Youth Culture*. Aldershot: Avebury.

Redhead, S. (1995) *Unpopular Cultures: The Birth of Law and Popular Culture*. Manchester: Manchester University Press.

Redhead, S. (1997) *Subcultures to Clubcultures: An Introduction to Popular Cultural Studies*. Oxford: Blackwell.

Redhead, S. (2000) *The Repetitive Beat Generation*. Edinburgh: Rebel Inc.

Reis, F. (2002) 'A Brazilian Hotline', *ECPAT Newsletter*, 39, April: 10.

Renold, E. *et al.* (2003) Images of abuse: a review of the evidence on child pornography summary of research and findings, *NSPCC Inform* October. www.nspcc.org.uk/inform.

Renshaw, J. (2003) The Audit Commission's review of the reformed youth justice system, *Criminal Justice Matters*, 54: winter.

Riles, A. (1993) Aspiration and control: international legal rhetoric and the essentialization of culture, *Harvard Law Review*, 106(3): 723–40.

Rimm, M. (1995) Marketing Pornography on the Information Superhighway: A Survey of 917,410 Images, Descriptions, Short Stories and Animations Downloaded 8.5 Million Times by Consumers in Over 2000 Cities in Forty Countries, Provinces, and Territories, *Georgetown Law Journal* (83): 1849–915. Reprinted in D. Wall (ed.) (2003) *Cyberspace Crime*. Aldershot: Ashgate.

Roche, J. (1997) Children's rights: participation and dialogue, in J. Roche and S. Tucker (eds) *Youth in Society*. London: Sage.

Rose, D. (1995) Back to jackboot justice, *Observer*, 12 March.

Rose, N. (1989) *Governing the Soul: Technologies of Human Subjectivity*. London: Routledge.

Rose, N. (2000) Government and control, in D. Garland and R. Sparks (eds) *Criminology and Social Theory*. Oxford: Clarendon.

Rutherford, A. (1996) *Transforming Criminal Justice Policy*. Winchester: Waterside Press.

Rutter, M. and Giller, H. (1983) *Juvenile Delinquency*. Harmondsworth: Penguin.

Saris, A. (2002) *The Rights of Child Victims and Witnesses of Crime: A Compilation of Selected Provisions Drawn from International and Regional Instruments*. Montreal: International Bureau for Children's Rights.http://www.ibcr.org/vicwit.pdf.

Save the Children (no date) *Children's Rights in the U.K.* Information pamphlet. London: Save the Children.

Select Committee on Race Relations and Immigration (1972) *Police/Immigrant Relations*. London: HMSO.

Sen, S. (2000) *Disciplining Punishment: Colonialism and Convict Society in the Andaman Islands*. Oxford: Oxford University Press.

Shelley, L. (2002) Crime as the defining problem: voices of another criminology, *International Annals of Criminology*, 39(1/2): 77–88.

Shelley, L. (2003a) The trade in people in and from the former Soviet Union, *Crime, Law and Social Change*, 40: 231–49.

Shelley, L. (2003b) Trafficking in women: the business model approach, *The Brown Journal of World Affairs*, X(I): 119–31.

Sibley, D. (1995) *Geographies of Exclusion*. London: Routledge.

Singh, J.G. (1996) *Colonial Narratives, Cultural Dialogues: 'Discoveries' of India in the Language of Colonialism*. London: Routledge.

Skelton, T. and Allen, T. (eds) *Culture and Global change*. London: Routledge.

Smart, C. (1976) *Women, Crime and Criminology: A Feminist Critique*. London: Routledge & Kegan Paul.

Smith, D.J. (1994) *The Sleep of Reason: The James Bulger Case*. London: Century.

Southon, J. and Dhakal, P. (2003) *Life Without Basic Service: 'Street Children Say'*. Nepal: Save the Children. http://www.savethechildren.net/nepal/key_work/street_children.html.

Sparks, R. (1992) *Television and the Drama of Crime*. Buckingham: Open University Press.

Stephens, S. (1995) Introduction, in S. Stephens (ed.) *Children and the Politics of Culture*. Princeton; Chichester: Princeton University Press.

Storch, R.D. (1980) The plague of the blue locusts: police reform and popular resistance in Northern England 1840–1857, in M. Fitzgerald, G. McLennon and J. Pawson (eds) *Crime and Society*. London: Routledge.

Strasburger, V.C. and Wilson, B.J. (eds) (2002) *Children, Adolescents and the Media*. London: Sage.

Takashi, M. and Cederlof, C. (2000) *Street Children in Central America: An Overview*. The World Bank Group. http://wbln0018.worldbank.org/.

Tate, T. (1990) *Child Pornogtraphy: An Investigation*. London: Methuen.

Taylor, I. and Taylor, L. (eds) (1973) *Politics and Deviance: Papers from the National Deviancy Conference (NDC)*. Harmondsworth: Penguin.

Taylor, I., Walton, P. and Young, J. (1973) *The New Criminology: For a Social Theory of Deviance*. London: Routledge & Kegan Paul.

Taylor, L., Lacey, R. and Bracken, D. (1979) *In Whose Best Interests? The Unjust Treatment of Children in Courts and Institutions*. Nottingham: Cobden Trust/MIND.

Taylor, M. (2002) The nature and dimensions of child pornography on the internet. University College Cork. http://www.ipce.info/library_3/files/nat_dims_kp.htm.

Taylor, S. (2003) The gangs of New Labour: yobs or just youth? *Criminal justice matters* No. 54 Winter.

Thornton, S. (1995) *Club Cultures: Music, Media, and Subcultural Capital*. Cambridge: Polity Press.

Thorpe, D.H., Smith, D.B., Green, C.J. and Paley, J.H. (1980) *Out of Care*. London: Allen & Unwin.

Tierney, J. (1996) *Criminology: Theory and Context*. London: Prentice Hall/Harvester Wheatsheaf.

United Nations (1990) *Convention on the Rights of the Child (CRC)*. General assembly resolution 44/25 20, November 1989. http://www.unchr.ch/html/.

United Nations (2002) *United Nations Committee on the Rights of the Child: Concluding Observations of the Committee on the Rights of the Child: United Kingdom of Great Britain and Northern Ireland*. Geneva: United Nations.

United Nations (2003) *Convention on the Rights of the Child (CRC)*. General comment No. 5, Committee on the Rights of the Child 34th Session, 19 September–3 October 2003, CRC/GC/2003/5.

Wakeford, N. (2000) Networking women and grrrls with information/communication technology: surfing tales of the world wide web, in D. Bell and B. Kennedy (eds) *The Cybercultures Reader*. London: Routlege.

Walklate, S. (1989) *Victimology: The Victim and the Criminal Justice Process*. London: Unwin Hyman.

Wall, D. (ed.) (2003) *Cyberspace Crime*. Aldershot: Ashgate.

Wall, D. (2003) Policing and the regulation of the internet, in D. Wall (ed.) *Cyberspace Crime*. Aldershot: Ashgate.

Welsh, I. (1993) *Trainspotting*. London: Secker & Warburg.

Williams, J. and Taylor, R. (1994) Boys keep swinging: masculinity and football culture in England, in T. Newburn and E.A. Stanko (eds) *Just Boys Doing Business? Men, Masculinities and Crime*. London: Routledge.

Williams, M. (2000) Virtually criminal: discourse, deviance and anxiety within virtual communities, *International Review of Law, Computers and Technology*, 14: 95–104.

Williams, M. (2001) The language of cybercrime, in D. Wall (ed.) *Crime and the Internet*. London: Routledge.

Williamson, H. (2004) Opinion: The plight of 'ordinary kids' in the media, *Young People Now*, 21 September. http://www.ypnmagazine.com/news/index.cfm.

Willis, P. (1977) *Learning to Labour: How Working Class Kids Get Working Class Jobs*. Farnborough: Saxon House.

Willis, P. (1990) *Common Culture*. Buckingham: Open University Press.

Willson, M. (2000) Community in the abstract: a political and Ethical Dilemma? in D. Bell and B. Kennedy (eds) *The Cybercultures Reader*. London: Routledge.

Wilmott, P. (1966) *Adolescent Boys of East London*. London: Routledge & Kegan Paul.

Windlesham, Lord (1993) *Penal Policy in the Making: Volume 2 – Responses to Crime*. Oxford: Clarendon Press.

Wullschlager, J. (1995) *Inventing Wonderland*. London: Methuen.

Young, A. (1996) *Imagining Crime*. London: Sage.

Young, J. (1974) Mass media, drugs and deviance, in P. Rock and M. McKintosh (eds) *Deviance and Social Control*. London: Tavistock.

Young, J. (1988) Radical criminology in Britain: the emergence of a competing paradigm, *British Journal of Criminology*, 28(2): 159–83.

Young, J. (1992) Ten points of realism, in J. Young and R. Matthews (eds) *Rethinking Criminology: The Realist Debate*. London: Sage.

Young, J. (1994) Incessant chatter: recent paradigms in criminology, in M. Maguire, R. Morgan and R. Reiner (eds) *The Oxford Handbook of Criminology*. Oxford: Clarendon Press.

Young, J. (1997) Left realist criminology: radical in its analysis, realist in its policy, in M. Maguire, R. Morgan and R. Reiner (eds) *The Oxford Handbook of Criminology*. Oxford: Clarendon Press.

Young, J. (1999) *The Exclusive Society*. London: Sage.

Young, J. and Matthews, R. (eds) (1992) *Rethinking Criminology: The Realist Debate*. London: Sage.

Zedner, L. (1994) Victims, in M. Maguire, R. Morgan and R. Reiner (eds) *The Oxford Handbook of Criminology*. Oxford: Clarendon Press.

Index

UNDERSTANDING DRUGS, ALCOHOL AND CRIME

Trevor Bennett and Katy Holloway

- What is the connection between drugs, alcohol and crime?
- What works in reducing drug and alcohol-related crime?

The book provides a succinct overview of current theory and research on the links between drugs, alcohol use and crime. It discusses the legal and social context of drug and alcohol use and identifies current levels of consumption. Focusing on the UK context, it also takes into account international research.

- Detailed review of the research literature on the connections between drug use and crime
- Examines the current government anti-drugs policy and assesses the effectiveness of programmes that have been used to reduce drug and alcohol-related crime.

The authors conclude that future government drugs policy should pay particular attention to the lessons learned from research on the connection between drug and alcohol use and crime. Ideal for criminology, criminal justice, social policy and social work students, this book is also a useful source for policy makers, the police, probation workers, social workers, drugs and alcohol counsellors, treatment agencies, sentencers, voluntary agencies, Drug Action Teams, and others with an interest in research on drugs and crime.

Contents

The nature of the problem – Policy context: from defining to reducing harm – Extent of drug misuse – Types of drug misuse – Explaining the drugs-crime connection – The statistical association: just coincidence? – The causal connection: more than coincidence? – The effectiveness of interventions – The nature of the solution.

c.160pp   0 335 21257 3 (Paperback)   0 335 21258 1 (Hardback)

INTOLERANT BRITAIN?
HATE, CITIZENSHIP AND DIFFERENCE

Derek McGhee

This fascinating book uses case studies to explore a number of high-profile and contemporary 'social problems' that exist in British society, including:

- Racism and institutional racism
- Ethnic and religious community segregation
- Social and institutional asylophobia
- Islamophobia and the incitement of religious hatred
- Homophobia and institutional homophobia

At the same time the book examines various legislative and strategic movements introduced to tackle these social problems, for example strategies to counter institutional prejudices (especially in policing), hate crime legislation, managed migration, community safety and community cohesion strategies. Throughout the book, McGhee contextualizes these strategies within the Government's wider project of attempting to revitalize British citizenship.

Intolerant Britain? is key reading for students on courses in sociology, social policy, politics, race and ethnicity studies, gender studies, media and cultural studies and criminology.

Contents

Introduction – Over-policed and under-protected – race and policing from Scarman to Lawrence – Trouble up north: building community cohesion in Bradford – Asylum hysteria: insecure borders – anxious havens – Faith-hate in post-9/11 UK – Building trust – policing homophobia – Beyond toleration: privacy, citizenship and sexual minorities in England and Wales – Cosmopolitan citizenship: new Labour – 'new' Britain – Notes – Bibliography.

192pp   0 335 21674 9   (Paperback)   0 335 21675 7 (Hardback)

UNDERSTANDING PUBLIC ATTITUDES TO CRIMINAL JUSTICE

Julian V. Roberts and Mike Hough

- Which factors shape public opinion of criminal justice?
- How do the views of the public influence criminal justice policy and practice?

This book provides an introduction to public attitudes towards criminal justice. It explores the public's lack of confidence in criminal justice processes, and summarizes findings on public attitudes towards the three principal components of the criminal process: the police, the courts, and the prison system. It examines the importance that people attach to different criminal justice functions, such as preventing crime, prosecuting and punishing offenders, and protecting the public.

Topics include:

- Youth justice and public opinion
- Public perception of restorative justice
- Penal populism and media treatment of crime
- The reliability of public opinion polls
- The drivers of public opinion

Understanding Public Attitudes to Criminal Justice provides an international perspective on the issues surrounding criminal justice and public opinion, drawing on research from a range of countries including the UK, the United States and Canada.

Key reading for students in criminology, criminal justice, and media studies, this book is also of value to researchers and those with an interest in crime and the media.

Contents
Acknowledgements – Introduction to Public Opinion and Criminal Justice – Public Confidence in the Criminal Justice System – Attitudes to the Police – Attitudes to the Sentencing and the Courts – Attitudes to Prison and Parole – Attitudes to Youth Justice – Attitudes to Restorative Justice – Conclusions – References

180pp   0 335 21536 X (Paperback)   0 335 21537 8 (Hardback)